KU-142-475

DISPOSED OF
BY LIBRARY
HOUSE OF LORDS

THE HARMONIZATION OF EMPLOYMENT CONDITIONS IN BRITAIN

Also by Alice Russell

POLITICAL STABILITY IN LATER VICTORIAN ENGLAND

THE GROWTH IN OCCUPATIONAL WELFARE IN BRITAIN

The Harmonization of Employment Conditions in Britain

The Changing Workplace Divide since 1950 and the Implications for Social Structure

Alice Russell

Lecturer in Economic and Social History
University of Wales
Aberystwyth

© Alice Russell 1998

All rights reserved. No reproduction, copy or transmission of
this publication may be made without written permission.

No paragraph of this publication may be reproduced, copied or
transmitted save with written permission or in accordance with
the provisions of the Copyright, Designs and Patents Act 1988,
or under the terms of any licence permitting limited copying
issued by the Copyright Licensing Agency, 90 Tottenham Court
Road, London W1P 9HE.

Any person who does any unauthorised act in relation to this
publication may be liable to criminal prosecution and civil
claims for damages.

The author has asserted her right to be identified
as the author of this work in accordance with the
Copyright, Designs and Patents Act 1988.

First published 1998 by
MACMILLAN PRESS LTD
Houndmills, Basingstoke, Hampshire RG21 6XS
and London
Companies and representatives
throughout the world

ISBN 0–333–71714–7

A catalogue record for this book is available
from the British Library.

This book is printed on paper suitable for recycling and
made from fully managed and sustained forest sources.

10   9   8   7   6   5   4   3   2   1
07   06   05   04   03   02   01   00   99   98

Printed and bound in Great Britain by
Antony Rowe Ltd, Chippenham, Wiltshire

Contents

1 Introduction

THE WORKPLACE DIVIDE AND THE 'BOURGEOIS WORKER'

Britain is generally acknowledged to have been a deeply class-conscious nation in the 1950s and 1960s. British society understood itself as being broadly divided into working class and middle class, and most individuals were acutely aware of their position in one or other of these two broad social strata. The existence of numerous levels within the stratification order had long been recognized, but the main split was always regarded as that which separated 'working' from 'middle'. Conventionally, the most important indicator of class position was occupation, and closely associated with this was total remuneration from work and the general standard of living and lifestyle which earnings permitted. In the workplace the main class divide was between manual workers on the one hand and non-manual employees on the other. The far-reaching social changes which have occurred since the Second World War, gathering momentum in the last decade and a half, have rendered the task of identifying class position progressively more problematic. The conventional concepts of class are of dubious relevance to the study of the social structures of the 1990s.[1]

During the quarter century following the Second World War the changing nature of the workplace divide and its implications for the British class structure were matters of debate and controversy amongst academics, journalists and political commentators. While some[2] were citing evidence to show that advanced sections of the working class were becoming 'bourgeois', others[3] were fulminating against the persistence of class inequality, and still others,[4] while recognizing the growth of working-class affluence, were denying that change could be convincingly represented as a process of working-class embourgeoisement.

The manual/non-manual workplace divide in Britain has deep historical roots. In times past, a combination of custom, practice, sentiment, labour market circumstances, the growing size of the firm, and change in the organization of production led to the emergence of non-manual layers above the level of manual grades, and to profound

differences in the payment structures, terms, benefits and conditions
of employment which became characteristically associated with each
of the two broad groups: 'non-manual work has carried with it an
assumption of higher status and better terms and conditions of
employment.'[5] As Lockwood,[6] Braverman[7] and many others have
argued, there were both operational and attitudinal assumptions at
the root of the divide. In the nineteenth century progressively larger
business enterprises in the growing industrial sector required increasing amounts of 'non-productive' labour to assist employers and
managers with bookkeeping, correspondence, design, merchandising
and supervisory functions, in circumstances which made it impossible
for the entrepreneur to cope single-handedly. The devolution of some
of these functions led to the emergence of bureaucratic hierarchies in
many firms, and at the same time there were growing demands for
non-manual or white-collar employees to work in the burgeoning
bureaucracies of central and local government and in the rapidly
growing legal, professional and financial services sector of the
economy.

These developments produced a hierarchy of responsibility and
control. Non-manual employees were expected to identify with the
managerially conceived objectives of the enterprise. Their loyalty,
commitment, and association with control functions gave them privileged status as a natural consequence. At a time when there was a
limited supply of recruits with suitable educational credentials for all
but the most routine aspects of office work, it made sound commercial
sense to provide preferential rewards as an aid to attraction and
retention of employees who were not readily replaceable. The hierarchical structure of bureaucracies created a career ladder, which
encouraged aspirations and effort by providing opportunities for
upward mobility. Competent and loyal performance at the lower
levels and demonstrable commitment to the goals of the organization
would lead to promotion. Thus, non-manual staff have traditionally
been expected to be motivated by something more than short-term
gain and cupidity. In industry, the employer regarded the commitment, discretion and loyalty of his office staff to be as important as
competence in the performance of work tasks. Similar distinctions
emerged in the public sector bureaucracies, such as the civil service
and local government, where a required commitment to the goals of
the organization was reinforced by the notion of 'public service ethos'.

The privileged occupational status of non-manual employees and
the associated rewards have not, of course, been inviolate. As

Anderson and Lockwood[8] have shown, the rapid growth of the clerical labour force as a result of changes in educational provision and the entry of women into the occupation in the later nineteenth and early twentieth centuries undermined the employment prospects and job security of youthful clerks with only minimal qualifications. This served to create a sense of distance between some clerical grades and their managerial supervisors. After the Second World War, the further growth of the non-manual labour force was accompanied by the development of 'credentialism', associated with the expansion of higher and further education; educational qualifications came to determine access to many higher-level non-manual jobs. This served to constrain promotion from the lower rungs of the ladder, and widened the distance between management and their salaried staffs. In the 1950s and 1960s, when some kinds of white-collar work were becoming routinized, monotonized and deskilled, when small offices with their close personal contacts were giving way to vast impersonal, sometimes open-plan, offices with clerical workers *en masse*, and when white-collar union membership was growing fast, some investigators were referring to the 'proletarianization' of the white-collar worker.[9]

Other investigators, whose research was concerned with change affecting the working class in the 1950s and 1960s, were claiming that some manual groups were becoming 'bourgeois'. Much evidence was adduced by proponents of the embourgeoisement thesis, most of it relating to earnings, expenditure patterns and political preference. This was an era of almost full employment, wage inflation, working-class affluence, 'never-had-it-so-good' living standards, and the spread of working-class Conservatism. The developments currently underway, it was alleged, represented the incipient decline and decomposition of the working class. The society of the future would be overwhelmingly middle class.

The concept of the bourgeois worker was not new; and the embourgeoisement thesis did not so much emerge as re-emerge in the quarter century following the Second World War. Engels, seeking to explain the willingness of recently enfranchized working men to vote for parliamentary candidates of the two middle-class political parties in the later nineteenth century, had acknowledged the growing significance of the British worker's craving for respectability and better social status, which produced an eagerness to adopt bourgeois social values, lifestyles and practical ideas. Engels had believed the bourgeois worker to be an essentially temporary sociological type, but the species apparently proved to be more durable than Engels had expected. To some observers, the distinction between the working class and the middle class was dissolving in the interwar years. George Orwell, for example, asserted that 'in tastes, habits, manners and outlook, the working class and middle class are drawing together.'[10] Similarly, their survey of the social structure of England and Wales led Carr Saunders and Caradog Jones to conclude that in respect of dress, speech and the use of leisure, 'all members of the community are obviously coming to resemble one another.'[11]

The theme was taken up with gusto in the 1950s and 1960s. Statistical evidence indicated a significant increase in the number of families receiving middle-range incomes, and some observers claimed that the traditional 'income pyramid', with a large percentage of the population located at its base, had been replaced by a diamond-shaped structure with a numerically dominant middle stratum containing highly paid skilled and semi-skilled manual groups along with various non-manual grades. It was claimed in *The Economist* in 1948 that the middle class was expanding 'as the wage-worker assumes bourgeois habits and standards.'[12] By the 1960s the overlap in manual and non-manual earnings was well documented. A publication, issued by the Central Office of Information in 1962,[13] disclosed that the main shift from low to middle-level incomes had occurred between 1949 and 1961, largely as a result of higher wage-earning on the part of manual workers. Routh's research[14] and COI statistics showed that there was now little difference in the average earnings of skilled manual workers and such non-manual grades as clerks and shop assistants. Millar, however, claimed that the convergence of earned incomes had gone much further; some manual workers earned as much as some managers, many school teachers and even some executives. The old incomes hierarchy, formerly one of the class system's greatest stabilizers, had been slowly but surely eroded. A low income could no longer be taken as an indicator of unskilled occupational status, nor a high income of professional rank. In times past, income level could generally be correlated with occupational grade, and so with class position; but the present situation was not so simple. There was no denying that there was still a very wide gulf between rich and poor, but level of earnings could no longer be taken as the main indicator of occupation and class position. There was now a broad band in the middle of the incomes structure which included professional people, industrial executives, and manual workers, and a very large section of the population fell into that group. Many skilled and semi-skilled manual workers had broken through the income barriers which once separated them from white-collar and professional people.

The much publicized homogenization of incomes was reflected in changing patterns of consumer expenditure. Since the Second World War manual workers had been acquiring consumer goods, including household durables, that had once been characteristic of middle-class households. The manual worker's inferior position in terms of economic resources and consumer power, once a defining characteristic of the working class as traditionally conceived, was rapidly disappearing. There was still severe economic deprivation for some, but it was no longer the lot of the mass of the manual labour force. Progressively more manual workers could afford to buy household equipment such as television sets, vacuum cleaners, washing machines, refrigerators and gas or electric cookers; and increasingly, too, they were invading the hitherto almost exclusively middle-class preserves of car and home ownership and holidays abroad.[15]

Abrams[16] observed in 1960 that in recent years there had been a spectacular increase in the proportion of British adults living in homes equipped with modern appliances. In the group covered by his survey, two-thirds of all persons eligible to vote were working-class by occupation, and half of these were skilled manual workers with earnings well above the average for all operatives. Between 1956 and 1959 this prosperous group had acquired consumer durables at a rate that far exceeded that of the population as a whole. During that period, ownership of refrigerators had almost trebled, from 6 per cent to 16 per cent of households; car ownership almost doubled from 18 per cent to 32 per cent; ownership of washing machines grew from 25 per cent to 44 per cent; and the proportion owning television sets increased by half, to reach near-saturation level at 85 per cent. Millar cited the example of a skilled engineering worker who was buying his own home, owned a car, washing machine, refrigerator, electric cooker and telephone, and regularly went abroad for holidays. Turner found that it was not uncommon for highly skilled workers in the car industry to play golf, pay for driving lessons for their sons and daughters, and eat out at restaurants. A substantial number of the Dagenham car workers covered by his investigation had moved to the recently built suburbs with the aid of mortgage loans, and had acquired fitted carpets, cocktail cabinets and tape recorders, in addition to the 'usual' kitchen appliances.

Evidence of material prosperity such as this lent substance to

Zweig's claim that large sections of the manual workforce found themselves on the move towards a middle-class style of living. Affluent manual workers had achieved economic parity with some sections of the middle class; the worker was more prosperous than ever before. Inquiries by Butler and Stokes[17] into political attitudes and behaviour disclosed that manual workers who received high earnings which permitted home-ownership had a tendency to describe themselves as middle class.

The emergence of the affluent manual worker was cited as an important factor in the long run of Conservative successes in general elections. When, by 1959, the Labour Party had lost three consecutive general elections by progressively wider margins, the embourgeoisement of prosperous elements within the working class seemed to explain Labour's defeat; highly paid groups were said to see themselves as 'merging with the middle class' and to be seeking consolidation of their 'new class aspirations' by voting Conservative.[18] Crosland believed that the forces of change were 'gradually breaking down the old barriers between the working and middle classes,' and that the Labour Party was losing support because people who would be objectively classified as working class in terms of occupation or family background had now 'acquired a middle-class income and pattern of consumption, and sometimes a middle-class psychology.'[19]

The embourgeoisement thesis was greeted with sceptism by critics who were unconvinced by the evidence upon which it rested. Goldthorpe and his colleagues argued that the emphasis placed on the increasing convergence of the consumption patterns of people in manual and non-manual employment had led to neglect of the fact that the two categories 'remain much more clearly differentiated when their members are considered as *producers.*' Despite the possibly levelling effect of some forms of advanced technology and modern employment policies, white-collar grades in general still had a superior work situation. By and large, their working conditions and amenities, employment security, fringe benefits, long-term income prospects, and promotion chances, were markedly better than those available for the vast majority of manual workers. Class position was not simply a matter of consumer power. The 'functions and status' of a group 'within the social division of labour' were still of paramount importance in analysis of the class structure.[20]

A detailed investigation of current differences in the terms, benefits and employment conditions of manual and non-manual grades, conducted in the later 1960s by Wedderburn and Craig, disclosed that the differences were substantial. The non-manual class could be subdivided into foremen, draughtsmen and clerical grades as one group, and the various grades of managers and professionals as another; and likewise the manual class could be separated into skilled, semi-skilled and unskilled grades. There were differentials in the employment terms and benefits of these several sub-groups; but the most marked disparities – which formed the 'great divide' – were those which distinguished all non-manual grades on the one hand, and all manual grades on the other. In certain respects, the gulf was 'very wide indeed'. Even where the two main non-manual groups diverged, they were 'still like each other more than they are like the manual workers.' With unequal treatment on the scale that their investigation seemed to show, Wedderburn and Craig believed that it was 'far too soon to talk of bourgeois workers.'[21]

Earned income continued to be a major differentiating feature, despite the recent appearance of the affluent manual worker. It was accepted that there was some overlap in the 'actual earnings' of some manual and non-manual grades, but there were great differences between the two in earning capacities, in longer-term income expect-ations, in dependability and stability of earnings, and also in payment structures, the pay period and method of pay. Non-manual workers characteristically received an annual salary which was paid in regular instalments regardless of minor fluctuations in the amount of work performed. It was not usual for the non-manual employee to suffer pay deductions for occasional lateness or, by arrangement with the supervisor, for absence for personal reasons. The amount of pay was regular, predictable and dependable. In contrast, most manual workers' pay was based on piece-rates related to the amount produced, or time-rates corresponding to the number of hours worked, so that earnings fluctuated in line with the individual's output or actual working hours. While take-home pay might be boosted by overtime working at overtime rates and by shift premia, bonuses and a variety of special supplements, it could fluctuate downward as a result of short-time working, temporary lay-off, and the withdrawal of overtime opportunities. Lateness and agreed time off for personal reasons tended to result in pay deductions. Non-manual employees usually received their earnings monthly, by cheque or credit transfer, whereas manual workers were usually paid weekly in cash via the pay packet. Most non-manuals were paid according to salary scales, with automatic, often annual, pay progression from the lowest to the highest point on the pay scale for the particular grade. The pay level might be relatively low in the early years of the individual's working lifetime, but it rose gradually with years of service and usually remained high in the middle and later years; and from time to time the pay scales themselves were raised. In contrast, the manual worker reached his or her peak earnings quite early. Pay increases, beyond the trainee period, were usually a matter of collective bargaining over wage rates. Earnings tended to level off in the middle years of the individual's employment lifetime, and then fall when age and declining physical strength led to an avoidance of overtime hours and an inclination to seek lighter work which usually carried lower rates of pay. Price and Price note that the effect of incremental salary scales, merit increases and career progression for non-manual employees was to link non-manual pay more strongly to age and experience, while the earnings capacity of manual workers was more closely linked to physical capability.

Differences in employment security for the two broad groups had implications for dependability of earnings. Non-manual employees could expect relatively secure employment for they were less vulnerable to redundancy, lay-off, and the effect of the trade cycle. In practice, it was the manual worker who was most immediately, most frequently, and most extensively affected by cyclical and seasonal fluctuations, structural change in the economy, and technological advance. In so far as non-manual employees experienced redundancy, they could expect preferential treatment in terms of period of notice, severance pay, and paid time off to find other employment.

There was a marked difference, also, in career prospects for the two broad groups. Again, there were implications for future earnings. Non-manual grades could reasonably expect to work their way upward to more responsible positions and a higher salary range; career development was sought by the aspiring employee and actively encouraged by employers. In contrast, the concept of career development did not generally apply in the sphere of manual employment, and there were relatively few opportunities for promotion to chargehand, senior operator, section leader or supervisor; the tendency was to voluntary job changing – but in response to opportunities for higher pay for similar work, rather than opportunities for promotion to a higher grade of work. There was little chance of moving from manual to non-manual employment.

During the 1950s and 1960s there were some improvements in working time, and manual workers were gaining some of the fringe benefits traditionally associated with salaried employment status, such as paid holidays, company-provided sick pay, and occupational pensions.[22] Even here, however, the status divide was still starkly visible. Non-manual staff typically had a normal working week of 38 hours or less and rarely worked overtime, whereas most manual workers had basic working hours of 40 or more, with actual working hours extended by often large amounts of overtime which in some organizations had become systematic or institutionalized. Shift work, generally confined to manual employment, meant that work was done at unsociable times, for it could involve night and weekend working, and even working on public holidays. The use of time clocks to record attendance and measure time spent at work was associated almost exclusively with manual employment.

Most manual workers had gained paid holidays around the time of the Second World War and their entitlements had increased by the mid-1960s; but most non-manuals had longer periods of paid holiday and, unlike manual grades, tended to have some choice about when holiday leave would be taken. Holiday pay for non-manuals consisted of normal salary, but for manual workers, although payment for the holiday period might include shift and other regular premia, it rarely took account of overtime pay, with the result that unless there was a special holiday bonus, holiday pay was lower than average take-home pay when the individual was at work. Occupational pensions, paid in addition to the state pension, were characteristic in non-manual employment. Proportional coverage was very much lower for manual workers, and pensions paid to the retired were meagre compared with those which the salaried could expect to receive. Some employers had pension arrangements for their salaried staffs but not for their manual work forces, while others operated separate schemes for the two groups, with superior provision for non-manuals. The pattern of sick pay provision was similar. The non-manual employee was more likely than the manual worker to be covered by a company sick pay scheme; and for the former, maximum entitlement was longer, sick pay as a proportion of normal take-home pay was higher, and sick pay was given from the first day of sickness absence whereas there were usually from three to five 'waiting days' before sickness benefit became payable for manual workers. Again, employers tended to operate separate schemes for the two groups.

Wedderburn and Craig found that manual workers were more closely bound by discipline than were salaried staff. Workplace rules affecting manual grades were stricter, disciplinary procedures more frequently operated, and penalties were more severe. Such differences of treatment reflected employers' assumptions about the behaviour and attitudes of the main groups on each side of the status divide. Manual workers on the shopfloor were believed to be less reliable, and to identify less strongly with the company and the employers' objectives than did their office staff counterparts. The former had to be more closely supervised and subjected to more stringent controls, because they could not be trusted to behave in ways that accorded with the company's interests. It was common practice in large firms to provide separate or segregated canteen facilities for shopfloor workers and office staffs, with better furnishings, fitments, service and choice of meals for the latter.

There were many contemporary critics of the prevailing state of affairs in the 1960s. Bugler,[23] writing in 1965, referred to the workplace divide as a form of 'industrial apartheid', the lingering legacy of a long-outmoded industrial system. The 'fundamental distinction', he argued, was 'hourly pay'. It was hourly paid workers who earned overtime, but the 'status benefits' available in lieu to staff – longer holidays, better pensions, better sick pay, a shorter working week, longer notice, and so on – were far more valuable. The 'great divide' in the workplace was evident also in segregation in car parking, canteen and dining room facilities, works entrances, washrooms, cloakrooms and toilet amenities; shopfloor workers had to punch a time card at the beginning and end of the day, while staff attendance was merely recorded by signature in the register on arrival. Bugler was angered by the myopic outlook of tight-fisted employers who, trapped in a time-warp of outdated practice, failed to recognize the longer-term advantage for all concerned of desegregating the workplace.

The foregoing comparison of the terms, benefits and conditions of employment characteristically associated with manual and non-manual occupational status in the 1950s and 1960s has focused on the relative advantages and disadvantages of the two broad groups. This is not to deny that, during the quarter century following the Second World War, changes had occurred which had had the effect of reducing some of the inequalities. Most of the improvements for manual workers were gained piecemeal in the process of collective bargaining between employers' and workers' representatives. These were years of generally tight labour markets and rapidly rising wages, and in such circumstances many manual workers reached an earnings threshold beyond which benefits were attractive as part of their pay increase. The wage level continued to be the main focus of negotiation, but the unions became accustomed to claiming or accepting improvements in working hours and other benefits, item by item, in what was fast becoming the 'annual pay round'. Since gains for non-manual grades were less spectacular in these years, the effect of improvements for manual workers was to reduce, though not yet to eliminate, the differentials between the two.

The average basic working week for manual workers fell from 48 hours at around the time of the Second World War to 40 by the end of the 1960s. For salaried staffs the basic week ranged from 35 to 38 hours, with 37½ hours common in the industrial sector by 1970. The working time differential was reduced in so far as *basic* hours are concerned, but it remained stark in other aspects – *actual* working hours, the *arrangement* of working time, *recording* of hours worked – and the manual wage-earner's basic working day still began earlier and ended later than the non-manual staff's. The manual worker's basic holiday entitlement had increased from one week to two by 1960, and by 1970 52 per cent had a basic entitlement of three weeks or more and 25 per cent received additional days related to length of service. Holidays for salaried staffs ranged from three to five weeks, so that, here too, the gap, though not totally eliminated, was narrower than it had been at the beginning of the Second World War when large numbers of manual workers had received no payment for any holidays taken.[24] There were major advances also in wage-workers' access to occupational pension schemes.[25] Total membership (manual and non-manual combined) of such schemes grew from 6.2 million in 1953 to 12.2 million in 1967, the greatest increases being in the number of male manual members; in the private sector coverage for these grew from 38 per cent in 1956 to 60 per cent in 1967, and in the public sector coverage reached 65 per cent. In 1961, around 92 per cent of persons in non-manual employment were covered by occupational sick pay arrangements, but only 44 per cent of those in manual work were covered. There was virtually no change in proportional coverage of non-manual grades in the decade up to 1971, but about 74 per cent of men and 48 per cent of women in full-time manual work had acquired membership of their employers' sick pay schemes by the beginning of the 1970s.[26] For employees in permanent full-time work, piecemeal progress has continued from the early 1970s to the present.

An alternative to the piecemeal approach began to emerge in the 1950s, to become more clearly evident in the 1960s and something of a trend by the 1980s. In the fifties decade some British employers began to put some of their manual workers on 'staff status' or 'staff grade'. This brought the terms, benefits and conditions of employment of the groups affected closer to those applying to salaried office staffs, though they were rarely equalized in all aspects. At the same time, and from the outset, a number of largely US-owned companies, such as International Business Machines and Texas Instruments which set up subsidiaries in Britain in these years, introduced 'single status' conditions which, by definition, did not discriminate according to occupational grade. During the 1960s a few British enterprises, such as Imperial Chemical Industries and Electricity Supply, embarked upon more ambitious staff status projects with the intention of bringing some, though not all, of the terms and benefits of their entire full-time manual workforces closer to those of their salaried staffs. In the late 1970s and early 1980s, many of the Japanese companies establishing new production sites in Britain brought with them their own version of 'single status'. By this time, the reduction of differences associated with occupational status – the traditional manual/non-manual workplace divide – had become the trend in some sections of the British economy, and, equally significantly, the terminology had changed. The term 'staff status' for manual workers gradually gave way to 'harmonization' of conditions for all permanent full-time employees, irrespective of collar colour. Some company spokesmen stated that the long-term objective was to provide 'common' or 'equal' terms and conditions. Many of these policies were not confined to the alignment of main fringe benefits such as holiday entitlement, sick pay and pensions, but went much further in that they sought to eliminate other differentials traditionally manifest in pay and grading structures, the pay period and method of pay, degree of employment security and, in some cases, career progression. In some cases, also, policy sought to establish common facilities and amenities, and a common approach to time-recording.

The new trend in personnel policy developed, grew, and gathered momentum during half a century in which there were major structural and cyclical changes in the British economy as a whole, transformation in particular industries and services, and upheavals in particular firms and their business strategies. At the same time, there were changes in trade unionism, in the unions' bargaining power, and in collective bargaining styles. These factors affected, and interacted with, innovations in personnel policy, sometimes reducing the pace of change and at other times accelerating it. They had implications for the manual worker as 'consumer', but the most profound effect was upon the manual worker as 'producer'.

OBJECTIVES OF THE BOOK

The purpose of this study is to examine the origins, growth and main features of the trend to equalize terms, benefits and employment conditions of manual and non-manual employees in Britain. That developments have occurred over a long period, characterized by dramatic change in economic circumstances, requires explanation. Some insights may be gained by ascertaining whether the rate of advance was constant and unbroken, or whether innovation occurred in waves or in short bursts. Pressures for change may have been dissimilar in different industries and services. It will be instructive here to discover whether developments have occurred in both public and private sectors, whether they are to be found mainly in new technologically advanced and expanding industries rather than in the older declining industries, and whether company size is of any significance.

Since 1950 there have been major changes in the organization of employment. In 1950s and 1960s permanent full-time work was more readily available for more people than ever before; retrospectively, permanent full-time work has been termed 'standard' or 'traditional'. More recently there has been a phenomenal growth in 'non-standard' or 'non-traditional' forms of employment, accompanied by a rapid and unprecedented increase in the number of women in the labour force. Two questions need to be raised here: what are the implications of these employment trends for the harmonization of employment conditions, and are men and women equally affected by companies' harmonization policies?

Moves to reduce or eliminate differentials have been underway in Britain for half a century or more as a long-term evolutionary process; but the establishment of subsidiaries in Britain by foreign companies, notably those with their main headquarters in the USA and Japan, on a scale sufficient to attract press comment and academic research interest, may have had some influence upon developments in British companies. Many of the migrants set up with advanced and highly developed personnel policies and practices. This raises a number of questions. Did British employers emulate practice in foreign companies setting up in Britain? Did foreign-owned companies in Britain introduce personnel policies identical to those of their parent companies, or was policy and practice adapted to the British tradition of industrial relations and collective bargaining? In what respects did the traditional British industrial relations system adapt to the innovative policies and practices of the newly arriving migrants from abroad?

There were major changes in government policy, reflected in legislation affecting both employers, workforces and the trade unions, during the period under review. Soon after the war the policy of the landslide Labour Government produced a vast expansion of the public sector with the nationalization of major industries and utility services, the creation of new social services such as the NHS, and the reorganization and expansion of others such as education. More recently the Conservative Government's policy for privatization resulted in a much pruned public sector. Under both Labour and Conservative Governments from 1959 to 1979 there were almost two decades of national prices and incomes policy; since then, the Conservative Government's economic policy has included deregulation, decentralization, greater responsiveness to market forces, and abandonment of national policy to hold down pay and price increases generally. Labour Governments passed legislation which in various respects strengthened the role of the trade unions; since 1979 successive Conservative Governments have passed a series of Acts to curb the unions' rights and immunities. In the years immediately after the Second World War, centralized industry-wide bargaining was paramount and favoured by government; national agreements came to be supplemented, and in some cases substituted, by local bargaining, and since the mid-1980s decentralized bargaining has been actively fostered by the Conservative Government. All of this raises the question of whether and how government policy impeded, facilitated, or actively promoted moves to reduce and ultimately to eliminate differentials in the terms, benefits and employment conditions of the two broad occupational classes.

Evidence strongly suggests that although the trade unions have always pressed for improvements in the total remuneration package and have met with some success in winning piecemeal gains for their members in the process of collective bargaining, the initiatives to introduce staff status for manual workers and to harmonize employment conditions has come mainly from employers. On the rational assumption that employers expected some benefit in return for what they were offering, we should attempt to ascertain why they proposed change, what gains and advantages were envisaged for the company, and what problems, pressures and considerations prompted their decision. This is not to suggest that all of the moves which occurred were the outcome of negotiation and collective bargaining with the trade unions. Evidence discloses that, in some cases, policy was introduced in non-union companies or companies which did not formally recognize trade unions for collective bargaining purposes. In other cases change was subject of prior discussion with workers' representatives, and sometimes involved preliminary trial and experimentation, ultimately leading to formal written agreements with the unions. In still other cases policy was introduced as a *fait accompli*, without reference to the unions or much by way of consultation with workforces. It was on this basis that ICI's staff grade scheme, introduced in the late 1920s and apparently the first of its kind, was put into effect; according to Reader,[27] the scheme was launched against the impotent hostility of the unions, though, no doubt, it was welcomed by workers who benefited from it. Employer initiative is still important in introducing change, but more recently some manual unions have pressed for staff status for their members or for the extension of a sectional policy to additional groups; and some of the unions have taken up harmonization as an objective to be sought at the bargaining table.

Employers who offered or conceded staff condition or harmonized terms and benefits to their manual workforces undoubtedly expected that certain quantifiable improvements would be forthcoming, but perhaps they sought qualitative gains also. Lower labour turnover, reduced absence rates, better time-keeping, higher labour productivity, and the like, are measurable; but did employers also seek less tangible improvements in qualities such as workers' morale, attitude to work, loyalty and commitment to the company, general *esprit de corps,* willing co-operation with management as opposed to grudging compliance under threat of sanctions, a sense of self-worth, a more gratifying self-perceived identity within the company's occupational structure, greater harmony in industrial relations, and a switch from an adversarial and confrontational stance in collective bargaining to a collaborative position based on joint problem-solving? There are clear implications here for productive efficiency. In order for a company to survive and prosper, businessmen need to be astute, practical and tough, for facts and figures have to be confronted as part of business strategy; but were managers in any sense idealistic, and did their business philosophy extend to generating a sense of higher status amongst manual workers by providing them with the practical gains of staff benefits? This suggests the need to consider what is meant by 'staff status', and why the term gradually fell from currency to be replaced by 'harmonization', 'equal status' and 'common terms and conditions'.

It is a well known fact that even the best laid plans can give rise to outcomes other than those sought and expected. In discussing moves to reduce the manual/non-manual differential, any pitfalls which subsequently became apparent but were unforeseen by management at the time, should be noted, along with potential problems which *were* anticipated and the pro-active measures taken to deal with them. What, for example, were the undesirable effects of abolishing clocking, abandoning the practice of deducting pay for lateness, and providing sick pay from the first day of sickness absence, and how did management seek to prevent abuse of new privileges?

Innovation in personnel policy often involved major adjustments for the workers affected: were the changes unreservedly welcomed by workforces, or were they greeted with caution, or suspicion, or even resentment? Did the new remuneration package involve certain losses which workforces regretted? Harmonization led to the erosion of long-established differentials in rewards, which had marked the traditional status divide in the workplace: how did the traditionally advantaged non-manual grades, white-collar office staffs, supervisors, lower levels of management and the salaried in general, respond when manual workers began to catch up?

There were also long-established differentials within the manual workforce, between craft and non-craft grades and between the skilled, the semi-skilled and the unskilled: did craftworkers fear the undermining of their craft status when all grades were to be treated alike, and did they favour staff status for themselves rather than harmonization for all? That employers expected something in return for their provision of improved terms and benefits suggests that there was a price to be paid by the recipients: what reciprocal concessions were required from unions and workforces, and did they regard the exchange as a fair deal under prevailing circumstances?

There are many variants of policy to reduce or eliminate differentials, and policies have changed in the course of time. Here, it is instructive to identify the main components of early staff-status packages, and to discover in what main ways the contents of the package have changed, and what new items have been added.

Lastly, we should re-consider that controversial type: the bourgeois manual worker. In the 1960s and early 1970s, critics argued that the embourgeoisement thesis was untenable, since it was based mainly on evidence of change in working-class patterns of consumption. Proponents of the thesis had focused on manual workers as *consumers,* and, in doing so, they had neglected the manual worker's position as *producer* and the persisting nature of his/her inferior terms, benefits and employment conditions *vis-à-vis* non-manual grades. Much change has occurred in the workplace since then. It raises the question: if the traditional workplace divide has been reduced or eliminated by improving manual workers' terms and benefits to bring them more, or completely, into line with those of salaried staffs, has the bourgeois manual worker arrived at long last? There is of course, the problem of defining the meaning of 'bourgeois'. The term was not entirely suitable, even when the controversy over the bourgeois worker was at its height. The whole debate reflected, and was strongly influenced by, the deeply engrained class consciousness of the period. The industrial system and the structure of the economy have changed a great deal since the mid-twentieth century: does this mean that the traditional British class system has disintegrated along with the outmoded industrial forms which supported it? Perhaps it is no longer appropriate to conceptualize today's society in terms of working class and middle class, or to think of inter-group relationships in terms of class conflict.

2 The Economic Context, Government Policy and Problems for Employers

INTRODUCTION

Change, development and transformation in the British economy during the second half of the twentieth century, and the wider changes in global economic circumstances, presented some formidable challenges for the Government, employers and workforces. The overall decline of Britain's manufacturing sector and her share of world trade was accompanied by the growth of the services sector, the gradual and then rapid spread of new information technology, a marked increase in jobs which were temporary or part-time, and a rise in the number of economically active women.

The quarter-century following 1950 was not only a period of consumer affluence, rising living standards and mostly near-full employment, but also of threatening inflation and recurrent balance of payments problems for the Government; and employers were beset by progressively more troublesome industrial relations. Britain's generally slower economic growth rate, compared with her main competitors, became markedly worse in the turbulent seventies; unemployment, which had begun to rise in the mid-1970s, escalated and remained high in the long-run recession of the following decade.

Successive Governments struggled with policies seeking to control wage and price inflation, to rectify payments imbalances and then to secure steady economic growth and employment creation, while employers endeavoured to increase productivity and price competitiveness, to curb labour costs, and to deal with the confrontational stances they encountered at the bargaining table. Traditional payment structures and long-established differentials in other employment terms and benefits came to be seen as anachronistic where technological advance affected job content, work tasks, duties and responsibilities. At the same time, employers began to find that the old craft divisions, job rights and trade boundaries, which were jealously guarded by unions and workforces as the means to employment protection, now served to frustrate innovation, impede improvement in business performance, and obstruct the kind of flexibility they needed to enable them to respond readily and cost-efficiently to changing market requirements.

It was the problems challenging them that caused employers to look for new approaches to personnel policy, to the organization of employment, and to reward for effort.

THE CHALLENGE OF ECONOMIC CHANGE, GOVERNMENT POLICY AND GLOBAL COMPETITION

The two decades from 1950 to 1970 have been described as the 'age of affluence'. Some of the achievements of the period were real, impressive, and historically unprecedented. The official unemployment rate was less than 3 per cent, and rose above 2 per cent in only seven years. Near-full employment and generally tight labour markets made labour recruitment and retention difficult for employers, and put the trade unions in a strong position to win wage increases which in the longer term contributed to pay and price inflation and pushed up production costs. There was plenty of premium-rated overtime work on offer, and progressively more job opportunities for women. Labour turnover, in years when the voluntary job leaver encountered no serious problem in finding employment elsewhere, made it difficult for an employer to construct stable, well-knit work groups and to foster a sense of identification with, and commitment to, the employing enterprise. It is unsurprising that employers were the more willing to make concessions and to offer incentives, and that workforces and trade unions made the most of the opportunities now available to them following the privations of postwar austerity.

Affluence was real enough in so far as the focus is upon the employment rate, earnings, consumer spending, and standard of living. The state of the economy, however, gave the Government and many economists cause for concern; for, despite the measurable increases in investment, total output, productivity and certain exports, the performance of Britain's economy compared unfavourably with the growth rates achieved by her main competitors. The USA, Japan and the major countries of continental Europe all had generally higher growth rates of real domestic product, investment, productive efficiency, technological advance, and exports. The shrinking of Britain's manufacturing sector was partly attributable to the kind of structural change characteristic of an advanced industrial economy, but in Britain's case it reflected her deteriorating position overall in international trade. Successive Governments sought to remedy the problem of sluggish economic growth, mounting inflation, and recurrent balance of payments deficits, with 'stop go' measures, later by prices and incomes policies, various kinds of credit control and the occasional devaluation of the pound. However, the Government-imposed 'stops' had the effect of inhibiting industrial re-equipment; high interest rates, credit restrictions and cuts in investment allowances acted as a damper on investment, and curbs on public expenditure meant that the nationalized industries had their investment programmes repeatedly cut or postponed. At the same time 'stop go' policies undermined business confidence and enterprise by making forward-planning difficult and the fulfilment of planned targets uncertain.[1]

Comparability studies, of the kind undertaken by Esso and ICI,[2] disclosed the problem of higher labour costs in Britain than in her main competitors; high labour costs, reflecting lax management and restrictive shopfloor practices, were said to push up prices, stifle innovation, obstruct the most efficient use of what equipment there was, and impede the introduction of new machinery.

The deceleration of economic growth, signs of which were already evident in the late 1960s, became more clearly apparent in the 1970s. These were exceptionally troubled years for the British economy.[3] The structural transformation, begun many decades earlier, continued; new and growing sectors did not fully compensate for the relative and absolute decline of the old staple and export industries. Manufacturing output per head, which had been growing at 3.5 per cent per annum from 1960 to 1973, grew at an annual rate of less than 1 per cent from 1973 to 1979. The decline in manufacturing output as a proportion of GDP was paralleled by a steep fall of employment in all manufacturing industries.

Wage and price inflation, which had caused concern in the preceding decade, became alarmingly high in the 1970s. Governments continued to attack the problem with a succession of incomes policies seeking to curb escalating wages. There were periods of 'pay freeze' and 'severe restraint' in the first half of the decade, but the effect was not so much to damp down wage increases as to cause negotiators to drop claims for improvements in those fringe benefits which counted as part of an annual pay settlement. There followed further pay policies; but the Government's 'guiding light' for voluntary moderation of claims, and attempts to set a 'norm' for permissible increases, provoked growing resentment from the trade unions. With the 1978–9 'winter of discontent', when disputes proliferated throughout industry, the unions would no longer tolerate Government intervention in pay bargaining. The Labour Government fell, and the incoming Conservative Government abandoned the kind of incomes policy which had been applied in various forms for almost two decades. Inflation was gradually brought under control, but there followed other problems with which the Government would have to contend: the rise of mass unemployment and the long-run recession of the 1980s when upturns in the economy were all too often short-lived until the more sustained recovery and stability achieved by the mid-1990s.

Government policy aimed after 1979 to promote an 'enterprise culture' and economic regeneration, by relaxing some of the institutional constraints upon the operation of market forces. To these ends the Conservative Government set out to denationalize large parts of the public sector, to discourage industry-wide collective bargaining and national agreements, to promote inward investment by offering generous grant aid to foreign companies establishing subsidiaries in Britain, to deregulate the labour market, to curb the activities of the trade unions by employment legislation restricting their rights and immunities, and to abolish the Wages Councils in 1993 following the curtailment of their functions in 1986.

The combination of high and persistent unemployment, ongoing change in the structure of the economy and gender composition of the labour force, and the phenomenal rise in the proportion of all economically active persons with jobs which were less than permanent or less than full-time, contributed to a steep fall in total trade union membership. After rising from around 9.25 million in 1950 to a peak of roughly 13.25 million in 1979, membership declined to about 10 million in 1990 before plummeting to some 7 million in 1996.[4] There was a parallel overall decline in the number of days lost through strikes. During the turbulent seventies, well over 10 million days were lost in each of six years; only in 1976 was there a loss of less than 6 million. Afterwards, there were only two years, 1980 with the last rumblings of the 'winter of discontent' and 1984 with the miners' national strike, when over 10 million days were lost.

Marked changes in bargaining styles occurred in these years, variously condoned, endorsed, or actively promoted by the Government. Industry-wide national bargaining and pay determination by statutory wage-regulating bodies where organization was weak or non-existent, which had been chivvied into growth by the Government much earlier in the century, continued to find favour in the 1950s. The amicable, fair and mutually advantageous industrial relations climate, which national negotiation was supposed to create, became progressively more elusive, however; the 1968 Donovan report disclosed the tensions between the formal system based on national agreements and informal shop-steward led systems at the local level. The significance of local bargaining, often disregarding what had been agreed at national level, grew during the 1970s, and industrial relations became explosive. At the same time, legislation relating to employment protection, minimum notice periods, and compensation for redundancy and 'unfair dismissal', brought more scope for trade union action and more obligations for employers. Some employers began to withdraw completely from national bargaining bodies.

The rapid withering of multi-employer bargaining and the system and structure of national agreements was actively favoured by Conservative Governments between 1979 and 1997, in the belief that the general unfettering of business enterprise from the constraints and rigidities imposed by industry-wide negotiation would lead to greater productive efficiency, a healthier economy, and employment creation. The Government's pro-business and anti-union posture was equally evident in the spate of legislation enacted to tame the unions by illegalizing certain of their activities and increasing their liabilities. A battery of legislation enacted during the 1980s and early 1990s in various ways pruned the unions' rights and immunities, curbed the activities of union officers and members, outlawed the closed shop, imposed a legal obligation of full ballots for election of union officers and prior to strikes, illegalized sympathetic striking, and increased the financial and other liabilities upon the unions in acting 'unlawfully'.

It was against the background of decentralization of business operations and industrial relations, privatization of large parts of the public sector, the breakup of former public monopolies into separate and autonomous units, deregulation of the labour market, and the taming of the trade unions, that marked changes in bargaining styles occurred within the context of an overall decline in national collective bargaining. Some employers chose to recognize and negotiate with a single trade union rather than a plurality of them; others opted for single-table bargaining, with all their recognized unions brought together in a single bargaining unit with a single annual settlement date. Many of these employing enterprises also had their own company councils; and where trade union recognition lapsed or was refused in a newly established firm, the company council might provide a forum for representation and participation of the workforce.

Privatization up to 1990 affected British Telecommunications, Cable and Wireless, Jaguar, British Gas, British Airways, Rolls Royce, the British Airports Authority, British Steel, Electricity Generation and Supply, and the Water Authorities; further moves affected the coal industry, the railways, and other public sector organizations. Privatized companies were now free to develop their own business strategies and industrial relations arrangements in a competitive market environment. The Government strongly advocated competitive tendering.

Increasing inward investment in these years led to the establishment in Britain of many subsidiaries of foreign-owned multinational companies. Some were of European and Scandinavian parentage, but the most conspicuous were those of US, Japanese, and, later, Korean origins. A number of US-owned companies, such as Ford and Johnson & Johnson, had established subsidiaries in Britain before mid-century; other spectacularly new migrants, such as IBM and TI, arrived in the 1950s to be followed later by many others, including Hewlett Packard, Digital, NCR, and National Semiconductor. The Japanese began to arrive in conspicuous numbers in the late 1970s and the 1980s: Sony, Toshiba, Nissan, Toyota, Matsushita, Komatsu, to name but a few. With their 'world class' manufacturing operations, these companies were at the 'leading edge' in terms of product and product design, production methods and plant layout, the technology they used, and their approach to personnel policy and human resources management.

Many of the innovations, both theoretical and practical, brought to Britain by the migrants have been shown to be of American origin;[5] but it was the effective operationalizing of ideas and 'foreign knowledge' by the Japanese, and the consequent spectacular success of Japanese manufacturers in certain global markets, that caused the 1980s to be termed the 'decade of the Japanese'. Many of the features of 'excellent' US companies, identified by Peters and Waterman[6] in the early 1980s, were also characteristic of notably successful Japanese companies; and similar practices were said to have been adopted and adapted in certain ways and to a certain extent by several British companies to produce the so-called Japanization of British industry.[7] Some multinationals of British origin, such as ICI and Pilkington, were quick to move with the trend; other British companies were much slower off the mark.

Companies with what became widely acclaimed as Japanese 'world class manufacturing standards' at the 'leading edge' of modern industry had certain common characteristics; these were identified by Oliver and Wilkinson as: techniques of total quality control (TQC) usually involving the operation of 'quality circles'; 'just in time' (JIT) production methods often in association with the 'Kanban' system; flexible production systems based on flexible labour utilization and deployment; use of advanced computerized information technology sometimes involving 'group technology' or 'cellular manufacturing'; careful recruitment, induction, training and retraining of employees; relatively secure employment with labour retention fostered by 'company culture' and provision of harmonized employment conditions along with career prospects; industrial relations conducted via a company council or negotiation with a single union; and extensive systems for communication.

The basic idea of TQC is that quality control is an integral part of total quality management rather than a separate function of a quality control department; faults are identified and rectified with minimum delay and waste at the time of their occurrence rather than after the event. In other words, total quality control is built into the process of production. Schonberger[8] attributes the Japanese willingness to adopt TQC techniques to: (a) resource scarcity in Japan which exerted greater pressure than in the West for techniques to eliminate waste in the form of scrap and parts needing rectification, and (b) Japanese cultural values which have not embraced the dysfunctions of specialization in the organization of work and responsibility. The total quality concept is antithetical to the principles of scientific management, which sees each individual as concerned solely with his or her own area of work. Feigenbaum defines TQC approaches as systems that 'enable marketing, production and service at the most economic levels which allow for full customer satisfaction.'[9] This suggests tightly integrated organization, with efficiency in the use of resources, sufficient flexibility to respond readily to market requirements and customer preferences, and the capability of producing competitively priced goods of the desired quality.

The concept of 'quality circles' is fundamental to the idea of total quality control, and is one of the characteristics of Japanese manufacturing most loudly acclaimed in the West. Fortune and Oliver[10] define quality circles as small groups, usually of between five and ten people led by a foreman or team leader, who meet regularly to improve productivity and quality in their work areas. Members of quality circles are usually trained in simple statistical analysis and methods of problem-solving. While cynics, such as Briggs,[11] have derided quality circles as merely another coercive instrument of management, Yap[12] has applauded them as the means to increase motivation and commitment; such groups operated as 'participative mechanisms' which encouraged shopfloor involvement and led to greater job satisfaction, good management–employee relations, increased commitment, improved moral, and opportunities for 'self-actualization'.

JIT methods, like TQC, have been widely represented as one of the main reasons for Japan's spectacularly successful performance in certain world markets in the 1980s. As Schonberger has explained it: 'The JIT idea is simple: produce and deliver finished goods just-in-time to be sold, sub-assemblies just-in-time to be assembled into finished goods, fabricated parts just-in-time to go into the sub-assemblies, and purchased raw materials just-in-time to be transformed into fabricated parts.'[13] The aim is to minimize waste of both materials and time, to ensure that production is both 'last-minute and profitable', and to release capital for other purposes. This means eliminating non-value-added functions such as storage and 'buffer stocks', inspection, and movement of parts and finished goods about the factory – which add to costs but not value. The Kanban method is a means of reducing the quantity of stock in the system and of ensuring that materials and components are 'pulled through' corresponding to the needs of final assembly.[14]

Successful operation of JIT/Kanban systems requires swift machine set-up and simple uni-directional material flows. There is virtually no margin for error. It is for this reason that JIT methods function most effectively within systems of total quality management. Since materials and components are used quickly at each stage, errors and faulty parts can be detected swiftly, and the cause identified and remedied with minimal delay so as to avoid costly hold-ups to production and stockpiles of defective parts that have to be scrapped. Commonly cited advantages of JIT systems are reduced production costs, more efficient use of working capital, reduction of waste, and swifter responsiveness to customer demands and changing market preferences.

Companies at the 'leading edge' were quick to introduce productive equipment based on micro-electronics and advances in computerization and robotics. In some cases plant lay-out was improved by 'group' or 'cell' arrangement, which simplified the work-flow and enhanced flexibility of production; and, in addition, a more effective lay-out served to minimize the time, distance, and potential damage involved in moving components backwards and forwards from one part of the factory to another. All of this required a flexi-ble workforce, provision for skill acquisition and enlargement, and an absence of strict job and trade demarcations; and it also needed effective team work of the 'quality circle' kind.

An important aspect of policy to create a stable, versatile and co-operative workforce was careful attention to the screening, induction and training of recruits. Satisfactory performance in written and prac-tical tests was required; but equally desirable was 'attitude': moderate views, a balanced personality, and an inclination to endorse the company's ethos, culture and philosophy. An attractive total remu-neration package was an inducement to company loyalty. Where productive efficiency depended upon flexible labour utilization and deployment, the old job and skill boundaries had no place; neither did the fragmentation of a company's workforce through representation of separate groups by different trade unions, each with its own list of bargaining priorities, its own annual settlement date, and insistence on strict demarcations. It was for this reason that some of the com-panies setting up on greenfield sites refused to recognize trade unions, least of all a multiplicity of them, for bargaining purposes, and instead set up a company council with internally elected representa-tives from each main area of the factory; others chose to recognize and deal with a single union representing most of the workforce. The third alternative, single-table bargaining with two or more unions, was more often found at brownfield sites, particularly where a major restructuring of operations occurred.

Where a company needed flexible labour deployment, it made little sense to have substantially different terms, benefits and conditions of employment for different groups of employees in its permanent full-time workforce. 'Single status' conditions, 'common' terms and benefits, or 'harmonized' conditions were administratively simpler; and, in combination with single-unionism or single-table bargaining, would prevent the *ad hoc* growth or re-emergence of the rigidities of job and skill demarcations and restrictive practices.

Some British employers had been moving gradually in this dir-ection for many years, of their own accord, in the changing circumstances they encountered. From the time when Britain could no longer claim to be the world's leading industrial nation, British manufacturers and their advisers looked towards their overseas competitors for ways and means of improving their own performance, first to the USA, then to Germany, and more recently to Japan. Although for much of the present century the USA has provided the most attractive manufacturing models, the recent arrival of the Japanese on the British industrial scene heightened British employers' interest in the kind of production methods and personnel policies that seemed to account for their Japanese competitors' spectacular success. The challenge of the long-run recession, the spread of microelectronics technology, and the innovative practices and policies of their foreign rivals, spurred wider and faster innovation by British employers.

PRODUCTIVITY, LABOUR COSTS AND INDUSTRIAL RELATIONS, 1950–79

During the interwar years of economic recession and mass unemployment, numerically weakened trade unions had had poor bargaining clout, and prevailing circumstances facilitated the enforcement of managerial will. By the 1950s, that situation no longer obtained. Near-full employment, resurgent unions, escalating wages, and the increasing frequency of strikes during the two following decades were all manifestations of the shift in the balance of workplace power in favour of workforces and the unions. Generally low levels of unemployment until the later 1970s produced tight labour markets, an availability of abundant overtime in some sectors, and increasing employment opportunities for both men and women. Voluntary job changing was relatively easy, but, when jobs were to be surrendered involuntarily, workforces were in a powerful position to resist and protest.

The unions' ascendant influence was evidenced in their ability to raise earnings. Wage inflation was a constant worry for employers and Government ministers. The widening gap between basic wage rates settled in industry-wide national agreements and take-home pay enhanced by local shopsteward bargaining reflected the reality of power on the shopfloor. The shift of power was not only from employers to unions, but also within unions from national to local levels. The interplay between the formal and informal systems of bargaining, identified in the 1968 Donovan Report,[15] was producing leap-frogging local wage claims, demands for the restoration of pay relativities that led to wage-drift, the raising of basic rates claimed in national agreements, and the introduction of a wide variety of pay supplements and premium rates which resulted in highly complex wage structures. The desirability of PBR payment systems was now being questioned. Critics alleged that for the worker they caused 'disturbing fluctuations in earnings' from week to week, fostered self-ishness and jealousy 'at the cost of loyalty and co-operation', and propelled wage settlement away from the 'safeguards of collective bargaining' and into the 'arbitrary arena of rate-setting'. The results were endless occasions for disputes which interrupted production, and the loss of management's control over labour costs.[16] It was being strongly urged by 1967 that managements encumbered by compli-cated PBR systems should change over to a payment structure based on a high time-rate with measured day work or, where MDW was unsuitable, to a high time-rate and more efficient supervision.

In some respects, workplace power also shifted as a consequence of technological advance. Although, with the development of more complex and automated industrial processes, some job functions were routinized or even displaced, [17] others became increasingly skilled, demanding and responsible.[18] In large-scale capital-intensive com-panies, such as Imperial Chemical Industries, technological progress was rapid and resulted in ever larger and more costly plant with more sophisticated and intricate instrumentation.[19] Mistakes in the pro-duction area could be alarmingly expensive. This underlined the importance of the training the worker received and the care he or she took over the job. Highly skilled key workers were not readily replace-able, even in circumstances of generally high unemployment; when the labour market was tight, craftsmen were at an especially high premium. Key jobs in production and maintenance functions were more demanding of training, expertise and experience. The theoret-ical knowledge and skill training required of engineering and electrical craftsmen involved in the operating and monitoring processes, and the skill levels of others involved in the work of dismantling, erecting, repair and maintenance of plant, were often much greater than the skills required for routine kinds of office work. That the vocational training of craftsmen was both prolonged and mentally demanding meant that they were not in abundant supply. Where labour efficiency and productivity were as much a function of years of experience as of quality and quantity of training, labour retention could improve a company's cost-effectiveness and high labour turnover could reduce it. The persistent presence in a firm's workforce of many recent recruits, even with good formal qualifications, would serve to limit the extent to which efficiency could be improved. Work study, job evaluation and work measurement exercises, conducted in some of the major capital-intensive industries in these years, were producing some illuminating results; in some cases the value of highly skilled manual work was considerably greater, and the work itself more responsible and challenging, than routine clerical and lower-grade administrative tasks. Where technology demanded both skill and some years of practical experience, the net result was greatly to increase the power of shopfloor work groups to make their presence felt.

There was another feature of industrial relations, inherited from the past, which restricted the extent and ease of adjusting to a new reality. This constraint was in the range of items which management and unions had elected to discuss in the process of collective bargaining. As Roeber argues, it had been largely management's choice that negotiations had been confined to pay and conditions, and this choice had its origins in management's traditional view of what were appropriate subjects for settlement at the bargaining table. Managers now found themselves to be locked into a position from which there was no easy escape. At shopsteward level the unions had 'unofficially' and 'informally' acquired power over matters not conventionally covered by the process of collective bargaining. Esso's decision formally to put on the bargaining agenda the matter of work practices at its Fawley refinery represented the institutionalization of an informal power reality. By agreement with the unions, Esso brought in consultants whose investigations disclosed that performance at Fawley, especially in the sphere of labour costs, was poor in comparison with performance at other Esso refineries. However, the changes needed at Fawley were obstructed both by the power of the unions to insist upon the observance of demarcations, manning levels and restrictive practices, and by management's practice of providing systematic overtime to make up earnings. Management and shopstewards jointly discussed alternative approaches to dealing with the problem, and a catalogue of proposals – 'The Blue Book' – was produced in 1960 with the objective of drastically reducing overtime, abolishing craftsmen's mates, cutting tea breaks, and applying other cost-reducing measures. In return for agreeing to these changes, the workers were to receive a pay increase totalling 40 per cent. This was a path-breaking agreement, generally acknowledged as the first 'productivity deal'.

That other such agreements followed is testimony to the fact that shopfloor power was a force to be reckoned with in many major industrial sectors. Initially, it is true, there were relatively few productivity agreements; McKersie and Hunter estimate that there were 4 in 1963, 14 in 1964, 28 in 1965, and 27 in 1966. Thereafter there was a sharp rise: 761 between January 1967 and June 1968, 1107 between July and December 1968, 977 from January to June 1969, and 874 from July to December 1969.[20]

The rise in the number of productivity agreements concluded was attributed to the Labour Government's prices and incomes policy in 1965. A Government White Paper, issued that year, stated that pay increases above the norm laid down in incomes policy were permissible: 'Where the employees concerned...for example by accepting more exacting work or a major change in working practices, make a direct contribution towards increasing productivity in the particular firm or industry.'[21] The incomes policy in operation in 1965 and 1966 seems to have provided relatively weak stimulus to productivity bargaining; the dramatic rise in the number of such agreements after January 1967 is attributed to the stringency of the statutory incomes policy introduced that year.

The apparent decline of productivity bargaining after 1969 was generally explained in terms of management's disenchantment with empty agreements, but Flanders offers an alternative explanation: that productivity bargaining's loss of favour was largely due to change in the Government's approach to incomes policy and the growth of unemployment.[22] The legacy of 'something for something' bargaining lingered on, even so, in the form of self-financing pay deals in the 1970s, and was widely evident in the two following decades in the numerous 'flexibility agreements' reached in those years. These facilitated important changes in working practices, in the spheres of working methods, machine operation, manning levels, break times, workloads, job content and hours of work; and they were conducive to change in payment systems and structures. The longer-term effect of incomes policy, even after its abandonment after 1979, was to establish the criteria upon which improvements in terms and conditions were permissible. Both sides stood to gain something from agreements of this kind. Combative stances and brutally confrontational displays of power did not disappear from the collective bargaining arena overnight, of course; industrial relations in the 1970s were more turbulent than ever. The seed was sown, however, to germinate in the future.

Restrictive work practices, the rigidities of job and skill demarcations, job rights and trade boundaries presented the most formidable of problems for employers seeking to introduce more cost-efficient production methods to improve price competitiveness and develop new product lines. Contemporary press reports tended all too often to castigate the unions and shopfloor workers who applied such sanctions as premeditatedly obstructionist and childishly petty-minded in their attitude to change and the need to move with the times; but, as the Donovan Commission acknowledged, there were perfectly logical reasons for all restrictive work practices. They did not constitute a 'single-minded conspiracy to hold up production,' but they did present 'a serious obstacle to productive efficiency.'[23] The main forms of restrictionism were identified as: strict observance of job and skill demarcations, institutionalized over-manning, systematic and often spurious overtime working, restrictions on entry, direct restrictions on output and the work pace, and hostility to technological change. The strike was most extreme of the workshop sanctions strategically used by shopstewards; others included sudden 'down tools' lasting for a few hours, overtime bans, 'laying back' on the job, 'working to rule', 'withdrawal of goodwill', the 'go slow', putting on the heat, and various tactics to waste management's time with trivia. Inevitably, there was tension between employers seeking to innovate in order to improve business performance and workers seeking to maintain the *status quo* in order to protect their jobs and to preserve them in a familiar and accustomed form. The building industry, vehicles, shipbuilding, marine engineering, and metals engineering were particularly affected by demarcation disputes.

Craftsmen had a long established historical tradition, and a well respected reputation, as guardians of skills against encroachment by untrained or unqualified people; and this had been condoned by employers as a means of maintaining quality standards. But practices which had once served the best interests of both employers and craft workers now functioned as impediments to industrial advance: 'Technological change seems to have been largely responsible for transforming what were once common sense divisions between crafts into restrictive demarcations.'[24] New technology, new divisions of labour, new specializations, new processes, all threatened the craftsmen's security; not only did changes undermine his employment protection, but they also affected his craft prestige, his earnings differential, his job satisfaction, and his occupational identity.

In several key industries endemic over-manning was the main cause of inefficiency in the utilization of labour; it served to maintain labour costs at a higher level than was necessary and practicably possible. In essence, over-manning was a matter of employing more manpower than was actually required for a job to be done. Over-manning meant that workers, in effect, were under-employed, though in full-time attendance and in receipt of full-time pay; it was deplored by H.A. Clegg as 'one of the major scandals of the British economy.' Hundreds of thousands of workers, he claimed, were being paid though 'doing nothing for a considerable part of their working time.' Craftsmen's mates, for example, were as much a symbol of the craftsman's status as an adjunct to his skill. The mates waited, sometimes for hours, until the craftsmen found something for them to do; and craftsmen often stood idle waiting for a member of another craft to do work which they themselves were capable of or could soon be trained to do.[25] Over-manning, like contrived overtime working, reduced productive efficiency, pushed up the wages bill and total production costs, affected the selling price of goods and services, and therefore put British employers at a disadvantage in both domestic and overseas markets. From the workers' standpoint, overtime was the most simple and direct means of boosting the level of take-home pay: 'Workers spin out jobs in order to obtain the premium rates paid for overtime. Such premia have become an integral part of the pay packet.'[26] By being permanently maintained at a high level, overtime had come to be built into a firm's wage structure and its labour policy, and it had become institutionalized in shopfloor practices, work habits and expectations.

Control of the work pace and restriction of output by workforces similarly served to inhibit management's attempts to improve efficiency. In some cases workers placed fixed limits on output from the machines they used; in other operations, such as packing, they set limits which were well below what, on measurable average, could be reasonably expected. Sometimes they set fixed times for jobs such as the oiling and cleaning of machines, without reference to any work-study measurement of the time actually needed to permit the job to be done.

Some restrictive practices were the time-worn legacy of tradition which had no place in the modern world; others were the result of lax management. Over a long period of time, Roberts observes, harassed management had gradually conceded to unions the right to regulate the entry of workers into particular occupations and the right to determine how they should be employed; under conditions of full employment, management had 'surrendered such rights to a greater degree than in any other advanced industrial country.'[27]

Productivity bargaining, directly and indirectly fostered by the Government's incomes policy, offered the means to gain work-people's acquiescence in innovations in manpower utilization necessitated by industrial and technological advance. Restrictive practices could not be eradicated unilaterally and at a stroke by the simple expedient of exercising management's traditional, but now circumscribed, 'right to manage'. In Gunter Frederick's words: 'Productivity bargaining is bargaining to make changes acceptable.'[28]

The significance of productivity bargaining in the history of the changing nature of the workplace divide is that such deals were the medium by which staff status arrangements for manual workers were introduced in a number of major employing enterprises. Proposals to put manual grades on to staff status sprang almost invariably from employers and their management consultants. Most productivity pacts were a simple 'Persian market' exchange of pay increases from the employer in return for concessions on working practices from workforces; but, as Bugler[29] noted in 1965, some employers were taking 'firm steps...towards diminishing, or even totally abolishing, the manual/non-manual distinction' in terms, benefits and employment conditions. Major moves were underway as part of productivity agreements in Electricity Supply, BEA, BOAC, Mobil Oil, Esso, Unilever, ICI and several chemical and engineering companies, to raise manual grades to staff status. The precedents set by these innovators established the 'probable pattern of development in much of British industry.'

RECESSION, UNCERTAINTY AND THE QUEST FOR FLEXIBILITY SINCE 1979

Labour mobility has long been recognized as a crucial factor in economic growth and development. Movement between sectors, enterprises, occupations and regions was essential to permit structural change in the economy as a whole. In the 1960s attention had focused not only on the problem of rigidity in national, regional and local labour markets, but also on constraints imposed on firms' internal labour markets by restrictive work practices and trade demarcations. Employers, as we have seen, were beginning to find ways and means to the relaxation of constraints such as these. With the economic downturn of the later 1970s and the onset of a recession that would persist for many years, employers, encountering ever keener competition for shrinking domestic and global markets, were faced with the need for change in their business strategies; and these, in turn, created a need for change in personnel policy and human resources management.

The experience of market uncertainties and volatility in the 1970s led to a widening recognition of the need for flexibility sufficient to permit a company to respond readily, rapidly and cost-effectively to capricious market demands. Labour flexibility, permitting freer interchange of tasks between different groups of workers, was by no means a new concept. It found much favour amongst employers in the early-1970s, and in the latter half of that decade they showed a renewed interest in productivity schemes and training arrangements to facilitate labour interchangeability.[30] The pressures to adapt intensified in the 1980s with the onward rush of new information technology, robotics, computerization and developments in microelectronics generally. The combination of the long-run recession and technological advance had the most profound of implications not only for employers' business decisions but also for their labour requirements. In 1984 Atkinson produced his model of the flexible firm and 'manning for uncertainty'.[31] The simple expedient of eradicating restrictive practices and dismantling demarcations was no longer sufficient in itself. What was needed now was a far more radical reappraisal, with training and retraining in new skills, new combinations of skills, dual or multiple skills, and greater adaptability on the part of both operatives and maintenance workers. The proliferation of redundancies caused by the recession and technological displacement, employment insecurity, and a persistently high level of unemployment prevailing generally, meant that employers were now in a powerful position *vis-à-vis* unions and workforces to implement policies to achieve their objectives.

Investigation carried out for NEDO[32] towards the mid-1980s identified three major pressures for change and two main facilitators of it. One pressure was employers' desire to consolidate productivity gains in response to the keenly competitive economic environment so as to enable them to take advantage of any upturn in trade. Their aim was to cut costs, especially the labour element of their costs. Reduction of capacity, plant closures and an associated shedding of labour provided opportunity for employers to make cuts in the most troublesome areas; restrictive work practices tended to be a major consideration in decisions concerning which plants to close. The second pressure was the volatility of markets; firms were apparently feeling the need to develop 'manning practices which enable them to adjust to larger and increasingly unpredictable fluctuations.'[33] The third pressure was technological change. The storm of microelectronics technology, which had been gathering in the 1960s, had reached gale force in the later 1970s and assumed hurricane proportions in the 1980s. This created a need for new manning practices to match the technology of the present and to permit accommodation to future technological advance. The effect of heightened competition during the recession was to encourage employers who could afford to do so to invest in more advanced equipment which enabled a much larger amount of work to be done by a much smaller workforce. If such systems were to operate with maximum efficiency, maintenance had to be sufficient to avoid frequent interruptions and prolonged breakdowns for down-time was more costly than with slower and less-integrated systems.

There had been pressures of this kind for many years, but they had intensified during the worst years of the recession and showed no sign of abating during upturns in trade. Better use of equipment was essential to improved cost-efficiency; as the Director General of the Engineering Employers' Federation stated in 1983:

> We need to make maximum use of plant and machinery by eliminating restrictive practices, by having full flexibility between and within trades and occupations and between supervisor and supervised... In order to make better use of plant and equipment, our member companies need to be able to adopt flexible working times when required.[34]

It seems unlikely, even so, that innovation in labour deployment and utilization would have spread so markedly without what Atkinson and Meager term 'two important facilitators': the state of the labour market and the state of industrial relations. The sharp rise of unemployment and its persistence at a high level, despite the recovery of output, produced generally slack labour markets, so that employers had little difficulty in recruiting locally certain kinds and quantities of labour, thus escaping the necessity to maintain headcount during troughs in the workload. Extra labour could be hired when, and for as long as, it was needed, on contracts designed for that purpose. Poor prospects in the job market undoubtedly encouraged the willingness of the employed to accept the changes in working practices sought by employers, and increased the inclination of the unemployed to accept work which was temporary or short-term. At the same time, with the decline in membership and weakened bargaining power, the trade unions were in a relatively poor position to resist, oppose or impede the changes in employment proposed by management. Employers who had declared numerous redundancies had experienced little difficulty in gaining workpeople's acquiescence in flexible working practices.[35]

The TUC recognized the inevitability of going with the flow of new computerized technology and the steady shift from traditional mechanical and electrical engineering to microelectronics; the aim was to control rather than obstruct innovation so as to protect jobs. It was recognized that traditional attitudes, methods, structures and skills were becoming less and less compatible with the needs of modern production. As Eric Hammond, general secretary of the electricians' union acknowledged:

> Technology has exploded on these old structures of status and pay, both between and within crafts. Production, process, and craft pay differentials, which largely reflected the old levels of skills, have now become outdated.[36]

That union's brochure contained the statement that:

> Technological progress is vital to industrial survival... Our concern is to ensure that it is successfully harnessed, not fearfully rejected by the industrial backwoodsmen in some short-sighted emotional spasm... Productive, profitable, and competitive employers offer better rewards and more long-term job security for their work-forces than those who stick to old-fashioned methods and products.[37]

Attitudes such as these were not confined to the craft unions. Joe Mills, a regional secretary of the TGWU, asserted at a conference on flexible manning that the unions were not opposed to the idea of flexibility 'provided that it does not threaten or replace existing full-time workers,' and provided also that employers made some concessions in return for workpeople's acceptance of it. The kind of concessions the unions had in mind were guarantees of job security, a 35-hour week, improved holiday entitlements, and the harmonization of manual workers' conditions with those of staff employees.[38]

The flexible manning of flexible firms created core and peripheral sectors of employment. The core group contained those involved in a firm's central or key activities; employees were functionally flexible and their employment was full-time and relatively secure. The peripheral sector was numerically adjustable, and contained groups with a high voluntary turnover and others engaged on contracts designed to permit the ready expansion and contraction of numbers corresponding to the rise and fall of demand for them. Firms with innovatory business strategies tended to use one or a combination of both types of labour flexibility.

The stable core group contained full-time permanent career employees who had access to primary labour markets within the firm. Employment security could be maintained in the medium term, since the number of core workers did not vary directly with changes in total output. Functional flexibility, which reinforced employment stability, was furthered by training, retraining and redeployment – a process which was facilitated by harmonized employment conditions, frequently involving salaried status with a degree of pay progression, plus a range of fringe benefits related to long service with the same organization. Manning adjustments in core employment tended to be qualitative rather than quantitative, resting on versatility and skill acquisition. Career advancement and promotion prospects were favourable; the level of earnings was set by an incremental payment structure, with upward progression determined by the acquisition and deployment of skills and acceptance of greater responsibility, rather than by length of service.

The peripherally employed fell into three main groups. One contained employees on permanent contracts but with much less job security than those in the core, and with few opportunities for career advancement and promotion. Flexibility was quantitative and achieved by expanding and contracting numbers through recruitment and severance. The skills involved were general rather than firm-specific, with jobs fairly readily mastered and requiring little training. Since the level of pay and other terms and benefits were generally inferior to what was available for core employees, the per capita payroll cost for the company was lower. A characteristically high level of voluntary leaving assisted the process of numerical adjustment.

A second peripheral segment, and one which again facilitated numerical adjustability and labour cost savings for the company, contained employees on contracts designed to make severance cheap and simple by avoiding some of the constraints and compensations fixed in legislation relating to redundancy and unfair dismissal. There was nothing illegal about contracts of this kind. The group included temporary workers, workers on fixed-term contracts, job-sharers, part-timers and government-subsidized trainees. The rise of temporary forms of employment, including trainees on schemes such as YTS, often functioned as a form of delayed recruitment or extended probation before permanent employment was offered. Pay, benefits and conditions were said to be 'less attractive still' and such workers had fewer statutory employment rights.

A third type of numerical flexibility took the form of out-sourcing, subcontracting and the use of the self-employed to deal with ancillary activities and fluctuations in the workload. None of this was new; the main change was the increased use of such resources. For employers a main advantage was that some of the risk and some of the costs were projected on to agencies outside the company. Here, the employment contract was replaced by a commercial contract; the usual terms, benefits and employment conditions settled by agreement in the process of collective bargaining were not part of these commercial contracts.

Peripheral groups tended to have low job security, restricted training and career opportunities, and substantially inferior conditions, especially with regard to paid holidays, sick pay and pensions. Peripheral employment was not confined to low grade manual work. Core and peripheral sectors each contained both manual and non-manual occupations; a new workplace divide was emerging and becoming more distinct than the traditional manual/non-manual division.

Core sectors contained managerial, administrative, certain clerical and also operative and craft maintenance grades. It was the individual and group versatility of operative and maintenance workers that was becoming increasingly important to improvement in the firm's business performance.

Several types of functional flexibility were identified by Kirosingh[39] at the end of the 1980s. One of these was trade flexibility. Flexibility between trades ranged from relatively small changes that broke down demarcations which were not based on the existing capabilities of workers, to much more fundamental change which involved the worker's acquisition of new skills and performance of a group of work tasks formerly considered to be the preserve of two or more different trades. Between these two extremes were changes to increase the overlap between trades.

Attention tended to focus mainly on engineering craftsmen, particularly those involved in maintenance, but agreements at Continental Can, Lucas Aerospace, Richard Sizer, and Westland had established more flexible manning or multi-machine manning among operatives, most of whom were classed as semi-skilled or unskilled. This was 'lateral' flexibility. There were other agreements which sought 'vertical' flexibility between semi-skilled operatives and the craft trades.

Agreements for downward flexibility, with craft workers taking on some semi-skilled functions, were more usual than for upward flexibility involving the semi-skilled in the performance of what are conventionally regarded as craft tasks. However, as Kirosingh observes, the 'simplification of diagnostic procedures and setting and re-setting, made possible by new technology, has meant that the jobs of operatives have become enriched.' An agreement at James Howden, reached in 1984, enabled operatives to carry out programme modification and debugging.

A proliferating number of agreements reached in the 1980s contained clauses relating to functional flexibility; and most of the negotiated changes came about through collective bargaining on other issues – such as union claims for shorter working time[40] and companies' proposals to harmonize conditions.[41] The CBI's information on collective agreements reached between 1981 and 1985 suggested that some 60 per cent of all manufacturing establishments had at least one flexibility clause in their pay settlements and that a substantial proportion had several such clauses. Agreements on functional flexibility appear to fall into three main categories. A large number of them were simply broad 'enabling' agreements containing a general commitment from the unions to co-operate in innovations sought by management. Other agreements listed specific changes in precise detail; and still others combined a few specific changes with a general commitment to greater flexibility in working.

The peripheral sector, mainly comprising groups in various kinds of 'non-standard' employment, had been growing since mid-century and formed rather more than one third of the country's total workforce by 1987. There was every likelihood of further increase in this sector, for, as Hakim[42] noted at the time, the business cycle appeared to have very small impact within the long-term trend and it could not be assumed that a future return to economic prosperity and full employment would reverse the growth of jobs which were less than permanent and less than full-time. The non-standard sector was, and still is, more heterogeneous than the standard sector in which employment is typically regular, stable and continuous.

The distribution by industry of all forms of non-standard

employment varied immensely; it accounted for over 40 per cent of employment in building and construction, retail distribution, hotels, catering, repairs, public administration, professional and scientific services, and agriculture; but it was less than 10 per cent in energy and water supply, chemicals, minerals extraction and manufacture, metal goods, engineering, and vehicles.

It is erroneous to assume that all non-standard kinds of work are menial, manual and low-paid, as investigations undertaken in the early 1990s by Hunter and MacInnes and by McGregor and Sproull have shown.[43] They identified two broad but distinct categories. One comprised skilled craftsmen, technically qualified personnel and professionals, and included draughtspersons, design engineers, architects, computer programmers, and self-employed people with specialist technical skills; most of these were males, working freelance or through agencies and earned relatively high incomes. The other broad category was larger and more diverse, and contained both manual and non-manual groups. Here, the skills were routine, general or minimal, and tended to be readily transferable, and women outnumbered men in jobs such as catering, cleaning and domestic work, shop work and the distributive trades in general, nursing and auxiliary services, and routine kinds of administrative, clerical and secretarial work. For some of these, pay could be very low indeed.

In general, the main advantage for employers, and disadvantage for non-standard employees, was that elements of the total remuneration package – such as profit-sharing, special bonuses, holiday entitlement, cover for occupational pension and sick pay, and other fringe benefits – were much less frequently provided. In other words, the employer could reduce fixed employment costs associated with standard employment, by offering non-standard employment contracts. Similarly, the employer who out-sourced certain functions to the self-employed, or to sub-contractors through competitive tendering by them, could avoid PAYE and NI costs. Some observers have deplored the growth of part-time and temporary employment, which carries fewer and weaker employment rights and protections; but, as Hakim notes, there is evidence that casts doubt on the assumption that permanent full-time work is the universal preference. There is little sign of contraction of the non-standard sector of employment with the economic upturn and falling unemployment of the mid and later 1990s.

3 Staff Status and Harmonized Conditions: The British Models?

INTRODUCTION

Employers and managers, it is generally accepted, have three main areas of responsibility: business performance to satisfy stock and share holders with attractive returns on their investments; decisions about the quantity, quality and type of goods and services they provide to satisfy customers, in the light of changing domestic and overseas market preferences; and the employment and remuneration of labour in the context of change both in the firm's employment requirements and labour market circumstances. Decisions are influenced by the rate and nature of technological advance, the changing framework of the Government's economic policy and legislation directly and indirectly affecting business activity, and the state of domestic and global trade.

Effective management of human resources has always been an important aspect of employers' strategies to improve business performance. In essence, this meant attention to recruiting, retaining or discarding, controlling, and motivating workpeople. Recruitment involved an ability to attract job seekers in sufficient numbers and of suitable quality to meet the firm's labour requirements. People with relevant skills, and especially the newer flexible skills demanded by advanced technology, were often difficult to find; and in circumstances of near full employment, even generalist skills and basic competence were not in ready supply. Retention called for the means to discourage voluntary leaving, particularly on the part of those who were most useful for the company's purposes and most difficult to replace; but change in markets, technology and the state of trade presented the problem of shedding labour no longer required, and of doing so against the opposition of trade unions and within an evolving legal framework which affected the employer's ability to hire and fire at will. While retention might be aided by an attractive total remuneration package, discharge of workers who had committed no

41

offence to warrant dismissal might be facilitated by engaging them, where appropriate, on contracts designed to that end.

Effective control of labour was a multi-dimensional problem. It came to involve flexible deployment and utilization of human resources, the means to raise labour productivity and curb labour costs, and the need to train and retrain people according to the demands of new technology, new production methods and new goods to be produced; it meant attention to absenteeism, time-keeping, manning levels, overtime working, restrictive work practices and skill demarcations, and the climate of industrial relations. At the same time there was growing recognition by the more progressive employers of the need for better means than money alone to improve people's motivation to work. The morale of the workforce has obvious, though unquantifiable implications for productivity; people who feel that they are appreciated, valued, and fairly treated are the more likely to work purposefully, willingly and co-operatively, and to feel an identification with the company, its ethos, and its objectives.

The long-established workplace divide, with manual grades treated differently and less favourably than non-manual staff, was alienating for those who were constantly confronted with their inferior status as second-class citizens. Their attitude and reactions might take the negative forms of apathy, indifference and a passive uninvolvement; or they might harden into the positive forms of embittered truculence, intransigence at the bargaining table, confrontational displays of power, and resort to strike action.

It was the experience of practical difficulties in recruitment, retention, motivation and control of their human resources that caused some of the more thoughtful employers to consider the possibility of putting manual workers on staff status. But if there was a strong element of practical self-interest in the innovations in personnel policy which employers introduced, there is also evidence of what Hand[1] identified in 1968 as 'a streak of idealism'. At least some employers and managers believed it to be 'genuinely anomalous' that there should exist in the workplace a class system which seemed to discriminate against and actively discourage the kind of worker-employer relations that might foster 'a sense of unity and common purpose.'

Early staff status schemes of the 1940s and 1950s tended at the outset to be sectional and selective in that they applied to individuals or small groups who were upgraded on the basis of long service and/or the value of their skills. Some of the staff status arrangements which followed in the 1960s were more ambitious in covering the majority of manual workers in permanent full-time employment, though more limited in providing some but not all of the terms, benefits and conditions available to office staffs. In the 1980s and thereafter it was more usual for employers and management consultants to talk in terms of the harmonization of conditions.

STAFF STATUS FOR SOME

In so far as British companies had status arrangements in the 1940s and 1950s, it was the selective scheme which was typical. The engineering firm, S. Smith & Sons (later Smiths Industries),[2] whose range of products included car accessories, aircraft instruments, clocks and watches, introduced a staff status scheme as early as 1946 for highly skilled craftsmen. In practice, this meant toolmakers. The scheme, Hand claims, was 'purely a matter of social policy', with the expectation of 'nothing in return for the company', but the fact that staff status was confined to the highly skilled, suggests that its intended function at this stage was as a merit award, reflecting the company's desire to acknowledge the special value it placed upon its craftsmen, and its need to attract and retain them in times of change following the Second World War.

There was a tendency, which became more clearly apparent in the 1970s, for staff conditions initially given selectively to one group, to be extended later to others. This was the path taken by Smiths Industries, for in 1960 staff status was extended to all employees with a specified minimum period of service with the company. This did not mean that most employees moved to staff conditions immediately, or even all at the same time, for the minimum service qualification differed quite substantially for different grades, and meant that a relatively large number of manual workers would remain on non-staff conditions for some time. In fact, some of them would remain there for a *long* time – and quite a few for the whole of their working lives at Smiths. The qualifying period of service was to remain at two years for toolmakers; for other skilled grades it was to be five years, but for the semi-skilled, unskilled and women it was to be as long as ten years.

Employees were not explicitly asked for anything in return, but the company nevertheless believed that the 'removal of illogical inequalities' could lead to improved industrial relations and a more stable labour force, and that, in time, better relations with the shopfloor and increased co-operation might result in greater effort in response to the company's enlightened attitude. The fact that the service qualification was as long as ten years for the semi-skilled, the unskilled and women, amongst whom frequent job changing is characteristic, strongly suggests that the company was seeking to create a stable labour force by encouraging and rewarding the loyalty and commitment of job-stayers. The opportunity for both male and female unskilled manual workers to attain staff status, as the company's chairman, Mr Ralph Gordon-Smith, asserted at the time, was 'something unique' in industry generally, and unprecedented in the engineering industry which tended to be 'traditional' and 'old-fashioned' in its attitude to the desirability of 'breaking down the distinctions in status between the white collar and the overalls.' There would be a cost to the company in extending staff conditions to larger numbers but, conjecturally, there would be gains: greater stability of trained labour, and more loyalty, commitment and enterprising effort. As the company chairman saw it: 'We must do what is conducive to get and keep the best.'

The extended scheme introduced by Smiths did not completely align all the terms and benefits of manual and non-manual grades, but it substantially reduced the differentials. Upgraded manual workers qualified for coverage by the staff sick pay scheme, which provided up to three weeks' paid sick leave per annum for those with less than one year's service, rising to nine weeks after six years' service. It was believed that the possibility of inviting increased resort to sickness absence was a risk that 'any forward-thinking management' had to take in introducing 'something which is theoretically right.' On gaining staff status the manual worker became eligible to join the same contributory pension scheme as the white-collar staff. The scheme's rules and regulations were identical for all, but office staff would generally receive a higher retirement pension because its amount was based partly on level of earnings and partly on years of pensionable service. Some of the manual grades had lower earnings than office staff and, with five or ten years of employment before acquiring staff status, would have a shorter period of pensionable service.

Holiday entitlement for all those classed as staff, whether manual or non-manual, was the same and better than for those without staff status. The former continued to be paid hourly rates rather than a weekly or monthly salary like the office personnel, but all received premium-rated overtime pay for any extra hours worked, and all were 'on the clock'. Desegregation of canteen facilities was underway towards the end of the 1960s, and the company had plans for further reduction of differentials. The gap between the two broad occupational groups was narrowing, and it was expected to have been 'closed completely in all respects' in a few years time.

Armstrong Patents and Fisons[3] were also early in the field in introducing staff status for certain manual grades in the mid-1950s. The main stated objective in both cases was to attract and retain skilled craftsmen by rewarding loyalty, long service, and the value of the work performed. Like the arrangement at Smiths, these schemes were unilaterally introduced by management and were not subject to negotiation and formal agreement with trade unions. Again, the criteria for selection of those to be promoted to staff conditions were decided by management. Common characteristics of those two staff status schemes were: improved fringe benefits and greater predictability and stability of earnings in the form of a 'manual salary' at Armstrong Patents and an 'assured wage' at Fisons.

The main qualifications for promotion to staff grade at Fisons appear to have been 'reliability', 'good regular service', and a minimum of three years' continuous employment with the company. Full-time workers and part-timers working at least 20 hours per week spread over five days were eligible. The company's intention, as explained in a booklet issued to all its employees, was 'to give appropriate status and better security of earnings than that provided by Social Security Benefits to those wage workers considered suitable by the management.' The scheme introduced in 1955 was rather limited in scope, but it set in motion a longer-term process which in the distant future would eradicate the workplace divide at Fisons.

At Armstrong Patents staff conditions were offered in recognition of special craft skills in order to encourage particularly valuable workers to remain with the company at a time of an acute shortage of the kind of skills required in the production process. Those raised to staff status received an annual salary paid weekly, a higher grade rate, and overtime and shift premia related to the new rate. They worked a basic week of 38.5 hours compared with 40 for manual grades and 37 for office staff. Their holiday entitlement was increased and aligned with that of white-collar grades; cover for sick pay became 'almost identical' to the arrangement for junior office staff, and the pension schemes for works staff and office staff were said to be 'similar'. These arrangements, like those at Fisons, would be improved, enlarged and extended in the future.

STAFF STATUS FOR ALL

Other British companies introducing staff status in these years undertook to apply their policies to all their manual workers employed in a full-time capacity. Again, change stemmed from management initiative. In some cases there was no direct union involvement in the decisions taken; in others the arrangement was subject to extensive consultation and negotiation with union officials. Whether there was union involvement or non-involvement in the wholesale approach appears to have depended on whether workforces were already extensively organized and whether management sought concessions in working practices as part of a productivity pact.

A typical example of a large company initiating wholesale change without formal negotiation and agreement with the unions was cited by the Industrial Society[4] in a report published in 1970. The company in question was a British firm of brewers with a workforce of around 1,500, relatively few of whom were union members. This was an old-established family firm in a semi-rural area. Its workforce comprised 1,150 hourly-paid manual workers (including 250 women), 210 clerical and administrative employees on weekly pay, and 140 managers and supervisors on monthly salaries. In 1967 the production director drew up a five-year programme for removing arbitrary differences between groups of workers, and 'considerable progress' appears to have been made by 1970.

One of the first changes was to abolish clocking and formally to describe the whole workforce as 'staff'. Management believed that there was 'no moral justification for expecting one class of worker to clock and not another'. Requiring manual workers to clock on and off suggested that they were not trustworthy, and management felt that this was 'the cause of a great deal of resentment' and was thus 'harmful to good relations'. When clocking was abandoned, responsibility for recording time worked, necessary for purposes of calculating overtime pay, was taken over by supervisors after preparatory briefing and a trial period of three weeks. Eighteen months later, morale was said to be higher and time-keeping 'not significantly worse'.

Other common conditions which had been established by 1970 included provision for redundancy and resettlement allowances. All were covered by the same pension scheme; except for top management who joined the scheme in their first year, all gained coverage after a qualifying period of two years' service. The sick pay scheme was common to all, although differences remained in the qualifying period of service required for membership and receipt of benefits.

Some differences remained but these were to be tackled in further stages of the five-year programme. Holiday entitlements differed and favoured more senior and longer serving employees. Canteen facilities were segregated, but management was anxious to introduce common dining room facilities with no status barriers on seating or menus. It was hoped also that a job evaluation exercise would ultimately lead to a common pay and grading structure with all employees paid monthly.

Union density was low, but management was open-minded about union membership. The intention was to continue to provide attractive terms and benefits so that employees would not feel a need for union representation through any sense of frustration but, rather, through a perceived need for an effective negotiating system.

The company already had a series of consultative committees for the factory workforce. Workers' representatives, supervisors and departmental managers met regularly every month, and the meetings provided the occasion for discussion, consultation and briefing. There was no comparable communication channel for office staff, but management was fully aware of the need, and intended to set up white-collar consultative committees similar to those in operation for works employees.

Another firm, whose policy applied across the board and did not involve negotiation and agreement with the unions, was a small chemical company[5] sited on a large industrial estate and surrounded by other chemical and allied companies of national repute. In contrast to its larger neighbours, the company employed a workforce of only 250. The Industrial Society found that 'the trade unions do not play an obviously significant part', and whilst managers 'do not have a deliberate policy of keeping the unions out, union growth is slow'.

The policy stemmed from management's decision to establish common terms, benefits, and conditions for all its employees. It was a decision taken early in the 1960s and implementation took five years to achieve. The practical objective was to recruit and retain a reliable workforce, but the policy was also a matter of principle reflecting management's belief that in modern industry there was no logical reason for maintaining differentials in terms and benefits related simply to collar colour.

Implementation of the policy was relatively trouble-free. This may be partially attributable to low unionization and to the fact that most of the company's employees came from a fishing or shipping background rather than from manufacturing industry. It meant that, although many had some difficulty in getting used to chemical smells and working indoors, they did not bring with them conventional shopfloor attitudes. It seems likely that, amongst people from such backgrounds, the regular working week offered by the company was prized: 'Free weekends are valued.' Much of the success in implementing the policy was due to careful preparation by management, a period of experiment, gradual introduction of change in orderly stages, and a shrewd approach to recruitment.

Most of the intended changes had been made by 1970. The company had a three 8-hour shift system and a five-day week. Basic pay was high, and, although gross pay was less than could be earned elsewhere in the area, this was compensated by the free weekend, which was valued. The non-contributory sick pay arrangement was identical for all; it was introduced initially for specific groups and over a two-year period was extended gradually to cover the whole workforce.

The next step was to remove clocking for those with at least one year's service, and to introduce a monthly pay period. Only about 2 per cent of employees objected to being paid monthly, and only 'one or two' took advantage of the abolition of clocking. The company's pension scheme, with the employee's contribution amounting to 6 per cent of salary, applied across the board. By 1970 there were common dining room facilities, with the same menus for all.

The company reported that, with the establishment of common terms and conditions, labour was being retained and productivity had increased, but the extent to which increased per-man output was attributable to the new personnel policy was difficult to quantify because productivity had been affected also by other variables such as changes in machines and supervision. Management was sufficiently satisfied with the effect of the policy as to reduce the service qualification for staff status from one year to three months. There had been 'some grumbles' from longer established office personnel about the narrowing of differentials; but their complaint that service and experience ought to be reflected in salaries seems to have been answered by the introduction of a job-evaluated payment scheme.

Other staff status schemes covering entire workforces were the subject of negotiation and agreement with the unions. These were characteristic of the 1960s, tended to be part of a productivity deal requiring reciprocal concessions from manual workforces, and, in the later years of the decade, were affected by incomes policy. The effect of changing technology upon job content and skill requirement, an associated need to reduce rigidities produced by demarcations and restrictive practices, together with the high-cost problem of overmanning and institutionalized overtime working, all served to focus management's attention on the possibilities of staff status as a means of resolving their difficulties. Upgraded conditions were offered as part of a 'trade off' for unions' acceptance of changes sought by management. Again, the effect was to provide manual workers with annual salaries and an improved range of benefits. Although manual workers did not necessarily receive a total remuneration package identical in all respects with that available to white-collar staff, the result was significantly to reduce the differential between the two broad groups.

During the later 1960s a number of companies were operating very similar staff status arrangements introduced via local productivity agreements. These companies were mainly in the chemical and related industries, where, as we have seen, status changes were already in progress without formal agreement with unions. The main lead in the chemical industry, in effecting status changes through productivity bargaining, appears to have been given by ICI in 1965; other companies followed with similar negotiated agreements in accordance with the guidelines on productivity bargaining produced by the Chemical Industries' Association in 1967 and agreed with the unions at national level.[6] The 1967 national agreement recognized the need for full productivity bargaining during the period of stringent incomes policy in order to counter some of the problems of a capital-intensive technologically advanced, science-based industry. The industry required higher levels of labour efficiency to make more effective use both of existing and new productive equipment. It required a labour force which had appropriate skills, was compliant in adapting to change and increasing its efficiency through work experience and retraining, and was disposed to remain with the company. Equally urgently, it needed a reduction of the high levels of overtime working which had become firmly rooted in many companies, and fundamental alteration to traditional divisions of work which by now were unsuited to complex technology. ICI's staff status policy is noteworthy for its vast scope and the sheer size of the employing enterprise to which it applied; if agreements in other chemical companies grabbed fewer and smaller headlines in the press, this is explainable in terms not of less imaginative concept, but of the relatively smaller scale of the companies in question.

Amongst companies in the chemical industry, which negotiated status agreements under the CIA's 1967 guidelines on productivity bargaining, were Philblack, Dow Corning, and Albright & Wilson.[7] The agreements ultimately covered all process and maintenance workers employed by each company, and provided annual salaries based on job evaluation to replace hourly rates, combined with improvements in sick pay, holiday entitlements and pension arrangements in return for acceptance of substantial reductions in overtime hours and acquiescence in more flexible working. These agreements were intended not only to create the practical conditions conducive to achieving the changes needed in working practices for increased efficiency, but also to improve industrial relations generally. Agreements at all three companies had the elimination of all but essential overtime as a stated objective. Since 'manual staff' would no longer be paid by the hour, some alternative provision for overtime compensation (bearing in mind the planned reduction of overtime) had to be incorporated into new job-evaluated salary payment structures. The manual workforces in question thus gained relatively stable earnings which did not depend upon, nor fluctuate greatly with, overtime working; in return they agreed to a range of flexibilities between crafts and jobs.

A few more staff status schemes were introduced during the 1970s; the rather slow rate of change is probably attributable to the restraints of prices and incomes policies imposed by the Government. With the abandonment of incomes policy towards the end of that decade, there followed a marked surge of interest in what was now termed the harmonization of conditions. Developments were not confined to a few prosperous sectors at the 'leading edge' of economic growth, but were to be found also in longer-established industries and in organizations struggling for survival in a progressively more competitive economic environment. Deregulation of the labour market and decentralization of collective bargaining in the 1980s removed some of the constraints which had inhibited companies' ability to adopt innovative approaches to personnel policy. Increasingly the focus of attention widened to take in the possibilities of harmonizing in the areas of pay and grading structure, method and frequency of pay, opportunities for pay and career progression, basic working hours, time-recording and procedures for monitoring time-keeping. Greenfield sites apart, the equalization of terms and conditions tended to occur as a process of gradual change; since costs to be borne by the employer had to be weighed against the benefits likely to be forthcoming to the company, 'little by little' was usually preferable to the 'one fell swoop' approach.

In its survey of fifty organizations, conducted late in 1993, *Industrial Relations Review and Report*[8] found that most of the recent moves towards harmonized conditions had occurred in the areas of method of pay, pensions and death benefits, sick pay and holiday entitlements. There had also been significant though less widespread moves in the areas of basic working hours, payment structures, time-recording, and amenities such as canteens and car parks. The harmonization process was still underway in four out of five of the organizations, and one in three had made their most recent moves during the last two years. Developments almost always took the form of improvement in manual workers' conditions to align them with those of the staff. In times past, officers and members of white-collar unions had complained vehemently about the drive to equalize conditions, since gains for manual workers removed differentials and had the effect of undermining the status and privileges of office staffs. Few employers seem to have met with such complaints in the 1990s – possibly because white-collar staffs were now reconciled to the inevitability of changing inter-group relationships, and perhaps because employers were incorporating some form of compensation for white-collar grades in their harmonization programmes ahead of implementation. Only seven employers covered by *IRRR*'s survey reported 'any white-collar resistance to "harmonizing up" for blue-collar grades', and in two of these cases the opposition was short-lived. The main reasons given by most employers for equalizing conditions were: 'to treat employees more fairly' and the need to 'ease the introduction of new working practices'; the main benefits were said to be: 'better industrial relations, employee flexibility, and simplified administration'.

Harmonization was very much a 'live issue' in the early 1990s. In twelve of *IRRR*'s fifty surveyed organizations, harmonization of all standard terms and conditions was reported to be complete; in another nine, including Ilford, Sutton Seeds, Whitbread, AAH Pharmaceuticals, British Pipeline Agency, Octel Chemicals, Warner Lambert, Medway Ports (Sheerness) and Filtrona (Jarrow), most terms had been equalized. The process was still underway in the rest, including, for example, Salt Union, Souplex, Marley Extensions, Fisher-Rosemount Systems, Lucas Aerospace, Wabco Automotive, Bass Brewers-Alton, and H.J. Heinz. Given the nature of trends in personnel management, it seems likely that organizations which have not yet adopted a harmonization programme for their permanent full-time employees will be considering the possibilities in the future.

THE PUBLIC SECTOR

Staff status arrangements and initiatives to reduce differentials between manual and non-manual grades were not confined to the private sector. Negotiated deals with these objectives were being reached in a number of public-sector undertakings including BEA and BOAC[9] as long ago as the 1960s. Electricity Supply, under public ownership at that time, was one of the 'front runners' with its 'Status Agreements' of the mid-1960s,[10] but in the closing years of the decade decisive moves were occurring elsewhere in the public sector.

Electricity Supply's lead was followed within a few years by moves in the Civil Service, the Atomic Energy Authority and the water industry. The motivating causes of change were similar to those which had spurred private-sector organizations into action. In all four of these major public enterprises the packages of improved conditions were negotiated with the unions in the process of productivity bargaining within the context of constraints imposed by incomes policy.

Change at the Atomic Energy Authority, the Civil Service, and water services was broached during a period of relatively stringent policy for prices and incomes. Public-sector undertakings were expected to set a good example to the rest by strict compliance with the spirit and letter of even 'voluntary' versions of incomes policy. Having this moral obligation imposed upon them, they bore the brunt of policy in ways, and to an extent, which could be more consciously evaded by the private sector. In each of these public sector undertakings innovation was part of a productivity agreement which was endorsed by the National Board for Prices and Incomes. The NBPI, in point of fact, was strongly in favour of moves towards parity of this kind, provided always that they were related to, and could be justified by, higher productivity which would hold down both unit costs and consumer prices. The NBPI's recommendation in each case was that the parity objective should be achieved through a process of gradual change with specific improvements made as and when circumstances permitted.

In Electricity Supply a major reason for the linked staff status and productivity agreement was the need to improve costs by the drastic reduction of overtime working and relaxation of demarcations. In water services there was the effect upon manual work of organizational and technological change, which affected skill requirement and led to increased employment in 'grey area' work such as testing, inspection, and maintenance. Technology was a particularly important factor in the case of the Atomic Energy Authority where rapidly advancing productive equipment demanded not only higher and new skills but also greater theoretical knowledge and reliability. A related causative factor in the case of the Atomic Energy Authority and the Civil Service was the need to appease discontent and grievance voiced by industrial workers about the inferior nature of their conditions when much of the work required of them was more demanding and of greater value than the routine work done by many white-collar grades. For the Civil Service there was also the problem of attracting and retaining industrial workers of suitable calibre.

The problems confronting Civil Service[11] management had been mounting rapidly during the early and mid-1960s. The extension of staff conditions to manual grades was recommended by the NBPI as one means of easing some of the difficulties. In its examination of efficiency and payment structures in the service, the Board concluded that there was little justification for the retention of current differences in terms and conditions. Its recommendations, which were outlined in two reports[12] on the Civil Service, published in 1966 and 1970, were premised on three main lines of argument. Firstly, the way in which the Civil Service had developed historically had produced certain anomalies which were now a focus of friction. Currently there were an estimated 30,000 employees classified as 'non-industrial' who were in jobs similar, if not identical, to jobs being done by an approximately equal number of workers classified as 'industrial' in other areas of public employment. Because the pay and conditions of industrials and non-industrials were determined separately and according to different principles for the two broad groups, people employed in identical or very similar work received different pay and conditions depending on whether they were officially classified as industrial or non-industrial civil servants. This anomaly was the root cause of much of the discontent which was now affecting the efficiency of the service. Secondly, the Civil Service, for essentially practical reasons, had been obliged to re-classify some key industrial posts as 'non-industrial' with preferential staff-like terms, benefits and conditions in order to attract and retain the required calibre of labour. This had resulted in further anomalies of classification and further inconsistencies in the total remuneration package received by similar groups within the same establishment. The whole set-up was cumbersome and was perceived to be unfair by those who felt that they were the 'victims of circumstance and mischance'. From their viewpoint, the differential was patently illogical. Thirdly, the NBPI asserted, there was the more general case for removing differences in terms and benefits:

> A policy for productivity, prices and incomes is concerned with modifying attitudes making for resistance to increased productivity ... It is concerned, therefore, with general reforms which may help to bring about changes in attitudes. We would suggest, as one such reform, the desirability of abolishing the division between 'staff' and 'workmen'. The division is increasingly outdated – it is related to a past when greater co-operation was expected from the 'staff' than from the 'workers'; it is arbitrary, and it can give rise to resentment. We consider that the Government, as the author of a policy for productivity, prices and incomes, should play a leading part in promoting the reform to staff of salary status, and should do so in relation to its own employees.[13]

In the public sector, as in private industry, it was in the 1960s that ideas were taking shape, plans were being drawn up, and first moves were being made in long-term policies to reduce and ultimately to eliminate the traditional class division in the workplace. Changes were set in motion in the 1960s, and practical advance followed in the 1970s – to the extent that incomes policy permitted. The NBPI reports sparked off a long-term programme of integration in the Civil Service. A degree of alignment had already been attained by 1974, despite the stringent incomes policy of the early years of that decade.

The path to equalization was not an easy one to follow where conventional industrial relations practice was firmly established. It was the traditional collective bargaining structure which hampered further progress in the mid and late 1970s. One factor which caused some difficulty in the achievement of full parity in the Civil Service, as in a number of other organizations with similar programmes, was multi-unionism. Different unions had different priorities and different orders of preference in what was to be sought at the bargaining table, and some union objectives were incompatible with the alignment of conditions across the board. While the aim of the Civil Service was eventually to remove all illogical and unjustifiable differences between industrials and non-industrials, IDS observed, it might be that equal status can never be achieved as long as the two groups exist as separate entities.

In the water industry, as in the Civil Service, the main developments occurred during the 1970s, but the motivating causes and the policy possibilities were largely the product of the preceding decade. A number of regional water authorities had already upgraded some of their manual workers to staff conditions by 1968, and these early sectional moves pointed the way to the more general change which followed. Moves to staff status reflected the demands of technology.[14]

A rising industrial and domestic demand for water, for better water quality and more efficient service, led to the introduction of new processes and more sophisticated equipment. This induced structural change in the industry and affected its labour requirements. Technological change increased the responsibilities to be shouldered by supervisors and it produced a need for proportionally more non-manual employees. The industry was transformed towards the mid-1970s by extensive re-grouping to create a network of fewer but larger undertakings with sufficient capital resources and professional expertise to cope with increased demand and the growing pollution problem. Within the overall decline of the size of the workforce there was an increase in the non-manual element. This shift, the NBPI observed in a report of 1970, resulted partly from the spread of staff status to skilled maintenance workers, waste inspectors and similar groups, but it also reflected the steady automation of treatment and pumping stations requiring technical grades of staff rather than semi-skilled operatives.

The main gains for those transferred to staff conditions were an annual salary paid monthly, a shorter normal working week with strictly limited overtime, and longer holiday entitlement with higher calculators for holiday pay. In addition, those classed as 'staff' received sick pay from the first day of sickness absence and had 'immediate' entitlement, whereas for other manual workers there were 'waiting days' before sickness benefit became payable and a service qualification of six months before becoming eligible for sick pay cover. Also, staff were covered by a separate pension scheme which provided a higher retirement pension and a larger 'lump sum' than were available under the local pension schemes for manual workers not on staff conditions. Clearly, there was much ground to be covered in the future.

In the Atomic Energy Authority[15] pressure for change came from technological advance which increased the responsibilities shouldered by employees, and from growing resentment about existing differentials. A working party, set up in 1965, reported that ill-feeling about differentials was unsurprising where industrial and non-industrial grades worked in close proximity and often in integrated units. The 'most out-dated and intolerable' differences, it was suggested, might be removed as part of a productivity package deal. Likewise, in its 1968 report on circumstances in the Atomic Energy Authority, the NBPI observed that: 'Differences in such matters as hours, sick leave, and holidays can become a serious grievance. In these circumstances, a gradual approach towards staff conditions should...form part of a comprehensive productivity agreement.'

Change began in 1969. By 1974 holiday entitlement for manual grades was the same as for non-supervisory office staff. Manual and non-manual staff were covered by the same sick pay arrangements; the remaining difference here was that for manual grades there was a service qualification of six months before benefit was payable but there was no service qualification for non-manual staff. It was anticipated that this difference would be removed in the 1974 pay round. Pension arrangements for the two groups were now 'almost the same'. All were covered by the same provisions for redundancy, transfer and travel. Clocking had been abolished in southern establishments but was still at the discussion stage in the north. Of the major items still outstanding, the difference in basic weekly working hours was expected to be the most costly, and therefore the most difficult, to remove.[16]

It was in the 1960s also that the British Airports Authority took the decision to move gradually to 'staff status for all'.[17] BAA was created under the 1966 Airports Authority Act, to develop, operate and maintain airport facilities, including buildings, runways, taxi-ways and roads, fire-rescue services, apron control, manning of terminals, and also trolley, porter and passenger security services. The degree to which terms and conditions were harmonized by 1981 had been facilitated by BAA's consultative and negotiating structures which, unusually at the time, brought together into one forum all ten of the manual and white-collar unions recognized by BAA for negotiating purposes for what amounted to single-table bargaining.

BAA's policy to harmonize conditions was based on the principle that 'illogical distinctions' should be eradicated. By 1981 harmonization had been achieved in the areas of payment method, overtime premia, coverage for sick pay, occupational pensions, and holiday entitlements. Clocking was abolished in 1971 and replaced by a common system of attendance recording. Subsidized restaurants at main airports were equally available to all employees; elsewhere, lunch vouchers were provided. Every employee was paid according to an incremental salary scale or range; but, while pay progression for white-collar grades was based on a combination of merit and length of service, for manual grades it was dependent on 'service subject to satisfactory performance'.

A similar philosophy was at the root of harmonization at North Thames Gas,[18] a regional division of the British Gas Corporation which was set up in 1973 to replace the former Gas Council and its area boards. With reorganization of gas services, the regional divisions became largely autonomous except in policy decisions involving national agreements. Roberts asserts that the organization's approach to harmonization stemmed from 'a moral standpoint that there can be no justification for discriminatory conditions of employment'. Differences in 'responsibility and contribution to the organization' should be reflected in levels of earnings, not in differentials in benefits.

A review of terms and conditions had been carried out in 1971, to identify what unjustifiable differences existed and to assess what would be involved in any action to remedy anomalies. Some differences, such as salaries and basic working hours, were tied to national agreements and were therefore outside the regional division's authority to alter them; but changes in other conditions could be implemented autonomously at regional level. Progress after 1973 had occurred on an *ad hoc* basis in the process of negotiation with the unions, rather than as a result of a pre-planned programme to phase out specific differentials by certain dates. A working party, set up by North Thames Gas in 1983 to review progress and to make recommendations for further change, referred to harmonization not just as a worthwhile end in itself, but as one of the factors in the divisional authority's overall strategic plan to achieve greater operational efficiency.

By 1983, when North Thames Gas had around 10,500 employees, including some 6,600 people in managerial and white-collar occupations and almost 4,000 craft and manual workers, variously represented by six different trade unions, considerable progress towards harmonized conditions had been accomplished. Clocking had been abolished. The move to pay by credit transfer, encouraged by a one-off lump sum payment for manual workers, was more or less complete. Cover for sick pay and personal accident was the same for all. Plans to merge the several different pension arrangements into a single common scheme were postponed for the time being in view of the massive financial outlay that would be required. Moves to harmonize service-related holiday entitlement and basic working hours were still unfinished. Proposals for an integrated pay and

grading structure and a monthly pay period had been greeted unfavourably by the manual unions; and directors and managers wanted
to retain their separate restaurant when the idea of single status
catering was put forward. Further advance to common terms and
conditions would require sensitive handling, but was believed to be
accomplishable in the longer term.

Public sector moves towards harmonized conditions were occurring
also in local government services. Sheffield City Council's 'people-
centred policy',[19] adopted in 1984, had single status as its ultimate
objective. The policy included a new industrial relations framework
for the authority and its multiplicity of recognized unions, better staff
training and development, and eradication of those differentials
which symbolized the 'relatively low and inferior status' of the
Council's manual employees. Differentials were said to have provoked a sense of 'understandable grievance, injustice and discontent'
amongst manual grades, and to have caused 'low self-esteem and little
job satisfaction', leading to 'disharmony in industrial relations'.
Consequently, there had been a negative effect upon the efficiency
and quality of the Council's services for the public. The new policy
aimed to address the problem of low pay, and over a five-year period
to eliminate the most resented differentials, beginning with basic
working hours, holiday entitlements, and sick pay.

It was towards the mid-1980s, also, that Braintree District
Council[20] adopted a policy for 'total quality management'. Harmonization of conditions, begun in 1989, aimed to ensure that employees
felt 'properly recognized and rewarded' for their co-operation in the
Council's initiatives to provide high quality services under competitive tendering required by the 1988 Local Government Act. In the
mid 1990s negotiation was underway for a complete single-status pay
and conditions package, to apply across the whole authority and bring
all Braintree DC's employees on to a single pay spine.

Harmonization of terms and conditions were set to spread further
in local government services in the 1990s. The 1992 agreement of
the national joint council for local authority manual staff contained
a commitment to review existing agreements, bearing in mind 'the
possibility of moves to single-status employment in local government'. By 1993, Warwick County Council had already harmonized,
or had firm plans to do so, in the areas of: basic working hours, basic
holiday entitlement, holiday pay calculation, special leave, pensions
provision, death benefits, redundancy scheme, and arrangements for
pay during sickness absence.[21] Where a decisive lead is taken by a

few pacemakers in a particular sector of economic life, others in the same sector tend to follow. It seems not improbable that in time harmonized conditions will become standard in local authority services.

AFTER PRIVATIZATION

Privatization did not result in a general reversal of policies, initiated during the time of public ownership, to reduce and in some cases ultimately to eradicate differentials. Harmonization was furthered in the water and electricity supply industries after privatization in 1989 and 1990 respectively, and it was initiated when British Rail Engineering[22] moved from public ownership to the private sector in 1989.

Privatization, decentralization and the demise of long-standing national bargaining procedures cleared the way for sweeping changes when the water industry[23] was split up into ten separate and henceforth autonomous water companies: Anglia, Northumbrian, North West, Severn Trent, Southern, South West, Thames, Welsh Water, Wessex, and Yorkshire. The new competitive environment spurred the water companies into looking for ways and means to reduce costs and to create an industrial relations framework which would facilitate increased efficiency, productivity, and commitment of their employees. Steps were taken to streamline bargaining arrangements with the trade unions, to restructure payment systems, to secure more flexible working practices, and to relate pay more closely to performance. Associated with these moves was a pervasive trend towards the harmonization of terms and conditions of employment.

The abandonment of the water industry's national bargaining arrangements, dating back to 1919 for manual workers, was the principal dynamic of change. Thames Water had already withdrawn from national negotiations in 1988, followed by Northumbrian, and the remaining eight authorities announced their intention to adopt domestic bargaining arrangements in 1990. This meant that each privatized company could develop an employment policy designed to meet its own specific business needs, free from the fetters of national-level industry-wide bargaining. Thames, Northumbrian, Yorkshire, and Welsh Water each adopted unified bargaining.

The establishment of single-table bargaining, with all the recognized unions negotiating as one body, was intended to make more efficient use of managerial resources, to remove a potential source of conflict, to facilitate major changes in working practices affecting large sections of the workforce, and to ease the process of harmonizing the terms and conditions of manual and non-manual groups. As Thames Water's management saw it, new technology and linked changes in working practices had blurred the traditional distinctions between staff, manual, and craft grades, and single-table bargaining would help to remove outmoded differences in terms, benefits and conditions of employment.

Moves towards simplified bargaining and payment structures and the elimination of status-related differences in the treatment of manual and white-collar employees were part of wider programmes seeking to eliminate traditional demarcations and to introduce more flexible working practices. Anglian Water's aim was to get rid of wasteful manning, inefficient working practices and outdated skill demarcations, and to introduce flexible working arrangements and multi-skilling. Severn Trent was seeking improved flexibility, team working and up-dated skills as part of its restructuring exercise. The objective at Yorkshire Water was to eradicate inefficiency. Welsh Water had embarked upon a skill development programme, involving new job designs and work organization in order to improve its employees' productivity and flexibility of working.

Proposals to move to harmonized conditions in the water industry predate privatization; there had been much regional commitment in the mid-1980s and even earlier in some cases, and transfer to the private sector provided a renewed impetus. Policy now typically focused on alignment of non-pay conditions such as working hours, holiday entitlements, pensions, and sick pay arrangements, but a number of water companies were each taking harmonization a step further by introducing a single integrated pay and grading structure. Northumbrian Water, for example, agreed a new harmonized package in 1992, which provided for 'common hours, holidays, sick pay, pensions, and the establishment of a single integrated grading structure covering all employees in the company.' Thames Water had proclaimed a commitment to the establishment of common terms and conditions for all its employees as part of the process of eliminating differences in the treatment of manual, craft, and staff grades. Welsh Water in 1991 reached an agreement with its unions to introduce common terms and conditions of employment for all employees by April 1993; the single-status programme included: single-table negotiating and consultative arrangements; a 37-hour working week across the board, with an early Friday finish and new working patterns;

common conditions, policies and procedures including holiday entitlement, pensions, sick pay, overtime and shift premia, notice periods, maternity leave and disciplinary procedures; monthly pay by credit transfer and consolidation of guaranteed bonus levels; an integrated payment structure; increased flexibility of working to improve productivity; and job security premised on the principle of no compulsory redundancies. Yorkshire Water's 1992–3 pay settlement included moves towards harmonization of terms and conditions; a job evaluation exercise had been carried out with a view to moving staff, manual and craft grades on to a new unified pay and grading structure by April 1993. North West Water set up a working party in 1991 to discuss a range of related issues, including moves to harmonized conditions, single-table bargaining, a new grading structure, progress to monthly pay, productivity improvements and flexible work practices.

While a major restructuring of industrial relations and reward systems occurred in the water industry in the early-1990s, developments following privatization of the non-nuclear sector of the electricity supply industry, though significant, were generally less dramatic, less pervasive, and much slower to take shape. In part this was because a process of harmonization had been underway in electricity supply since the 1960s,[24] when the industry was under public ownership; much had already been accomplished, though harmonization was still incomplete when the industry was privatized in 1990. The most rapid and spectacular change occurred in PowerGen. For the non-nuclear sector of the electricity supply industry,[25] change represented a break with the highly centralized collective bargaining system which had existed in the industry since nationalization in 1947. Of the nineteen electricity companies created in 1990, only PowerGen had settled with the unions by the end of 1992 to introduce single-table bargaining, an integrated payment structure, and harmonization of most of the outstanding differences in terms and conditions. Policy was under serious discussion by the other companies, and evidence suggests that, in contrast to PowerGen's 'big bang' approach, change would take a more gradualist path elsewhere.

The delay in reforming industrial relations and reward systems in the industry as a whole is not altogether surprising. Privatization radically altered the industry's structure and business strategy, and government policy favouring deregulation raised major issues which would have to be addressed by both management and trade unions. Change had implications for industrial relations arrangements, not only for the privatized companies but also for their newly established subsidiaries; serious thought had to be given to the management of existing 'core' business activities in the context of growing competitive pressures and the need to consider the interests not only of employees and customers but also of shareholders.

In retrospect, it appears that, although there were some notable moves in Britain to reduce the differentials which marked the workplace divide during the two decades of near full employment, the rate of change in that direction slowed down during the 1970s. There was a renewal of interest in such policies and an acceleration of the trend to harmonized conditions during the years of high unemployment in the 1980s, which showed little sign of abating in the 1990s.

4 Single Status in Britain: The American Models?

INTRODUCTION

In Britain, single-status conditions, the most advanced of the policy variants, were to be found earliest and most characteristically in British subsidiaries of largely American-owned companies with their main headquarters in the United States. It would, of course, be erroneous to assume that all, or even most, American companies operated single-status policy in the USA; and it is equally mistaken to infer that all American-owned companies in Britain were single status companies. Even so, the trend was already established and would gather momentum. That advanced American practice in the 1950s and 1960s was more fully developed than advanced British practice is partially attributable to the fact that the leading edge of the US economy was technologically ahead, and the associated rate of business investment was higher. Something is owed also to the attitudes of American managers and workforces. Managers were more willing to experiment with innovative ideas, and, although unionism had a long pre-history in America by this time, workplace divisions and industrial relations were less powerfully defined by the kind of class attitudes which were deeply entrenched in much of British industry.

Historically, America was also typically in the van in development of management theory; a number of major advances – Taylorist scientific management before the First World War, Mayoist human relations in the 1930s, and now the motivational theories of the behavioural scientists such as Herzberg, Likert, MacGregor and Maslow – all originated in the United States. It seems likely that, with less emphasis in the USA than in Britain upon state provision for social insurance, company-provided welfare came much more to the fore. A few of the most advanced and progressive American companies set up operations in Britain in the 1950s and 1960s, and undoubtedly the personnel policies already in operation in the parent company had some influence upon the approach adopted in subsidiaries in Britain and elsewhere. Some of these subsidiaries were non-union companies; others, more obviously where take-overs or mergers were involved, adapted their policies to the British industrial relations pattern. Equally with British-owned companies operating in Britain, all were affected by the constraints of British incomes policy; but the fact that the 'front-runners' had put their policies into effect well before the more rigorous phases of incomes policy in the later 1960s and early 1970s, meant that they did not encounter the kind of externally imposed difficulties which beset ICI and Electricity Supply at a crucial stage of innovation in personnel policy.

THE EARLY MODEL

Three British subsidiaries of largely US-owned multinational companies – Texas Instruments, International Business Machines, and Smith, Kline and French – appear to have provided single-status terms and conditions from the commencement of operations in Britain.[1] Both IBM and TI produced and marketed microelectronic equipment; SKF produced ethical pharmaceutical goods. All three companies were capital-intensive, used the most advanced technology, and required highly trained and highly qualified personnel. Their technology and skill requirements were not typical of British industry in general in these years. Each company employed disproportionately large numbers of managerial, technical, research and white-collar staff relative to the size of their manual workforces. The fact that all three began operations in Britain on greenfield sites enabled them to avoid the kind of resistance which might have been encountered in introducing radical change at an established site with a legacy of traditional workplace practice based on the British style of industrial relations and collective bargaining. Professional, managerial, research and technical grades were not strongly pro-union in attitude, even in years when union membership was rising rapidly amongst the rest of the British working population. It seems probable that people recruited to work for the new companies in new premises producing new goods and services were predisposed to accommodate to a new style of personnel policy, and to accept means of pay determination without representation by trade unions for negotiating purposes. That all three set up on greenfield sites enabled the companies to start with modern purpose-built premises so that personnel policies as well as the lay-out of buildings could be designed with a single status philosophy in mind.

TI (UK)[2] was established in 1952 and patented the first integrated electronic circuit in 1958. The company's growth throughout the 1960s was largely based on the production of mainframe computers and electronic calculators. With a combined workforce of roughly three thousand by the end of the 1960s, TI had three main sites in Britain: general headquarters at Bedford, the main manufacturing unit in Plymouth, and a smaller establishment in Croydon dealing mainly with geophysical exploration equipment. There was some manufacturing at Bedford, but the site functioned essentially as TI's technology and business centre, employing over 800 graduate technologists, technicians and engineers, and roughly 350 operatives. IBM (UK)[3] was established in 1951 and by the end of the 1960s had two manufacturing sites, a development laboratory, and sales offices in over forty locations. The company specialized in sophisticated office equipment and became a leader in the development of computer hardware and software. The two manufacturing sites – one at Greenock in Scotland and the other at Havant in Hampshire – had a combined workforce of around four thousand. Of this total, about one-third were blue-collar workers and the remainder, plus staff at other locations, included researchers, electronics specialists, administrative and managerial personnel, clerical staff, sales representatives, and systems and customer engineers.

Management philosophy at both TI (UK) and IBM (UK) was based on the principle of equality: that all employees should have common terms, fringe benefits and conditions of employment, with level of earnings as the only differential. TI's policy came to embrace the motivational theories of Maslow and Herzberg;[4] IBM's reflected the rationale that there was no justifiable reason, whether economic, social or cultural, for the maintenance of differentials other than in levels of pay and where differences were an integral part of the work undertaken – company cars for sales and maintenance personnel whose jobs involved travelling, for example. These exceptions apart, the principle of equality did not preclude the possibility that some might be slightly more equal that others; for single status applied to all groups except for higher management and executive grades, whose conditions were superior.

Personnel policy in these companies was precedent-setting, yet for all that it was innovatory, the underlying objectives were similar to those which motivated the less spectacular staff status policies which a few British employers were introducing at the time: the recruitment, control and motivation of employees and the cultivation of a company-focused identity and ethos. New motivational theories provided philosophical justification; the practical means were now packaged under a new label, and drew upon new ideas about job enrichment, job satisfaction and participatory management, but none of this disguises the similarity of intention. TI's corporate personnel policy explicitly sought to avoid 'artificial barriers' in the workplace, and to treat people in 'an equitable, reasonable and responsible fashion'; single status, it was believed, created a 'flexible and satisfied workforce', helped to 'attract and retain the right sort of labour', and fostered 'co-operation and team spirit'. Problems were said to be more readily resolvable in an atmosphere of 'us' rather than 'we–they'. An IBM spokesman reported that single status was effective in 'removing a potential cause of de-motivation' and in 'improving employee loyalty' to the company and 'commitment' to its objectives; above all, it served to 'help productivity', and in the longer term was 'good for business'. Management at both companies took the view that the 'gap in status' between staff and manual grades was 'outdated and indefensible'.[5]

TI (UK)'s management believed that all employees, regardless of conventional collar colour, should have staff conditions, in recognition of the responsibilities accepted by the people employed in the entire range of the company's activities. Just over half of the 1,750 employees at the company's air-conditioned factory were women and girls; these were covered by the same staff conditions as the men, and so also were some 120 female part-time workers on the evening shift.[6]

Physical conditions at the workplace reflected TI (UK)'s philosophy, in that there was a conspicuous absence of the usual status symbols with degree of status reflected in thickness of carpet, quality and design of furniture, size of desk, nameplates on doors and pictures on walls. All furniture and fitments were purely functional. Offices were open-plan in design in order to improve communication, to avoid artificial status barriers, and to make it easier for people to approach each other. The only employees with separate offices were those whose jobs required privacy, such as departmental managers and personnel officers. There were no status distinctions in the design and use of cafeterias, cloakrooms, coffee bars, car parks and entrances. These were equally available and accessible to everyone. There was no separate directors' dining room with waitress service; all employees mixed freely at lunch time in the self-service canteen.

Apart from shift workers on a basic 37.5-hour week, everyone else had a basic week of 39 hours worked over five days with an early Friday finish. The 39-hour week maintained the single-status concept, but it was something of a compromise; for manual grades it was shorter than the 40 to 44-hour average basic working week in manufacturing industry in the mid 1960s, but for clerical and other non-manual groups it was longer than the standard office hours generally worked elsewhere. However, TI's management expected that the working week would be shortened before long. There was no requirement for any of the company's employees to clock on and off. Good time-keeping was taken on trust and was the individual's responsibility. Even so, the company's handbook warned that: 'If you are late ... you are required to sign in at the plant entrance. Repeated lateness is difficult to explain, and you will be requested to take corrective action.'[7]

For pay purposes, all TI (UK)'s employees were covered by an integrated salary structure which made no conceptual distinctions between manual and non-manual occupations as such. There was no 'rate for the job' for any group of employees; instead there were job-evaluated grade-related salary bands. This functioned as a merit pay system; performance, and salary advance, were assessed by a formalized appraisal process conducted twice yearly. All salaries were paid monthly, usually by credit transfer into the individual's nominated bank account. Regulations regarding overtime, the recording of overtime worked and the rate of overtime pay applied across the board.

Fringe benefits at TI (UK) were provided on a similar basis for all employees. Holiday entitlements were service related, no additional days being given for rank. At the end of the 1960s the average entitlement was four weeks. The company's non-contributory pension scheme covered all employees, and was designed to give a long-serving scheme member a monthly retirement income amounting after 35 years' service to roughly 60 per cent of former monthly earnings. TI (UK)'s sick pay scheme was common to all its employees; the scales of benefit made no distinction for occupational grade and were dependent entirely on years of service. At the lower end of the scale, employees with less than three months' service were entitled to a maximum of two weeks' sick leave on full pay and a further two weeks at half pay; at the top of the scale employees with five or more years of service had annual entitlement to a maximum of sixteen weeks of sickness absence on full pay and a further ten weeks at half pay. The company supplemented this with a private medical insurance scheme which included cover for hospital treatment; membership was not compulsory, but in practice had been taken up by at least 90 per cent of the workforce. In addition, TI (UK) provided a life assurance scheme and a profit-sharing scheme.

Single status was enhanced by the means and style of communications. The company did not recognize trade unions nor use conventional forms of collective bargaining. Instead, the aim was to provide conditions which were 'better in all respects than the union minimum', and to have extensive two-way communication channels both with individuals and groups. Management conducted an annual attitude survey by anonymously completed questionnaires, had a sophisticated suggestion scheme, and operated an 'open door' policy.

Since its foundation, TI (UK) had been free from strikes. Its experience of operating single status conditions was that the policy had helped to promote good industrial relations and to avoid potential causes of dissatisfaction. Considerable flexibility of labour had been achieved without demarcation problems.

Robinson's investigation disclosed that, in general, the people employed by IBM (UK) and TI (UK) had had little difficulty in accepting, and accommodating to, the exceptional working conditions found in these two companies. They were vastly different from conditions prevailing generally in British industry at the time, and undoubtedly their acceptability owed a great deal to the fact that they were superior. Apart from a clean, pleasant working environment and above-average fringe benefits, both companies had effective management structures, with highly qualified supervision and the widespread application of such controls as job evaluation, work study, management by objectives and, at TI (UK), job enrichment programmes. Great importance was attached to people and communications. Single-status conditions may have facilitated an acceptance of sophisticated controls such as these, producing concomitantly high productivity and good industrial relations. Problems of labour turnover and absenteeism were not completely removed, but the companies attributed this to local labour market conditions and attitudes prevailing externally in local communities rather than to dissatisfaction with single status as such.

American companies at the cutting edge with production sites in Britain were not necessarily anti-union in principle. The British style of trade unionism and collective bargaining was felt to be inappropriate in business circumstances which were very different from those which prevailed in British industry generally. Trade union structure, with members of the workforce organized by different unions – general, craft, and white-collar – separated the various occupational grades; and, in defining job functions and trade boundaries that created differentials, it was at odds with the tenets of single-status philosophy. Systems which were well-entrenched in traditional indus-tries were not necessarily well-suited to new industries. Effective means of communication were given high priority, but the channels, both formal and informal and relevant to the individual, the group, the department and the company as a whole, were company-specific and management-designed. It helped, no doubt, that management and workforces in these 'new' companies, were relatively young, and that the main centres of operations were not in Britain's traditional indus-trial regions with strong legacies of working-class consciousness and deep traditions of unionism. Something may be owed also to the priva-tions of the war years and the experience of several years of post-war austerity; the offer of superior conditions and clean, modern, well-equipped work premises had its attractions. Moreover, all three of these companies had disproportionately large numbers of managers, supervisors, administrators, technicians, graduate researchers, sales personnel and clerical staffs; amongst these groups unionization was not widespread in Britain as a whole. The very fact that these com-panies were American may have led to the expectation that things would be different, and to a predisposition on the part of recruits to accept the unconventional.

The approach adopted in the early years by TI and IBM is evident in later migrants setting up in Britain in similar or closely related manufacturing sectors: Digital and Hewlett Packard, for example.

THE ADAPTED MODEL

It would be erroneous to assume that all single-status American companies in Britain were non-union companies. There were some whose policy and practice were in various ways adapted to the British industrial relations scene. This tended to occur when a company in a long-established industry moved to a greenfield site or when British companies were subject to American take-overs. Both circumstances suggest a break with the past. Dow Chemical and Porvair were both taken over by American corporations. The decision to introduce single status at Porvair dates from the time of its move to King's Lynn in 1966, and its policy was built into the company's arrangements for collective bargaining in 1970 when a pay and procedure agreement was signed with the AUEW and ACTSS. To maintain the single-status concept, the agreement contained a statement of principle, that it was 'highly desirable that issues affecting the total employee force should be discussed with representatives of both unions as a single body rather than with each representative separately'. This would appear to be hinting at the kind of 'single-table' bargaining which became widespread in the later 1980s. Dow Chemical's Norfolk plant remained non-unionized in these years, but operative grades at the Barry plant in South Wales were organized by the TGWU. It seems likely that this reflects the different industrial pre-histories and different industrial relations traditions of the two regions. Single status at E.R. Squibb (UK) was introduced two years prior to the move to a new greenfield site in the mid-1960s, and was further developed during the following years.

E.R. Squibb (UK)[8] was part of the US-based Squibb Corporation, producer of pharmaceuticals and patent medicines, with its headquarters in Princeton, New Jersey. It therefore had certain characteristics in common with SKF (UK). In addition to links with the United States and similar market products, E.R. Squibb (UK), like SKF (UK), used advanced, highly automated technology in a capital-intensive environment, employed large numbers of skilled and highly trained personnel, and had a single status philosophy. The Squibb Corporation's British subsidiary was unionized, however. Single status was not introduced at the outset, and the transition to common terms and conditions was not accomplished in one move. The first steps were not taken until 1964–5, and other changes were made in association with the transfer of production to a greenfield site two years later.

The company had been manufacturing in Britain since 1949 at Speke in the Liverpool area. With market demand rapidly outrunning production capacity at Speke, the production plant and research facilities were moved in 1967 to a greenfield site at Moreton in Cheshire.

The British subsidiary disclaims any influence from its parent organization in the United States upon its decision to move to single status. The decision was not taken until the mid-1960s, when management had come round to the view that there was no logical reason for differential treatment of manual and non-manual grades. The first changes, made in 1965, affected the holiday period, holiday pay, sick pay arrangements, and occupational pensions. Further changes flowed from the move to the Moreton site in 1967.

At the time of the move, attention focused on payment methods, clocking, and working hours, where the manual/non-manual differential was starkly visible. Manual workers were required to record their attendance and amount of time worked by clocking on and off, were paid a weekly wage in cash, and worked a basic 40-hour week plus overtime at premium rates; in contrast, non-manual staff worked a basic 35-hour week, received salaries paid monthly either by credit transfer or in cash, did not usually work overtime but received no overtime pay in so far as extra hours were worked. In 1967 some manual grades were moved to salaried status, with earnings paid monthly either in cash or by credit transfer. At the same time, payment for overtime at premium rates was abolished, but payment for six hours' 'guaranteed' overtime was built into the new salary structure.

Basic fringe benefits were equalized. Entitlement to basic and service-related holidays was the same for all. Under the terms of the sick pay scheme, the relatively few who were weekly paid did not qualify for benefit until completion of one year's service. After one year their benefits were the same as for other manual and non-manual groups, all of whom had coverage from the commencement of employment with the company. The scheme allowed up to 13 weeks of sickness absence per annum on full pay (less NI benefit) plus up to 39 weeks on half pay. All employees were covered by the company's non-contributory pension scheme, which provided retirement pensions related to level of earnings and years of service. The scheme also provided disability pensions for employees who became chronically sick or disabled, and benefits for widows and dependants in the event of a scheme member's death in service or in retirement. Linked to the scheme also was a life assurance arrangement which provided a lump sum benefit equal to ten times the 'potential pension' in the case of the death of a male employee but, contrary to the company's single-status philosophy, only five times the 'potential pension' for a female employee. Given the expansion of operations, redundancy had not so far proved to be much of a problem, but the company had a severance scheme covering all employees and providing amounts of severance compensation related to length of service. The amounts were roughly twice the minimum sums statutorily required under the Redundancy Payments Act. The company had a single-status canteen.

By the end of 1967 many of the terms, benefits and conditions of employment were common to both manual and non-manual employees. The differential in normal working hours remained, however, and this issue, along with overtime, caused a certain amount of friction. Dissatisfaction first surfaced when manual workers, aggrieved about the overtime arrangement under salaried status, began to press for the re-introduction of overtime working at overtime rates. This pressure was associated with, and reinforced by, the spread of union membership and claims for recognition of the union for collective bargaining purposes. The company had always recognized the craft unions representing tradesmen but, up to the time of the move to Moreton, it had not conducted negotiations with unions representing non-craft workers or white-collar staff. In response to union demands, in 1972 the company agreed to recognize the TGWU for semi-skilled and unskilled manuals and to set up a Staff Association for clerical, administrative, supervisory and other staff. Recognition of the TGWU was shortly followed by the re-introduction of premium rates for overtime, at time-and-a-half from Monday to Friday and double time at weekends.

The overtime issued was resolved relatively quickly, though the new arrangement was a partial reversal of one of the purposes underlying the introduction of manual salaries, which was to make the payment system for manual workers similar to, and part of, that which already applied in the case of non-manual groups. It is, perhaps, unsurprising that, in years of rapidly accelerating wage inflation in Britain, the unions should focus on the overtime question as a means of keeping in step with, or even ahead of, increases in earnings elsewhere.

The question of basic working hours was less readily dealt with. What is clear in the early 1970s is that the unions cared less about the ideal of single status than about the practicality of getting the best possible deal for their members. Having ignored single status relative to overtime, they now pressed single status relative to basic hours, which amounted to the re-establishment of one differential in the sphere of working time and the elimination of another differential in the same sphere. In 1974 E.R. Squibb (UK) was faced with claims from the TGWU, the AUEW and EETPU for a reduction in basic weekly working hours to 35, in line with non-manual staff. This meant a 5-hour reduction to the basic working week, and the implications for overtime are only too obvious. Even so, in October of that year, mindful of its single-status policy, the company agreed to reduce its manual workers' basic working week from 40 to 37.5 hours as part of the annual settlement, and as a first step towards the establihment of a common working week. On this occasion, there was no adverse reaction from the Staff Association.

During the years which followed, the TGWU and the craft unions repeatedly pressed their claim for a 35-hour week in line with office staff. Finally in 1979 the company and the three unions agreed a package, which included a 15-month pay settlement, an indexation clause, and a two-stage reduction in hours. These were to be cut from 37.5 to 36.5 in October 1979 and thence to 35 in December 1980. However, E.R. Squibb (UK) required something in return for the equalization of hours. Attached to the agreed reductions were specific requirements: continuing union co-operation in the use of work study methods, strict compliance with specified contractual hours and agreed breaks, and no increase in unit costs as a result of the hours reductions (a reaffirmation of certain flexibility clauses and regrading arrangements originally agreed in the 1978 settlement). None of this was unique to E.R. Squibb (UK); it was part of a general trend in British industry. Reciprocal concession such as these were becoming common in many companies in many different industries in the later 1970s, and even more so in the early 1980s in years when widespread hours reductions for manual workers were breaching the 40-hour barrier which dated back to the mid-1960s.

The equalization of working hours at E.R. Squibb (UK) was a triumph for the unions, and a major achievement for the company, given its single-status philosophy. The company appears to have been one of the first to set the manual workers' normal working week at 35 hours. Other companies with longer term commitments to provide common terms and conditions found it relatively simple to equalize fringe benefits such as holidays, sick pay and pensions; equalized working hours and integrated payment systems were more problematic.

Manual groups at E.R. Squibb (UK) were well pleased with the hours reduction, but white-collar staff greeted the equalization of the normal working week with consternation. There was an immediate and insistent response from the Staff Association for some form of compensation for the loss of the hours differential – either a corresponding reduction in office hours or extra pay. The company was resolutely opposed to both; a straight pay increase would be very costly, given the numbers involved, and a reduction in staff hours was not only contrary to its commitment to single status but would adversely affect administrative efficiency. There were protracted and difficult negotiations on the issue during 1979. Eventually, an agreement was reached to introduce a totally performance-related incremental pay system. The pay increases which this permitted for office staffs served to pacify their resentment about working hours.

Despite the costs and the problems encountered, E.R. Squibb (UK) maintains its belief in the value of single status; difficulties were resolved by discussion and negotiation, without resort to industrial action. Although the company would not go so far as to claim that its generally good industrial relations record is entirely attributable to the removal of differentials, it firmly believes that the policy has contributed significantly to a generally improved climate of relations.

Porvair and Dow Chemical,[9] like E.R. Squibb, both had some unionization and both moved from a conventional British set-up to single-status conditions. It goes without saying, that this is more difficult than starting from scratch on a greenfield site. Unlike the other British subsidiaries of largely American-owned companies we have considered so far, both were British companies which were taken over by American corporations. Dow Chemical's single status policy was largely an import from its 'new parent' company, but Porvair disclaims any US influence on its move to single status, which began prior to the take-over. Both companies were part of the chemical industry, and the British chemical industry was already moving in the general direction of staff status for manual workers by the end of the 1960s. Policy had been formulated much earlier at Imperial Chemical Industries, and it seems not unlikely that both Porvair and Dow Chemical were influenced by policy resolutions and guidelines for productivity bargaining produced by the Chemical Industries Association in 1967.

Change at an established site seldom occurred in one big move. Implementation of decisions taken in the 1960s was often delayed until the 1970s, and practice was often updated or amended during the following decade. Even Dow Chemical (UK), with a conviction imported by its parent company that the only differential should be in levels of money earnings, did not attempt the move to single status all in one go. The single status decision was taken at the time of the take-over in 1969; some differentials had been eliminated or substantially reduced by 1974, leaving other disparities to be removed later. That most of the planned changes had been achieved within such a short space of time and with minimal disruption in industrial relations suggests that the company was led by an effective and dynamic management team.

By the mid-1970s all Dow Chemical (UK)'s employees received annual salaries, paid monthly. Basic weekly hours of work still varied: 42 hours at manufacturing sites, and 36 or 38 at sales offices. At the Barry plant time off in lieu was given instead of payment for overtime hours, but at the Norfolk plant overtime pay had been retained, and applied to operators, laboratory technicians and shift foremen. Annual holiday entitlements had been equalized at four weeks. All were covered by the same sick pay scheme and the same occupational pension scheme. Notice period was dependent on length of service. Other common conditions included a subsidized canteen or luncheon vouchers, subsidized membership of BUPA (private health-care), travel allowance, accident insurance scheme, and the option to join the stock purchase scheme. All salaries were reviewed annually. Office staff employees were eligible for 'merit' payments, and the company hoped to extend this to operating staff at some future date. Clocking had been abolished at the Norfolk plant but retained at Barry where the TOIL system was in operation. All employees, roughly 600, were covered by these conditions.

Change at Porvair provides another success story. The company was engaged in the manufacture of 'porvair', a man-made plastic material used for a wide range of consumer and industrial goods including shoe uppers, lightweight cases and bags, footballs, and equipment for liquid and gas filtration and pneumatic air silencing. Until the take-over in 1969 by the US-based Imnont Corporation, the company was part of the Choride Group, trading under the name of Porous Plastics Ltd.

The proposal to introduce single status conditions dates from Chloride's decision to move production of porous plastics from its Dagenham 'Dagenite' factory to King's Lynn in 1966. The proposal was adopted prior to the purchase of a controlling interest by the US corporation, but it was in line with the personnel policy and practice of the new parent. Relocation provided the occasion for a 'fresh start', and management believed that single status would create a good industrial relations climate at the outset. Highly automated capital-intensive production required round-the-clock shift working. A small nucleus of employees transferred from Dagenham, but most of the workforce was recruited locally in the King's Lynn area. Unionism did not accompany the move, but with growing pressure for trade union representation at the new site, the company agreed to recognize ACTSS, the TGWU's white-collar section, for industrial operatives, canteen and other manual grades and the AUEW for engineering craftsmen. Under the recognition agreement a Joint Factory Committee was set up for single-table bargaining in order to maintain the principle of single status.

Most basic terms, benefits and conditions were equalized on re-location. All employees were put on salaries, paid monthly by credit transfer, and the company provided short-term financial assistance to ease the transition to the new pay period. Normal weekly working hours were equalized at 36.25, worked over a 7.25-hour five-day week. No one was required to clock on and off; individuals were put on trust for their own attendance and time-keeping. The shift supervisor was to keep a register of attendance for entirely practical safety purposes in order to record who was where in the plant so that in the event of fire complete evacuation could be ascertained. When overtime was worked both manual and white-collar grades received the same premium rates of time and a half on weekdays and double time on Sundays. Equalized also were shift allowances, cover for sick pay and pensions, holiday entitlements, redundancy terms, notice periods, and arrangements for authorized absence for personal reasons. The cafeteria was equally available to all.

Single-status practice at Porvair was maintained and improved from the time of the US take-over. By 1980, holiday entitlements had been substantially increased, an annual ballot of employees was conducted to choose the weeks of holiday closure, and there was a new arrangement to ensure fair allocation of the available overtime. After many years' experience of operating single-status policy, management believed that the company had benefited from a good industrial relations atmosphere, a low rate of labour turnover and absenteeism, responsible time-keeping, and a co-operative workforce.

LATER MODELS

Some US-based companies with single-status policies set up subsidiaries in Britain more recently, and a number of those which had been established in Britain for many years moved to single status more belatedly. The latter group, which included Beckman Instruments, Eaton, and Johnson & Johnson, for example, appear to have made moves towards harmonized conditions as a practical response to problems encountered rather than as a matter of principle or company philosophy.

Beckman Instruments[10] had been manufacturing electronic components at its Glenrothes site in Fife for several years before taking the decision towards the end of the 1970s to phase in single-status conditions. Until 1979 the company had made little conscious effort to reduce differentials, but that year more decisive steps were taken to reduce the 'them and us division' implicit in differing terms and benefits. The workforce was densely unionized; around 90 per cent of the manual workers were members of the AUEW's engineering section and some two-thirds of all non-manual grades were members of TASS, the AUEW's white-collar section. Moves at Beckman occurred at a time when the AUEW was bringing the staff status issue into sharper focus. The union's claims for staff conditions were considered at length in the 1979 national engineering pay review discussions and the Engineering Employers' Federation had proposed a joint working party on the subject. A recent NEDO report on engineering skill shortages had pressed the point that differentials were a source of grievance amongst skilled craftsmen over their status and rewards *vis-à-vis* white-collar grades; the report went on to advise the development of policies to reduce existing differentials as one means of reversing the outflow of craftsmen from engineering firms. In 1979 the EEF endorsed the principle of moves towards harmonized conditions.

The main objectives of Beckman's policy to phase out differentials in the longer term appear to have been to improve industrial relations, to foster greater co-operation, to raise morale, and to retain craftsmen by providing them with a total remuneration package which acknowledged the value of skill and degree of responsibility shouldered, regardless of collar colour. In 1979 the company abandoned its 'typically British' bargaining arrangements involving separate negotiations at different times in the year for each of the two main bargaining groups and, by agreement with the unions, introduced single-table bargaining with one annual settlement date in order to facilitate the process of harmonization.

Beckman had had common holiday and pension arrangements for some time. The new drive for harmonization, begun in 1979, that year produced an integrated job-evaluated pay and grading structure covering all employees up to management level, and the extension to manual grades of 'staff rights' to authorized time off without loss of pay for visits to the doctor, the dentist and other 'personal purposes'. For the time being, the differential in basic weekly working hours, with a 40-hour week for all manual grades compared with 35 hours for office staff, would remain. Alignment of sick pay, redundancy arrangements, notice periods and other employment terms was to be tackled in the future. The integrated pay and grading structure, with job-evaluatedly equal manual and non-manual functions located in the same salary band, provided a good foundation upon which to build up the rest of the harmonization policy.

The objectives of Eaton's[11] radical three-year agreement of 1986 to move towards harmonized conditions were more specifically detailed than those given in Beckman's agreement. Eaton's general aim was to create a framework which would enable the company both to raise productivity and to 'eliminate potential sources of friction'. The deal was an important part of the company's survival strategy in the context of recession, but it also sought to resolve the kind of industrial relations problems which had been recurrent at the manufacturing site throughout the 1970s and beyond. Eaton, a largely US-owned multinational company producing vehicle components, had acquired its Newton Aycliffe plant in Britain in the mid-1960s, and had all the problems characteristic of the British engineering industry in those years: job demarcations, low productivity, industrial disputes and a moribund payment structure. In 1983, with a workforce reduced from over 7,000 in 1978 to less than 400, the site was on the brink of closure. The company had already gained union agreement to an itemized list of flexible working practices in 1983, in exchange for an explicit commitment from management to the principle of harmonization and new arrangements for greater employee involvement and communication.

The 1986 agreement took the form of a single-union deal between Eaton and the AUEW. It provided for the introduction that year of an integrated payment structure, no-strike arrangements, complete flexibility in labour utilization and deployment, and first steps towards harmonization: the abolition of clocking, common lay-off and redundancy arrangements, and alignment of sick pay provision for manual and office staff grades. The elimination of the remaining differentials would be addressed in the future and in the light of success of the business survival plan.

Eaton's agreement with the AUEW was of a type generally characteristic of newly established concerns with greenfield sites. As *IRRR* noted, however, at Newton Aycliffe Eaton had 'anything but a greenfield site' and its industrial relations were 'steeped in the traditions of the engineering industry'. Yet Eaton, like certain other companies driven to innovation in order to survive, succeeded in 'greenfielding' a brownfield site.

Johnson & Johnson[12] had had manufacturing and distribution centres in Britain even longer than Beckman and Eaton. Its UK subsidiary, established in 1924 to produce and sell its specialized health care goods more widely in British and European markets, was one of its first ventures outside the USA and Canada. The combined pressures of technological advance, and the need to raise productivity and resolve industrial relations problems, produced innovation in production methods and collective bargaining; and these changes, in turn, led to the adoption of a policy to harmonize the conditions of manual and non-manual grades.

By the early 1970s, with rather limited capital investment during the preceding two decades, much of the existing manufacturing plant needed to be replaced and premises were in need of refurbishment. Productivity and profit performance were unsatisfactory, and these problems were exacerbated by industrial relations which were adversarial, highly structured and influenced by national agreements. The company recognized four unions, had no less than thirteen separate negotiating groups, and at least four different settlement dates in the year. For management, collective bargaining was a complicated and time-consuming process. Outmoded payment structures and elaborate incentive payment schemes caused friction in negotiations, and uncompetitive pay rates caused disputes over earnings. Dissatisfaction amongst the workforce led to high labour turnover, and the unions' insistence on job and skill demarcations contributed to the problems of over-manning and low labour productivity.

The company took the decision in 1977 to deal with the more pressing of these problems. As a proportion of total output, commodity products were reduced in favour of fewer high-added-value speciality products. The company increased investment and upgraded plant and facilities; and manufacturing costs were lowered by the mechanization of many of the existing handwork tasks. Job evaluation techniques were applied to rationalize pay structures and to establish competitive pay levels. The company withdrew from the NJC and set up its own company-wide panel to bring together all the negotiating groups and to reduce the number of settlement dates. At the same time, steps were taken to develop a programme of employee-management participation and involvement in each plant. There were some job losses, but the 25 per cent reduction in the size of the workforce and rising investment in manufacturing capacity were associated with improvements in the morale and efficiency of those who remained, and produced a 37 per cent increase in productivity from 1977 to 1984. Apart from the revision of pay structures, there were moves towards harmonization in the areas of pensions, sick pay and provision for redundancy; holiday entitlements were in the process of being harmonized across plants and grades, and there were some moves towards the standardization of working hours.

By 1982 the size and composition of the workforce had changed and substantial improvements in performance had been achieved. It was clear, however, that in the near future the company would need even greater labour flexibility, and further gains in productivity. It was proposed, as part of the second stage of the company's programme, that a policy for further harmonization should be pursued. The central feature was to be a single integrated job evaluation system with a comprehensive salary structure, along with a profit-sharing scheme to replace individual bonuses. The separate unions were urged to discuss the proposal at joint meetings, with a view to moving to single-table bargaining in the near future. Negotiation through a single bargaining unit, representing all grades below management level, would facilitate the removal of remaining differentials in earnings-related sick pay arrangements, attendance recording, basic working hours, and shift premia; and it would ease the move to salaried status and monthly cashless pay for manual grades in line with the office staff. Productivity was to be further raised by the introduction of flexible working practices in combination with training and retraining of employees.

Johnson & Johnson viewed harmonization as a means to a number of ends: improved industrial relations, the removal of outmoded differentials, readier adaptability to market and technological changes, and better business performance.

In contrast to these longer established subsidiaries of US-owned multinationals, which moved to single status many years after commencement of production in Britain, Continental Can (UK)[13] set up manufacturing sites in continental Europe and Britain more recently, and began with purpose-built premises on greenfield sites and common terms and conditions from the outset. Continental Can, part of the US-based Continental Group Inc., established its first British subsidiary in the Wrexham area in 1980 to produce cans with the most advanced technology available at the time, which would involve round-the-clock operation and shift-working. Continental Group Inc. was not necessarily committed to a single-status philosophy wherever it operated, but at the Wrexham site the personnel director was keen to establish common terms and conditions as the basis of good industrial relations practice and as a means to discourage the emergence of 'us and them' attitudes. With single status in view, but mindful of a local industrial relations tradition, the company decided to recognize a single union for collective bargaining purposes. To recognize a multiplicity of unions would raise the immediate problem of job rights and trade boundaries; yet to begin without recognition of a trade union, in years when union membership at around thirteen million nationally was at an all time high, was to risk an *ad hoc* growth of a diversity of unions within the plant and the consequent emergence of demarcations. Such a situation would jeopardize the fully flexible working practices which cost-conscious management regarded as essential for productive efficiency, for effective utilization of present and future technology, and for rapid adjustment to changing market demands. The requirement of fully flexible working, commitment to retraining, and acceptance of mobility between jobs and departments, were written into the 1979 recognition agreement with the TGWU.

Continental Can introduced an integrated job grading and salary structure covering the entire workforce up to management level. This would facilitate flexibility in labour utilization and deployment. All those covered by the integrated grading structure had equal terms and benefits, with level of earnings as the only differential. Everyone received an annual salary, paid monthly by credit transfer. All were covered by the same arrangements for sick pay, pension, holiday entitlement, lay-off, notice period, and overtime and shift premia. No one was required to clock on and off, except for purposes of calculating any overtime worked. There were no pay deductions for short, infrequent and explained lateness. A scheme for private health care, designed by PPP, was equally available to all. Car parking arrangements and canteen facilities also came within the single-status concept.

The conditions offered by Continental Can were intended to attract, retain and motivate a 'stable, responsible and efficient labour force', to foster a company culture and identity, and to encourage commitment to managerially defined company objectives. The company aimed 'to motivate employees by treating them as responsible individuals'. That Continental Can adopted similar policies at the outset when it established other greenfield manufacturing sites in Britain later in the 1980s, suggests that its intended policy objectives were being achieved. It was a policy which provided scope for some input from the union, for management responded positively to the TGWU's proposal for a revision of the grading structure on its evidence that certain anomalies had emerged.

Cross International,[14] like Continental Can, established its British subsidiary with management commitment to the principle of common terms and benefits from the start in 1970, but subject to the controls of Government-imposed incomes policy, which were stringent in the early 1970s, management had less freedom for implementation and development of its philosophy. The company was perfectly willing to recognize trade unions, but ballots of employees to determine their wishes indicated that the vast majority preferred representation through the two joint negotiating committees for manual grades and office staff, which the company had established at the outset.

The British subsidiary of the US-owned multinational was established in the Merseyside area to produce special machine tool systems; the British site would provide the company with readier access to European markets and enable it the better to meet the current demand for its products from car manufacturers in Britain.

With the main exceptions of basic working hours and notice periods, most terms and benefits were single-status from the start. All employees below management level were covered by an integrated payment system with performance-related salary scales and salaries paid monthly by credit transfer into the individual's bank account. Arrangements for holiday entitlement, pensions, canteen, car parking and 'social facilities' were the same for all; everyone was required to clock on and off. The sick pay differential was of a minor nature: office staff received sick pay from the first day of sickness absence but manual grades only from the second. This differential was removed when management agreed to sick pay from the first day for everyone, but it was replaced by another: manual grades would continue to be required to produce a medical certificate after one day's absence while, at the request of the office staff committee, a medical certificate would be required of non-manual grades only after three days. Another differential emerged in response to pressure within the manual grades negotiating committee: from the mid-1970s manual workers were paid fortnightly and their salaries would become entirely grade-based instead of performance-related. Other differentials, obtaining at the outset, remained for the rest of the decade. Office staff worked a basic 37.5-hour week compared with the basic 40-hour week plus substantial amounts of overtime worked by manual grades; office staff had a minimum notice period of one month compared with one week for manual grades.

This was near-single status rather than complete single status. Management's response to the grievances voiced within the negotiating committees prevented friction over certain aspects of single status from precipitating a walk-out. The company's sensitivity in taking employees' views into account, in adapting to local conditions, and in deciding on complete single status as a longer-term goal, contributed to a good industrial relations record.

A co-operative work force and an absence of strikes and overtime bans were particularly important for a company operating in a highly specialized field in which product quality and ability to meet delivery dates, especially in exports, were crucial. Though the UK market was depressed in the early 1970s, Cross International succeeded in performing profitably and competing effectively in European markets. The company won the Queen's Award in 1974.

In retrospect, what can be said of the American companies' approach to the elimination of status-related differentials in their subsidiaries in Britain? It is sometimes assumed that IBM provides *the* American model, but, in point of fact, case studies show that there are numerous American models. In large part this is the result of the combined effects of company philosophy, type of product and technology, changing product market circumstances, the local economic and social environment, local labour markets and cultural tradition. Several companies, such as IBM, TI, Hewlett Packard and Digital, had greenfield sites, were non-union concerns, and had what amounts to complete single status from the outset. Others, such as Continental Can and Eaton, recognized and dealt with a single union. Still others, such as Beckman Instruments and Johnson & Johnson, recognized more than one union, though the tendency was to negotiate with them jointly in one bargaining unit. While some introduced harmonized conditions all in one go, others on brownfield sites proceeded more slowly. What all have in common is a willingness not only to take the calculated risk of innovation, but a willingness where necessary to adapt, change and develop their arrangements. The advanced practice of single status was brought to Britain, not by the Japanese in the late 1970s and 1980s, but by the Americans as long ago as the 1950s. The American approach, in being sensitive to British localism as well as mindful of and responsive to major external developments and the international dimension, is infinitely more varied and more flexible than the Japanese approach, possibly because the Americans are involved in a more diverse range of industries in Britain than are the Japanese.

5 Single Status in Britain: The Japanese Models?

INTRODUCTION

The 'Japanese economic miracle' was a cause of wonder for Western observers for many years. The 1980s have been termed the 'decade of the Japanese', and if Japan's economic performance attracts less sensational publicity in the West in the 1990s, the explanation may lie in the fact that exhaustive investigation and media coverage during the preceding decade have left few further dramatically new features to be uncovered, or because Japan's economic growth is now less spectacular than it was a few years ago.

It would be erroneous to assume that the ideas so successfully applied by the Japanese in Japan, Britain and elsewhere were exclusively, or even largely, Japanese in origin. Towers, Wickens, Oliver, Wilkinson and others remind us that 'many of the "imports" from Japan are of Western provenance.'[1] Non-unionism, enterprise unionism, company representation committees, and the like, have deep historical roots in the industrial relations tradition of the United States.[2] Graham[3] asserts that British managers had been experimenting for some time with techniques to gain the kind of cost-pruning advantages to be derived from Japanese Just-In-Time methods. Flexible working is generally acknowledged to be a vital element of JIT systems; but, again, British manufacturers had been seeking greater flexibility in manpower utilization and deployment for several decades: through productivity bargaining in the 1960s, self-financing pay deals in the 1970s, and flexibility clauses attached to broader agreements in the 1980s. JIT techniques, Graham argues, are not 'uniquely Japanese'; manufacturing managers in the western world had long ago recognized the inefficiencies caused by specialization, which were encountered 'in both craft and Taylorist manufacturing systems', and had sought a relaxation of demarcations 'without this being seen as a copying of practice in Japan'. Oliver and Wilkinson observe that the Japanese 'borrowed many of their ideas from the West', including group technology and quality circles.[4] The basic idea of 'cell' or 'group' technology, Graham claims, was being tried out in the Soviet Union in the 1950s, and was in evidence in the USA and Germany long before it came to be publicized as Japanese. Quality circles, which developed in sectors of Japanese industry in the late 1950s and 1960s, stem from the ideas of American statisticians, W.E. Deming and J.M. Juran, who promulgated their theories during visits to Japan in 1950 and 1954, respectively; likewise, the Japanese methods of total quality management are derived from the ideas of the American theorist, A. Feigenbaum.

When Peters and Waterman[5] went in search of excellence at the beginning of the 1980s, they found that many of the techniques, which others were describing as Japanese, had been in operation in several US manufacturing concerns for some time. Even so, if many of the theories, methods and concepts did not originate in Japan, it was the Japanese who were most fervent in their application. Leading manufacturers in certain sectors of Japanese industry were demonstrably proficient in operationalizing new ideas and drawing on 'foreign knowledge'. Company councils, a high degree of face-to-face communication, and harmonized employment conditions may be characteristic of major Japanese corporations, but they are not culturally unique to Japan. Moves to harmonize terms, benefits and conditions were underway in the USA, Britain, Germany and certain other European countries long before such practice received widespread publicity in the West as typically, and erroneously by some as singularly, Japanese in form and style.[6] While the Japanese apparently continue to look at Western ideas in the ongoing refinement of their own systems, it is increasingly to Japanese organizations that the West has looked in recent years for lessons in international competitiveness.

Innovation in manufacturing and personnel practice occurred in some British companies without conscious emulation of the Japanese; but with the spectacular success of newly established subsidiaries of Japanese companies in Britain, several British employers embarked upon innovations which were openly acknowledged to be emulative of the Japanese approach.

The remarkable performance of the Japanese in certain world markets was attributed, in part, to 'progressive' personnel policies, such as 'single status terms and conditions, consultative management styles...employment guarantees, and company-based welfare schemes.'[7] The company's commitment to providing lifetime employment security, occupational welfare, company-sponsored social amenities, and formally structured pay and promotion systems, was said to encourage a reciprocal workforce loyalty to the firm, to reduce labour turnover, and to facilitate flexible labour deployment. Employers were said to be consequently the more disposed to treat labour as an asset rather than a cost, and to be the more willing, therefore, to expend time, effort and funds on training and developing their human resources. Dore[8] argues that lifetime employment and paternalistic welfarism were not necessarily culturally determined characteristics. Something may be attributable to Confucianism and the feudal ideology of 'loyalty to one lord', but more is owed to the state of trade and the state of the labour market and their effect upon business decisions. Lifetime employment is neither a legal nor contractual obligation, and it is not available to all Japanese workers. It is a matter of company policy, and is effective only to the extent that prevailing economic and labour market circumstances permit. Like the developed countries of the West, Japan has relatively large numbers employed in jobs which are less than permanent and less than full-time. Guaranteed employment and well-developed occupational welfare systems tend to be found mainly in large manufacturing concerns which the more readily permit labour redeployment within their own organizations. In the later 1980s, with growing competition from rapidly industrializing East Asian countries, anti-dumping reactions in Europe and the USA, and a strong yen, there were redundancies in Japan's steel, shipbuilding, and coal industries; and a slower rate of economic growth made it more difficult for companies to guarantee employment.

Company welfarism developed in Japan, not so much as a manifestation of cultural tradition but rather as a conscious management strategy to attract, retain, motivate and control labour. Littler argues that, as long ago as the 1920s, employers saw paternalistic welfare policy as 'a panacea for all the ills of industrial capitalism', and more specifically as 'an alternative to Western-type class struggle'.[9] Somewhat sweepingly, Pascale and Athos[10] claimed early in the 1980s that the Japanese version of paternalism as a strategy of personnel management was 'desirable'; it offered benefits and advantages all round, and was 'potentially transferable' to the West. Briggs[11] and other critics remained sceptical about the 'all round' nature of the advantages thus provided.

JAPANESE COMPANIES IN BRITAIN

Japanese-owned subsidiaries in Britain began with certain advantages, as did many of their American precursors. Most were set up on green-field sites, engaged a relatively high proportion of 'green labour', and commenced with union recognition agreements containing important concessions – on flexible working, for example – already secured. It may be the case, as Pang and Oliver[12] argue, that recruits were disposed to acquiesce in 'alternative ways or working' because the 'very Japanese-ness' of the new enterprises aroused an expectation that working conditions and practices would be different from traditional approaches. From a more realistic viewpoint, however, workpeople's willingness to accept new working methods and conditions probably owed a great deal to the high levels unemployment prevailing generally in the late 1970s and during most of the following decade, and to unemployment rates well above the national average in some of the regions where the Japanese chose to establish their manufacturing and assembly plants. Compliance, even in districts with strong traditions of working-class consciousness and trade union involvement, is unsurprising from people whose only real alternative to the jobs on offer was the dole queue.

Moreover, the likely compliance of prospective workforces was largely pre-ascertained by careful screening, testing, selection and induction policies, which were as much concerned with applicants' attitudes as with relevant skills. Initial recruitment was followed by a probationary period of employment, with intensive preparation and training. Recruitment officers looked for a willingness to work flexibly, to co-operate in training and re-training programmes, to adapt to an environment of ongoing change and continuous improvement, and to identify with the company's objectives. The creation of a community of interests and sense of commitment were further fostered by extensive consultation and communication systems, by single-status employment conditions, and elaborate mechanisms for resolving differences and avoiding industrial action. Single-union deals, with provision for binding pendulum arbitration, have come to be regarded as a characteristic of Japanese industrial relations practice in Britain.

Japanese and other foreign-owned firms with production sites in Wales were reported to be generally well satisfied with their business performance in terms of productivity, employee motivation, and industrial relations. ACAS[13] claimed, however, that none of this could be 'attributed to any imported managerial sophistication.' In most cases the Japanese, American and European companies in question had not embarked upon industrial relations practices which were 'entirely foreign' to British experience. At an early stage most had appointed British personnel management teams to search out and adapt best British practice to the needs of the particular company. The result was 'a blend of the practices which have been proven within the UK and usable strands of their native philosophies'. The greenfield locations of most Japanese companies had presented the same opportunities for them as for British enterprises in a similar position. Greenfield sites had facilitated flexible working arrangements, greater employee involvement, moves to single status, and more effective methods of quality and cost control. Ready access to British and European markets, financial incentives from the British Government, and the regional supply of a 'suitable workforce' were key considerations in Japanese companies' choice of location. Several companies recognized no union; most of the rest recognized a single union. In association with a checklist of 'issues for new investors in Wales', ACAS recommended that employers should 'consider harmonized single-status terms and conditions, and a workforce with a "team spirit" based on employee involvement and flexibility'.[14]

Certain common characteristics were disclosed by *IRRR*'s 1990 questionnaire survey of the employment policies and practices of well over a hundred Japanese companies in Britain at that time. All expected their employees to be flexible in their working practices, and multi-skilling, evident in all but one firm, was the most common form of flexibility. The vast majority had implemented team or group working (80 per cent), JIT manufacturing techniques (75 per cent) and measures to encourage employee involvement and/or participation, such as quality circles and consultative councils (80 per cent). A similarly large proportion provided harmonized terms and conditions, security of employment and continuous training. Although personnel policies were claimed to be generally in line with those of the Japanese parent companies, managements in the British subsidiaries stated that they alone had ultimate responsibility for the formulation of policy at British sites. Only half of the firms recognized a trade union, and in all these cases single-union deals had been reached, mostly with the EETPU. Unions appeared to stand a better chance of gaining recognition if they were seen as being 'moderate' and had been granted representation rights by other inward investors.

The flexible working practices implemented by Japanese companies in Britain involved performance of some unskilled tasks by craftsmen, and multi-skilling to enable employees to cope with a wide range of work tasks, such as electrical isolation, oxyacetylene and arc welding, pipe-fitting, operation of turning, milling and grinding machines, sheet-metalworking and diagnostic/maintenance work, without demarcations of any kind.[15] Japanese companies were able to take advantage of greenfield sites and local pools of skilled labour to adopt multi-skilling from the outset, while their British counterparts on brownfield sites were struggling to negotiate agreements allowing more limited flexibilities.

There were marked differences in the nature of team working. At one extreme it took the form of self-contained groups of multi-skilled workers operating their own 'mini factories', with team responsibility for output, quality standards, and achievement of financial targets; at the other it involved little more than team briefings by supervisors and some job rotation. There were variations also in the extent and style of employee involvement and participation. The most common form was found to be quality circles; at Komatsu and certain other companies there were full-time 'QC facilitators' who had responsibilities for training, administration, back-up resourcing, and publicity. Consultative groups and advisory boards were in existence in many companies, but there were considerable differences in the nature and extent of their powers and duties. *IRRR* notes the incidence also of suggestion schemes at Aiwa, Daiwa Sports and Matsushita Graphic, of work improvement teams at Calsonic Exhaust Systems (UK), of review councils at Hashimoto and Matsushita Electronic Magnetron, and of 'various forms' of participation at Nissan.

A very large proportion of the Japanese companies in Britain provide single-status conditions of employment or common terms and benefits, but personnel policy did not generally extend to providing lifetime employment as such; nor was recruitment largely confined to school, college and university leavers seeking first jobs. Although 'raw' recruits were preferred for production work, most companies required managers with experience. Pang and Oliver discovered little evidence of the transfer of seniority-based pay and promotion systems from Japan to the West. The main determinants of promotion were performance and qualifications; pay was determined in ways similar to those operating in comparable British companies. Greater attention was given to training in Japanese companies in Britain than in many British companies, but it was more restricted than in the parent companies in Japan. There was some emphasis on induction, and on on-the-job training which was most intensive during the employee's first year of employment with the company. There was continuous training in general and transferable skills, and job rotation to facilitate flexibility was common.

The general consensus amongst investigators was that Japanese management methods were being adapted and adjusted to the British manufacturing and industrial relations environment, rather than being imported wholesale. As the Japanese deputy managing director of Matsushita expressed it:

> We understand that this is Britain, with a totally different history and traditions, and therefore the Japanese have deliberately sought not to impose the Japanese way of doing things, but rather to evolve, in consultation with the employees, a system which actually works.[16]

The generally successful performance of Japanese companies in Britain owes less to the enforcement of practices and techniques which operate in Japan, than to a willingness to adapt, adjust and re-fashion the means and methods. This is an important dimension of flexible operation; and it has to be remembered that, even if we take Government grant aid into consideration, those Japanese companies which set up production in decaying industrial areas with a deeply rooted working-class culture and strong union traditions succeeded in the least auspicious of social contexts.

Nissan[17] at Washington, Tyne and Wear, formally opened in September 1986, was claimed to represent the heaviest financial commitment of a Japanese company in Britain to date. In the North East, Nissan had the advantage of starting from scratch, with working practices based on the principles of 'teamwork, quality consciousness, and flexibility'. Under the terms of the company's single-union recognition agreement of 1985, the AUEW gained sole bargaining rights in a deal cutting 'right across traditional demarcations' and establishing 'working flexibilities until now unknown in the British car industry'. A number of agreements of this kind had already been reached elsewhere, such as the 1981 deal between Toshiba and the EETPU. The Nissan agreement was path-breaking, however, in that it was reached and implemented in an industry with a long and still prevalent tradition of multi-union bargaining and strict demarcations. *IRRR* found no single element in the deal that was 'especially novel or, indeed, distinctively "Japanese"', but the total package and the interrelatedness of its various features represented one of the 'most sophisticated expressions so far of the "new style" industrial relations' pioneered recently at greenfield sites; and by the current standards of the indigenous UK motor vehicles industry, it was 'unquestionably unique'.[18] Nissan's decision to recognize a single union was taken in the belief that a policy of non-unionism would result in the haphazard informal growth of multi-unionism, consequent pressure for bargaining rights from several different unions and the emergence of demarcations which would undermine the principles of labour flexibility and common terms and conditions of employment.

Apart from sole bargaining rights for the engineering union, the agreement made provision for a Company Council, of management and directly elected workforce representatives, to function as the main forum for consultation and negotiation. There was an arrangement, in the event of a difference remaining unresolved by the Company Council, for referral of the issue to ACAS for 'compulsory conciliation' with the option of 'binding pendulum arbitration'. The clause relating to 'complete labour flexibility' was accompanied by the requirement of employees' commitment to accept technical change and to undergo any training or retraining deemed necessary by the company. The agreement proposed to set up a very simple job grading structure with no rigid job definitions, along with a salary system with broad salary bands and merit-based pay progression for all employees. Single-status terms and benefits included no clocking, payment of salaries monthly by credit transfer, plus common basic working hours, holiday entitlement, sick pay and pension arrangements, overtime premia, notice period, and redundancy compensation.

Membership of the union, which had sole representation rights for all up to senior management level, was not compulsory, and the agreement, in fact, explicitly ruled out the operation of any form of closed shop. Membership of the single union was actively encouraged, however, for the company believed that a high level of involvement was important to the long-term success of the agreement; if some employees were to join other unions, the result might be an *ad hoc* growth of job and skill boundaries, which would undermine the teamwork ethic and the principles of labour flexibility, the integrated pay and grading structure and common employment conditions, even though the other unions in question had no recognized bargaining position within the company.

Following the appointment of a few key managers in 1984, recruitment of other employees was a carefully constructed exercise phased over eighteen months. The process of selecting supervisors was necessarily rigorous, for this group would have a crucial role in establishing and maintaining a consensual rather than adversarial industrial relations climate in the plant, and in ensuring effective communication with production workers. Supervisors were required to be both technically competent and capable of effectively motivating people. The recruitment of production staff, including team leaders, manufacturing operatives, and technical maintenance grades, was an equally rigorous procedure, based on detailed application forms, aptitude tests, tests of verbal/oral skills, numeracy and mechanical comprehension, and informal group discussions with supervisors. Short-listed candidates were subsequently recalled for further tests in practical skills, designed to assess manual dexterity, ability to follow instructions, work quality, and time taken to complete set tasks; in addition, there were tests of attitude, outlook, personality and ability to co-operate.

Nissan had the advantage of beginning with purpose-built premises designed with an equalized conditions philosophy in mind, carefully screened recruits already committed to fully flexible working, extensive structures for employee participation, acceptance of binding pendulum bargaining to settle differences unresolved by direct negotiation, and a 'guaranteed week' arrangement to cover specified periods should work be unavailable for the full 39-hour working week. The latter provision was put into operation for a short time during 1996. Overall business performance was such as to permit the company to expand its operations in the North East and to increase the size of its workforce from the relatively small numbers with which it began in 1986.

Toshiba Consumer Products (UK),[19] though producing different goods, nevertheless had much in common with the approach adopted by Nissan. The company was set up following the closure of Rank Toshiba's Ernsettle and Redruth factories which had produced television and audio equipment. Closure was said to have been caused by the onset of the economic recession, high UK inflation, and the effect of strong sterling upon markets, but soon after settlement of financial matters between Rank and Toshiba, Toshiba announced its intention to take over the main Ernsettle manufacturing unit and to recommence production, mainly of colour TV sets for the UK domestic market. The 'fresh start' in 1981 would involve some fundamental changes in industrial relations and working practices, which would become more 'typically Japanese' in style.

Industrial relations at Rank Toshiba had not been a main cause of the closure, but a high level of union membership and traditionally structured collective bargaining had presented management with problems which were difficult to resolve. A complexity of different basic pay rates and a variety of bonuses had been negotiated with no less than six different unions representing separate occupational groups within and between the two manufacturing sites, each bargaining unit having its own annual settlement date. Skilled and semi-skilled production operators were represented by the AUEW and EETPU, specialist operatives by FTAT, and clerical supervisory and technical engineering staffs by APEX, ASTMS and TASS, respectively. The distinction between manual and non-manual grades was clearly marked by different terms and conditions of employment for the two broad groups. Skill traditions, union demarcations, job rights and trade boundaries constrained the extent to which flexible working could be realized.

There were fundamental changes when Toshiba Consumer Products was set up, following the gutting and modernization of the main manufacturing site. With the fresh start in 1981, a single union, the EETPU, was recognized for collective bargaining purposes; the framework agreement provided harmonized conditions for all permanent full-time employees, an advisory board structure for employee involvement in all the company's activities, and pendulum arbitration as the final stage of procedure for the resolution of differences. At the time, this system of arbitration was hailed as 'novel for the UK', a 'revolutionary change of approach', and was described by Roy Sanderson, national officer of the EETPU, as representing 'some of the best industrial relations practices to be found anywhere in British industry and some that are quite new and point the way to the future.'[20]

With the streamlining and modernization of production, 'suitability for the new jobs in a new work environment' was the company's main consideration in recruitment of employees. Toshiba required people who had a willingness and competence for fully flexible working, to the point where clerical grades could be called upon to perform operative tasks and operatives could undertake clerical work. All would have responsibility for their own maintenance functions on a 'work and check' basis. In the course of an intensive and rigorous interviewing process, evidence of commitment and co-operative attitudes was as important as indicators of the technical ability of those selected. Acceptance of flexible working practices was made explicit in the company's agreement with the single union which was to represent all employees up to supervisory level. The arrangement was wide-ranging in scope, and provided for a high degree of interdepartmental co-operation. The relevant clause in the agreement specified 'complete flexibility of jobs and duties...both within departments and between the various departments'. In return, the company recognized and accepted 'the need for training and retraining in the broadening of skills and in the new technological developments as they affect the company's efficiency as a manufacturing operation'.[21]

Harmonized terms and conditions of employment applied across the board. All employees received monthly salaries, paid by credit transfer into a nominated bank account. A totally new integrated and simplified grading structure was introduced; regardless of collar colour, employees up to supervisory level were assigned to one of four broad grades according to the number of skills which individuals could exercise. Salary progression within the grade, and promotion to the grade above, depended upon skill acquisition through the company's training programmes. A basic 39-hour working week was common to all. Clocking was required of everyone working overtime, and everyone up to the grade of supervisor was eligible for the same premium rates of pay when extra hours were worked. A new dining room, with no segregated seating areas, was run on the single-status principle. All employees were covered by the same arrangements for sick pay, pension, holiday entitlement, notice period and redundancy compensation. Everyone, including the managing director, was supplied with a company uniform and name badge, to be worn at all times on the work premises.

Accompanying these innovations was total reorganization of the traditional machinery for consultation and communication. The working day on the factory floor began with a five-minute meeting of supervisors and work teams to discuss the previous day's production, any problems that had emerged, and ways and means of resolving them. There were also 'small circle activities' at other times during the day. These were enhanced at company level by a new advisory system to provide representatives from all sections of the workforce with the opportunity of influencing company policy and company performance.

Provision for pendulum arbitration sought to avoid industrial action and breakdown in industrial relations. The procedure allowed for the joint reference of an unresolved issue to an independent arbitrator; both parties would present their case and the arbitrator would find in favour of either the company or the union. The arbitrator was not permitted to 'split the difference', and both parties had to abide by the decision. The clause was 'novel' in Britain at the time, and was clearly intended as a last resort after all attempts at compromise had failed. Its main function was to encourage both sides to explore every possibility of reaching a compromise, to discourage excessive and frivolous demands, and to minimize the risk of industrial action.

Toshiba's management was undoubtedly aware that employees' willingness to accept the new work environment, methods and practices owed something to the 2,500 redundancies which had followed the closure of Rank Toshiba, and to a local unemployment rate of around 14 per cent at the beginning of the 1980s. Retrospectively, a certain amount of optimism was justified, however, for the workforce had increased from about 300 in 1982 to around 800 by 1990; and if industrial relations were not entirely trouble-free, neither were they catastrophically turbulent. Many of the techniques applied at Toshiba, such as the harmonization of manual and non-manual conditions, were already well known in Britain and had already been introduced by several British companies; others, such a small circle activities and pendulum arbitration, owed more to Japanese or US practice. The company disclaimed 'any "parent pressure" of a direct kind'; but management, even with a great deal of freedom to map out their own strategy, was almost certainly indirectly influenced by Japanese ownership and their knowledge of Japanese practices which produced 'world class manufacturing standards'.

Komatsu,[22] in contrast, acknowledged that the policy applied at the British manufacturing site was consciously intended to be in line with that operated by its parent company in Japan. Komatsu, ranking financially after Caterpillar on the international scene as the second largest manufacturer of earthmoving and construction equipment in the late 1980s, had been pursuing a policy of setting up offshore manufacturing sites since the early 1970s. In order to relate production more effectively to market needs and to gain a more competitive international position than was possible from its home base in Japan, Komatsu established factories in Brazil, Mexico and Indonesia, followed later by manufacturing sites in the USA and the UK. In the mid-1980s Komatsu chose to set up production in the UK at Birtley near Gateshead in the North East, at a site recently vacated by Caterpillar. This was an area which offered the advantages of a large pool of skilled labour, suitable transport and technological resources, a grant from the British Government of 15 per cent of approved capital expenditure, positive attitudes on the part of local union officials, and suitable local suppliers. Like other Japanese companies already established in the UK, Komatsu wanted to introduce single-union representation, pendulum arbitration, single-status terms and conditions of employment, and mechanisms for employee consultation and involvement. By 1990 the company employed a workforce of over 400; the main characteristics of its operations were JIT methods, quality circles, multi-skilling, skilled/unskilled flexibility, mechanical/electrical flexibility, security of employment, common terms and conditions, continuous training, and employee involvement/participation.

A start was made on preparing the site in March 1986; at this time the company had an 'abandoned shell of a factory', a Japanese managing director, a British personnel officer, and an understanding with the AEU for single-union representation. By September, after a rapid start-up, around 50 locally recruited employees with the assistance of 30 Japanese advisers had assembled five hydraulic excavators from training model kits brought over from Japan, and the move to full production was scheduled for the end of the year.

For all staff, whether managers, supervisors, office personnel, or production workers, the main focus of initial training was on the additional skills needed for effective working in small teams with maximum flexibility and job responsibility, rather than on the basic skills needed for the job in question. Applicants for jobs were put through a searching selection procedure, involving aptitude tests and 'pencil and paper psychological tests' designed, in part, to identify attitudes supportive of teamwork and flexibility.[23] There was a ten-week induction period for new recruits, and some of the locally recruited supervisors were sent to Japan for four weeks of specialist training at the parent company. The flexibility clause to Komatsu's framework agreement with the AEU stated that there would be 'interchangeability and mobility of labour' between jobs, duties and departments; 'complete flexibility' would be enhanced by training 'in the broadening of skills and in dealing with new technology developments to improve efficiency and profitability'.

Single-status terms, benefits, and employment conditions were listed in Komatsu's *Company Handbook* as:

single-status contract of employment;
subsidized canteen facilities common to all employees;
free company uniform;
company social club;
paid overtime;

25 days of annual paid holiday;
free life assurance;
free private medical scheme;
company pension scheme;
no time clocks;
no deductions for short occasional lateness;
monthly salaries;
common company sick pay scheme;
39-hour basic working week.

An integrated pay and grading structure was set up, along with performance review and career appraisal systems. The latter served four
main purposes: (i) to provide potential for career development across
the company; (ii) thus to provide an incentive element of pay, which
is related to quality and competent performance as opposed to crude
measures of speed and quantity of output; (iii) to encourage supervisors and team leaders to be responsible for development of their
own and their work group's skills; (iv) to provide an assessment of
managerial and labour efficiency.

The ten characteristics, identified in 1990 as typical of Japanese companies operating in Britain,[24] were: multi-skilling,
skilled–unskilled flexibility, mechanical/electrical flexibility, teamworking, JIT methods, security of employment, single-status terms
and conditions, continuous training, policies similar to parent
company, and structures for involvement/participation. To these
might be added quality circles, single-union recognition, and pendulum arbitration. Of the 25 companies covered by *IRRR*'s survey, the
full complement of characteristics was found in nine cases:
Matsushita Electronic Magnetron and Matsushita Electronic, both
set up in the 1970s, and Calsonic Exhaust Systems, Fujitsu
Microelectronics, Hashimoto, JVC Manufacturing, Komatsu, Nissan
Motor Manufacturing, and Sanyo Industries, all of which were set up
in Britain in the 1980s. In four other companies there was only one
'missing' characteristic. Omron Electronics and Seiko Instruments,
established in 1987 and 1989 respectively, did not have formal
arrangements for involvement; Matsushita Communication
Industrial, established in 1988, did not use JIT methods; and
Diaplastics, established in 1987, did not provide continuous training.
Only four of the 25 Japanese companies did not provide single-status
terms and conditions of employment.

JAPANIZED COMPANIES IN BRITAIN

British manufacturers, struggling against ever keener competition in global markets, were not unnaturally interested to discover the key to success; and it is unsurprising that their attention during the 1980s should turn to the Japanese. A WRU discussion paper,[25] issued by the Department of Employment in 1986, noted that some British employers had already effectively applied certain 'Japanese ideas', such as quality circles, statistical process control, and new methods of product design; but it warned against the assumption that simply 'copying the surface features...their excellent production engineering disciplines, or their good approach to production planning' would ensure an improved manufacturing performance on the part of emulators.

A similar view had been jointly expressed by union and management representatives of Thorn EMI Ferguson following visits to Japan in 1978 and 1983.[26] They concluded that one of the most important factors underlying the success of Japanese companies was management's ability to draw upon employees' ideas, to win loyalty, commitment and a sense of involvement on the part of the workforce, and to treat labour as 'people' rather than as a 'factor of production'. Long-term survival and prosperity required an ability to 'compete in the field of employee commitment'. This, *IRRR* believed, was one of the most important of the lessons to be learned from Japan. With this in mind, British employers were urged seriously to consider: (i) the elimination of status barriers in the workplace; (ii) an approach to 'work structure' which provided employees with 'meaningful roles' and allowed them to make a 'positive contribution' to the success of the company; (iii) training programmes for the development and succession of management; (iv) effective 'two-way communication' on the company's performance, policies and future; (v) encouragement of individuals to shoulder greater responsibility for work quality, their working environment, and 'factory house-keeping'.

Negotiation with a single union, often an 'enterprise union' specific to the company, which was appropriate in Japan, was not such a practical proposition in most long-established British companies with their traditions of multi-union recognition and separate bargaining units for different grades. The way forward was to adapt existing bargaining structures to a changing manufacturing environment, rather than to impose the Japanese approach and risk turbulent industrial relations.

The British could, however, learn something from Japanese

employers' practice of designing workforce training schemes for: (i) developing craftsmen with the multi-skills required by sophisticated machine technologies; (ii) developing new skills for new roles in an environment of technological advance; (iii) achieving a high level of safety consciousness and safety standards; (iv) fostering sound labour relations based on formal industrial relations training.

Several British companies were introducing Japanese-style methods and practices in the 1980s, though relatively few adopted the whole Japanese package. Lucas Electrical,[27] for example, applied the 'recognizably Japanese' practices of JIT production, total quality control, the grouping of factory machining processes into 'product families', a flexible manufacturing strategy to match market needs, elimination as far as possible of non-value-added activities, and a personnel policy with harmonized conditions in view.

Some change in British car-producing companies was set in motion by Nissan's arrival on the British manufacturing scene.[28] Nissan's distinct advantages, which included complete labour flexibility, a keen and committed workforce, the most advanced technology available at the time, cost-effective production methods, stylish product design, and promising order books, were highlighted in the press; and the effect was to spur some of the long-established companies to introduce change in their manufacturing processes and working practices.

Innovation at the Rover Group had begun some years earlier and was pushed much further with Nissan's arrival in the North East. Rover's management had been in consultation with Honda in years when the company was suffering damaging competition from overseas car manufacturers. By 1986 the Rover Group was in the process of a fundamental transformation. Many of the new practices to be introduced were reported as being 'very similar to those already existing in Japan'; the 'whole British car industry' was said to be 'attempting to emulate certain Japanese practices'. Single-status terms and employment conditions were a significant feature of Rover's survival strategy. The removal of 'them and us' distinctions was intended to foster greater co-operation from the workforce and to boost motivation. The unions were broadly in favour of the proposed changes. The personnel officer predicted that full harmonization would be accomplished by the end of the decade.

In 1987 Rover announced that, in order to facilitate functional flexibility, it intended to recruit 'better educated people for production jobs'. Job applicants were to undergo thorough testing, not only for manual skills and dexterity but also for attitudes and aspirations compatible with company culture. An induction and preliminary training programme, focusing on work quality, was set up that year. Like a number of other car producing companies, Rover introduced quality circles and team briefings, termed zone circles and zone briefings in Rover's case, as means to greater employee involvement, participation, and direct communication.

A degree of Japanization produced a certain amount of improvement in manufacturing performance, but Smith's[29] investigation led him to conclude that Rover had not yet succeeded in creating a company culture of shared aspirations and commitment to common objectives. He found the shop stewards anxious about losing their influence, and the workforce compliant rather than committed to the company and its objectives. After initial enthusiasm, workers felt frustrated by management's apparent uninterest in the ideas and suggestions put forward by team members. These responses may, of course, have been coloured by the job insecurity prevailing at the time, both in the car industry and in the region, which was hardly conducive to optimism. Despite some disenchantment with the changes in production methods and working practices, the harmonized conditions were broadly greeted with approval.

British Leyland, Vauxhall, Talbot and most other motor vehicle manufacturers were seeking to introduce flexible working practices and to reduce differentials in terms, benefits and employment conditions in the 1980s as means to greater productive efficiency and cost-competitiveness.[30] Despite some opposition from the trade unions, flexible working had been implemented at most of British Leyland's manufacturing sites by 1983 and, with a new job evaluation scheme, some 500 different job classifications were condensed into five broad grades company-wide. Responsibility for work quality and inspection of product was transferred to operatives during the next two years. The formation of work teams provided opportunity for progression within the team, from materials handler to operator, to quality controller, and to maintenance. Rotation of some tasks and delegation to the teams of some responsibility for maintenance and quality control represented a significant break with past Fordist-style production characterized by the fragmentation and specialization of support functions. Japanization would be pushed much further in the 1990s, when Leyland Trucks was established following a management buy-out of the trucks division of Leyland-DAF in 1993.[31]

Japanization was not, of course, confined exclusively, or even mainly, to the motor vehicles industry; it was apparent at Thorn

Lighting,[32] a subsidiary of the Thorn EMI Group, when in the late 1980s new technology was introduced and restructuring was undertaken in response to market pressures. Operating on a brownfield site, the company succeeded in moving from 'a position of inefficiency, poor customer services and financial weakness to "world class manufacturing" status'. Thorn replaced outdated practices by production methods based on flexible working, cell-based manufacturing and JIT controls, and made decisive moves towards harmonized conditions as part of the overall streamlining programme. At Thorn's largest manufacturing plant at Spennymore in the North East of England, production of goods ranging from light fittings to 'white goods' had changed little during the preceding two decades. During the 1970s, when the company had no difficulty in selling all it could produce, there had been little incentive to change; and restrictive practices had emerged in the context of multi-unionism. Four unions, the EETPU, AEU, GMB and TGWU, represented the hourly-paid, and TASS and APEX were recognized to represent monthly-paid staff below management level. Union density was very high and there was a large number of separate bargaining units with different settlement dates. During the difficult years of the 1980s, while many competing companies adapted in various ways to progressively keener competition, Thorn stood still and missed global market opportunities.

Prior to restructuring, the company had had a complex job evaluation system which produced 950 job descriptions and 100 pay grades for the 2,400 employees in question. Though industrial relations were generally good, the existence of a large number of individual bargaining groups meant that much of management's time was absorbed in dealing with the unions rather than managing the business. Pressure from customers for delivery dates to be met had caused management to use bonus incentives and higher wage rates to secure employees' co-operation in achieving production targets. The payment structure had resulted in accelerating wage drift. Thorn remained relatively labour-intensive in years when competing companies were introducing the technology of the future and winning markets at Thorn's expense.

With a change in senior management, a thorough business review was undertaken, and in 1987 it was decided that the company should sell off the appliances manufacturing facility and confine its Spennymore operation to production of commercial lighting fittings, electronics, mouldings and wound gear. Many changes were needed to achieve the new management's objective of creating a 'world class manufacturing' operation. New technology was one of the most urgent requirements, and this necessitated an agreement with the relevant unions to 'crew new CAD/CAM machinery with multi-skilled craft operators' who would be able to change tooling and set the computer numerically controlled system. In 1988 management designed a five-year human resources and working practices strategy, which involved cell-based manufacturing, JIT methods, team work, total 'preventive maintenance', and continuous quality improvement.

The various stages of the production process were grouped into cells, with teams of employees given responsibility for production of 'product families' from start to finish. Components not produced within the cell were subject to strict JIT and Kanban controls. A 'typical' cell was made up of thirty or forty employees working a one, two or three shift system. Where, owing to changes in product demand, full crewing was not needed, employees would be redeployed to other cells or operations, as appropriate. All of this was in sharp contrast to the company's earlier production methods. Formerly, factory lay-out had been tailored to deal with high-volume long-run production. Separate processes – pressing, painting, assembly etc. – had been carried out at different locations on the site; and this had involved movement of components to appropriate areas, delay in waiting for supplies in some cases, and unnecessary stock-piling in others. New technology, cell manufacturing and JIT methods greatly reduced waste, speeded up production, and eased scheduling problems.

Team-building courses with feedback sessions were arranged in consultation with shop stewards, in part to prepare for the re-deployment of inspectors and the move to a system of 'total quality control', 'right first time', and quality assurance measures based on statistical process control. Shift supervisors' responsibilities included maintenance of production levels and quality, monitoring of raw materials supply according to Kanban principles, and ensuring machine efficiency. At the start of each shift there were short team briefings to discuss the previous day's production along with ideas for problem-solving and continuous improvement. The elimination of three tiers of management left a much 'flatter' structure – managing director, manufacturing manager, cell manager, and first-line supervisor.

The company reported marked improvements following implementation of the new policy. Machine downtime to change tooling had been halved; investment in quick-change tool retrieval equipment and the removal of inspection substantially reduced changeover time;

average monthly scrap costs had been cut by two-thirds; and cell manufacture economized on both time and space. The whole process of change had been greatly assisted by extensive communication exercises and full involvement of the unions and workforce. The agreement with the unions provided for the harmonization of conditions, and included a new streamlined pay and grading structure to accommodate craft flexibility.

Two companies, both US-owned, which had successfully introduced the Japanese style of JIT production by 1990 claimed that the process had been facilitated by the adoption of measures to transform management's and employees' attitudes and working practices. These measures included: improved communication, management training to improve accountability to the workforce, flexible and simplified payment systems with few differential rates, extensive and intensive training to equip workers with the skills needed, and harmonized terms and conditions of employment.

JIT working was introduced in 1989 at its Basildon plant by York International,[33] the US-owned manufacturer of industrial refrigeration and heavy air conditioning equipment. To overcome employees' hesitancy about the new system, the company took prior steps to gain the active involvement and commitment of the workforce by seeking the co-operation of the unions (GMB and AEU) and by organizing briefing groups to discuss the proposed changes. Further to allay suspicions and to promote active co-operation, York International arranged for groups of employees and union representatives to visit other companies already operating JIT systems.

One of the factors which encouraged acceptance of JIT methods was the upgrading of many employees and the prospect of higher pay as their skills increased. The company already had an integrated pay and grading structure, with opportunities for individuals to reach the highest level within their grade on satisfactory completion of training modules. In 1990 the company set up a working party to discuss the introduction of a merit-linked reward system based on performance appraisal.

The company had operated a profit-sharing scheme, covering all employees, since 1988, and some months after implementing JIT methods it went ahead with its proposal to harmonize terms and conditions for all employees and to adopt certain other measures to enhance employee relations. With the harmonization of conditions relating to sickness absence, sick pay was increased from 85 per cent to 100 per cent of basic salary; the two 'waiting days' were abolished so that sickness benefit became payable from the first day of absence. The practice of 'docking' pay for lateness was abandoned and employees, now given the option of making up the time lost, generally chose to do so. Paid absence was allowed for purposes such as medical and dental appointments. Evidence suggests that the new working methods and improved terms and conditions worked to the general satisfaction of the employees, and management believed that the system accounted for the company's vastly improved performance.

It was towards the end of the 1980s also that McDonnell Douglas Information Systems,[34] a US-owned computer manufacturing company, introduced JIT systems at its Hemel Hempstead plant. This company had the advantage of learning from, and avoiding, some of the problems encountered by its sister plant in the USA. That plant's experience showed that good communications and training were essential to the effective operation of JIT methods; the system had broken down at the US site because communication between management and employees was deficient, and the 'Kanban' system had not been explained sufficiently clearly for correct stock levels to be maintained.

Teamworking, as in other companies implementing JIT methods, was regarded as fundamentally important. Team members would meet regularly to discuss ideas, problems and solutions, and anyone, including top managers, could be brought in to assist where the group felt that there was a need. Management was reluctant to use the term, 'quality circles', as 'the company did not wish to suggest a "Japanese" approach'. Their main function was to enhance communication, to ensure that any impediments to the effective working of the system would be dealt with immediately, and to permit new ideas to be implemented without delay.

The company believed that, in general, employee motivation and job satisfaction had increased with the broadening of skills to cover a range of tasks required by flexible working; in so far as problems arose here, they stemmed not so much from employees' dissatisfaction with the principle of flexible working as from disappointment at having to perform a wider range of 'merely repetitive' tasks, despite their retraining. In order to encourage acceptance and co-operation, McDonnell Douglas restructured its pay and grading system. This reduced the number of job grades, rationalized the salary structure, and improved pay and conditions generally. With the adoption of the principles of single status, the whole workforce received the same terms, benefits and employment conditions.

Long-established companies were not alone in seeking Japanization, or a degree of it; new concerns were also affected. Dundee Textiles,[35] a joint venture involving two Japanese companies, Kurabo and Toyo Menka, and the UK-based Tootal Group, is a case in point, but even here the approach was partially rather than completely Japanese in style. DTL was set up on a greenfield site in North East Scotland, with production of dyed fabrics scheduled to begin in 1990. In the context of shifts in market preference from large runs of single fabrics to smaller runs and greater variety, the new company's production methods and technology were designed to cope efficiently with present and future market demand. The location was chosen because of the quality of the local water supply, proximity to European markets, and the availability of suitable labour in the area. The most advanced computerized technology would enable the company to produce faster and at lower unit cost than its main competitors.

DTL's employees would have single-status terms and conditions of employment, a performance-related salary system, job security, continuous training, and the means to develop interpersonal skills. A three-stage recruitment process sought to select from amongst job applicants those who could most readily identify with a company culture embracing 'hard work, flexibility, and open communications'. The training schedule included some in-house instruction, appropriate courses provided by the Scottish College of Textiles at Galashields, and, for some employees, visits to fabric-dyeing firms in Japan, France, and Switzerland. Both basic and advanced courses in technology would be provided. In addition, DTL was to offer training for personal career development, and 'life-long learning opportunities' to reinforce employment security by permitting flexible utilization and deployment of human resources.

Harmonized conditions, salaried status, team work, and fully flexible working practices would apply from the outset. Teams would consist of around ten skilled and semi-skilled employees who would be 'fully interchangeable' within the limits of individual competence, with both horizontal and vertical mobility and job rotation once the plant was fully operational. Production methods and personnel policy meant that supervisors and team leaders would have heavier duties than would normally be shouldered by such grades, for they would have responsibility for the efficiency of the work team, salary administration, performance appraisal governing salary movement, and identification of training needs.

In the early 1990s DTL appears not to have recognized a trade union for collective bargaining purposes, but there were extensive two-way communication systems at all levels; and an 'open-door' policy gave all employees the opportunity to discuss work-related matters directly with management.

DTL, while acknowledging the valuable input of its Japanese partners in the formulation of employment policy and business strategy, considered that it would have been impossible to transfer Japanese methods wholesale to the British manufacturing scene. It had therefore sought a combination of the 'best elements' of the Japanese approach and features of British practice derived from Tootal's own business experience. Similarly, in their survey of change in the five-year period up to 1986 in 66 manufacturing concerns, Oliver and Wilkinson[36] concluded that, although 'a fundamental transformation' was being attempted, there was little evidence that firms were embracing the whole Japanese package or operating any element within it in an entirely unmodified form. Only 34 per cent of the 'Japanized' companies covered by their survey had introduced JIT methods and the Kanban system, but 60 per cent or more had team work, flexible working, quality circles, statistical process control, and total quality management. As large a proportion as 80 per cent had single-status facilities, and 74 per cent provided harmonized terms, benefits and conditions of employment. It had been easier to introduce such methods and practices at greenfield sites with relatively young recruits than at brownfield sites with workforces already acculturated to traditional manufacturing methods, working habits, and industrial relations systems. Change was nevertheless advanced, and a fundamental reversal of the trend seemed unlikely.

Wood's[37] comparison of practices in Japanese-owned companies and firms without any direct Japanese involvement in the early 1990s confirmed that the former were 'significantly more likely' to: (i) use team briefing, quality circles, performance assessment, merit pay, and temporary staff as 'buffers'; (ii) select staff on the basis of trainability and commitment; (iii) have flexible job descriptions, career ladders, and regard for job design; (iv) attempt to guarantee employment and avoid redundancies; (v) eliminate status differentials. Intense Japanese competition in certain global markets had 'probably contributed' to the adoption of a range of new manufacturing methods and working practices in Britain; but 'at least as influential' had been the 'new economic realism' in the outlook of British manufacturers and trade unions as a result of the long-run recession of the

1980s and the Conservative Government's belief in free market forces.[38] Lack of competitiveness meant closed plants and lost jobs.

There was some conjecture in the West about the implications for world trade of the slowdown in Japan's economic growth rate in the early and mid-1990s; and there was comment about the effect of the 1997 financial fiasco upon stock markets and upon Japanese firms and their workforces. Crisis in some of the so-called 'tiger economies' of South East Asia made matters worse. It seemed likely that Japan's employment practices, in particular, would be ditched as it reached economic maturity and encountered set-backs. British employers were advised to be 'wary of imitating practices that are only appropriate in a climate of ever-increasing growth'.[39] Even so, moves in Britain to reduce status-related differentials and to harmonize employment terms and benefits have occurred during the last half-century in periods of both prosperity and recession. The beginnings of change pre-date the application of Japanese manufacturing methods by British companies and the establishment of significant numbers of Japanese companies in Britain's shrinking manufacturing sector. Japanese manufacturing methods are not a pre-requisite of harmonized terms and conditions of employment. Further harmonization in Britain seems unlikely to be directly affected by the fortunes of Japanese manufacturers, whether in Britain or Japan.

6 New Technology and Harmonization

INTRODUCTION

The imperative to improve competitiveness and cost performance focused employers' attention on the possibilities of what has been termed 'the new technology'. For a country like Britain, with a long history of industrialization dating from the mid-eighteenth century, there is nothing novel about the idea of technological change. However, recent developments in microelectronics, producing computer and information technology, have been claimed to be 'sufficiently distinctive, dramatic, and far-reaching' as to represent a 'new technological revolution'.[1] The microprocessor-based applications of the computer and telecommunications equipment have produced the latest and most remarkable phase in the automation of work. Microelectronics technology, McLoughlin and Clark note, radically enhances processing power, greatly increases the speed with which information is processed, vastly improves reliability and flexibility, and substantially reduces costs in relation to processing power. With advances in computer hardware and increasingly powerful software, the potential application of microelectronics is enormous.

The introduction of early computer technology on the shopfloor dates from the 1950s, but progressively more sophisticated and 'user friendly' versions have become available since then. The principal development was in the use of an electro-mechanical technique known as Numerical Control (NC) to control the action of metal-cutting machine tools. The main advantages of this technique were an improvement in the quality of the product, reduction in scrap rates, and saving on production time.

Developments in microelectronics have led to the appearance of the more advanced technique of Computer Numerical Control (CNC) which, by permitting programming directly at the machine, offers much greater flexibility than the NC predecessor. Along with developments in CNC technology there have been advances in industrial robotics, followed by Flexible Manufacturing Systems (FMS).[2] FMS allows groups of CNC machine tools and robots to be centrally linked by a computer which contains all the relevant design and manufacturing information to control machining operations. Further developments expected in the mid-1980s included a fully computer-integrated manufacturing system (CIM). There were parallel and equally spectacular developments in office technology, which affected the work of managers, administrative personnel, and secretarial and clerical employees. Surveys undertaken by the Policy Studies Institute showed that the adoption of microelectronics in production processes was spreading rapidly in the 1980s.

Technological advance raises productivity, but it also affects the work tasks and job content of the firm's employees. One effect is to eliminate or reduce the number of complex tasks requiring manual skills and dexterity; another is to generate more complex tasks which require theoretical knowledge, mental problem-solving abilities, interpretational skills, and an understanding of system inter-dependencies.

Management tends to regard new technology as the means to greater consistency and predictability of operations by placing less reliance on the human factor. This is not necessarily a manifestation of Taylorist strategy to deskill and downgrade work tasks. Certainly some deskilling occurs with routinization and simplification of functions, but Braverman[3] has perhaps overstated the extent and degree to which new technology has produced this outcome. There is a great deal of evidence that, for some groups at least, new technology and new ways of organizing production require training and retraining either in new skills, or new combinations of skills, or overlapping of skills.

New technology may therefore exert contradictory pressures; it may deskill work tasks in so far as they become simplified and routinized, but it may raise skill requirement by demanding greater mental ability to permit the most effective use of new equipment. As Buchanan argues, 'Sophisticated, flexible and expensive equipment needs sophisticated, flexible and expensive people to operate it.'[4] A similar argument may be applied to the design, construction, repair and maintenance of the equipment. New technology tends to necessitate the redesigning of work, and this kind of innovation is most effective where it is introduced as part of an integrated package. Several observers[5] have pressed the importance of linking changes in job content and work organization with changes in payment systems; this would seem to be inevitable where new skills or combinations of skills cannot be readily accommodated within traditional job classifications and their associated pay and grading structures. For example, 'the creation of integrated grades of machinist-programmers' would require the creation of an integrated payment system which recognized both 'changes in the pattern of required skills' and the need for 'smooth progress from jobs which predominantly involve machining to those which place greater emphasis on technical programming tasks'.[6] Traditional piecework systems (PBR) were being replaced by measured day work (MDW) in the 1960s. The new technology of recent years has decisively broken the traditional kind of direct link between individual effort and output; and since quality and quantity of output tend to derive from the performance of the work group as a whole, 'payment systems may have to be designed around the need to encourage flexibility and adaptability', with incentive schemes such as profit-sharing, employee share-holding, and merit-rated or performance-linked pay systems.[7]

New technology has raised new bargaining issues for the trade unions. Barnett suggests that the unions have been the 'strongest single factor militating against technological innovation and high productivity' in Britain's economic decline since the time of the Second World War.[8] This may be true for the 1960s; the Donovan Commission disclosed that restrictive practices and demarcations were widely observed and well-entrenched, and many of the productivity agreements reached at national level were not effectively implemented on the shopfloor.[9] It is generally accepted that Britain's economic growth rate has been unspectacular during the last half-century, but McLouglin and Clark question whether responsibility for the slow rate of technological innovation lies entirely with the unions. As these writers point out, the TUC has consistently subscribed to the view that rapid technological advance is necessary for economic growth and international competitiveness. Restrictive practices have not proved to be immutable in the 1980s and 1990s; managements have not been generally discouraged by union action from proceeding with plans to introduce new equipment; and employees have been largely willing to accept the inevitability of new technology. In a deteriorating economic environment after 1979, with escalating unemployment, proliferating redundancies and few job opportunities, there were recurrent technology-related disputes, but these occurred mainly in printing, motor vehicles and on the docks; and such incidents do not seem to have deterred employers who wished to introduce new technology from proceeding with their plans.

There is much evidence of restrictive practices, but there is much evidence also of unions' willingness to reach formal agreements on flexible working, the relaxation of demarcations and co-operation in retraining. The extensive technological displacement of labour in certain industries, such as telecommunications, was much regretted by the TUC; but the main response was not to press affiliated unions to obstruct technological advance, but to urge them to seek 'new technology agreements' in order to bring some control to a runaway situation. Nor does responsibility for the observance of restrictive practices lie solely with the unions; the emergence of shopfloor sanctions is at least partially attributable to managements' willingness to condone or overlook them. The existence of trade unions is not a major obstacle to innovation, for, as the Workplace Industrial Relations Surveys disclosed, manufacturing establishments which recognized trade unions for collective bargaining purposes were more likely than non-unionized companies to have introduced advanced technology.

The TUC's initiative for new technology agreements had lost its momentum by the mid-1980s. In part, McLoughin and Clark argue, this was attributable to an unfavourable economic environment and a political climate hostile to the unions. Having encountered scant success with agreements to control the pace and method of technological innovation in employing enterprises, the unions concentrated, as in times past, on negotiating the price for acceptance of change, focusing on higher pay, improved terms and benefits, shorter working hours, and guarantees of job security. This outcome was not attributable to unions' apathy about the idea of new technology agreements, but to employers' concern to defend 'managerial prerogatives' and to confine decision-making on capital investment to those with expertise in the relevant spheres. Few new technology deals were reached in the 1980s, but there were innumerable agreements containing clauses which linked changed payment structure, reduced working hours, or harmonized conditions to acceptance of flexible working and training necessitated by more advanced technology.

Employers' decisions to invest in new technology were taken with one or other of three main aims in view, Buchanan and Boddy suggest. In some cases there were 'strategic objectives'; the intention here was market-orientated, the purpose being to improve product quality, expand market share, and maintain market lead. Others had 'operating objectives', which were technical and performance-related, and intended to improve product flexibility and reduce plant running and labour costs. Still others had 'control objectives', the goal being to reduce reliance on human intervention and the associated uncertainty, to extend management control over workflow, and to increase both the amount of performance information available to managers and the speed of its delivery.[10]

The extent and manner in which new technology affected workforces appeared to depend upon the economic circumstances of the firm and the type of technology introduced. Where a firm's product market was relatively young, its main aims in introducing technological innovation were likely to be higher product performance and greater share of an expanding market rather than lower production costs. Firms in this situation were likely to adopt policies to develop workforce skills and expertise to gain improvements in quality and to develop new products. In maturing product markets, the aim of the firm in introducing new technology was likely to be improved efficiency and continuity of production in order to increase sales. Here, manning policy was likely to seek greater managerial control over work and employee acceptance of ongoing technological change. Where a firm operated in a mature product market, it tended to introduce new technology to reduce production costs in order to maintain competitiveness. A policy to raise labour productivity and improve manpower utilization, perhaps involving reduction in headcount and a restructuring of the labour force, might be adopted where labour costs were the main cause of concern.

Towards the mid 1980s, when Atkinson and Meager were developing their model of the flexible firm, Child[11] identified four directions in which firms' labour policy was moving in response to new technology. Firstly, when new technology was substituted for human effort in order to set up completely automated production processes, there was a reduction in the amount of direct labour used. Secondly, new technology permitted some kinds of work to be subcontracted outside the organization. The most frequently cited example of this is employment of professional and managerial staff on contract and working from home with the aid of computers linked to the company's central office. Thirdly, new technology could produce greater flexibility in labour utilization and deployment by breaking down traditional horizontal and vertical skill demarcations, expanding the range of tasks which individual workers could perform, and/or increasing the amount of discretion left to workers in the performance of tasks. Fourthly, new technology downgraded some jobs by deskilling the work to be done and increasing managerial control.

The introduction of new computing and information technology,

McLoughlin and Clark claim, may 'enable managers to develop labour regulation policies' which produce a 'radical restructuring of an organization's labour force'; and it is one of the main factors contributing to more flexible forms of work and employment.

More was needed, however, if new technology and flexibility were to be really effective in improving business performance. Workpeople's co-operation and their commitment to the organization's objectives were crucial. The 'us and them' syndrome of British industry, the traditional workplace divide, and combatively oppositional stances in industrial relations, all needed to change. Earlier production methods had dictated clearly defined and separate roles for manual workers, supervisors, clerical staffs and administrators; but new technology was blurring many of these distinctions and outmoding traditional differences in terms, benefits and conditions of employment.

NEW SITE, NEW TECHNOLOGY AND HARMONIZED CONDITIONS

New technology was one of the factors which influenced the Pilkington Company to create a functionally versatile workforce on harmonized terms and conditions, with an integrated job-evaluated payment structure which facilitated flexibility and teamworking. By the late 1970s, while continuing its glass-making activities, the company was diversifying into other product markets with production centres dispersed throughout the country. All of this suggested the need for a policy of decentralized bargaining to permit terms and conditions to be negotiated at site level. Policy focused on site identity, integrated payment structures, and single-table bargaining, and an opportunity to put these ideas into practice presented itself at Pilkington's new Greengate works to be built on a greenfield site. Construction of the new plant began in 1978, and, from the outset, the aim was to 'combine the latest "float glass" technology with modern industrial relations procedures and practices.'[12] Advanced technology and flexible working at the new factory, which opened in April 1981, resulted in substantially higher productivity than was being achieved at the older sites. By 1984 Greengate's 404 employees were producing 5,000 tonnes of float glass per week, whereas at the older St Helen's plant 680 employees were producing only 1,800 tonnes weekly. The new factory provided the opportunity for Pilkington to introduce completely new work practices, new negotiating arrangements, and a pay and conditions package which was quite different from arrangements elsewhere in the company.

The harmonization of conditions meant that all employees, both manual and non-manual, had the same conditions of service, including holiday entitlement, sick pay and pension coverage, and access to single-status canteen facilities. All received monthly paid salaries based on a common job-evaluated pay and grading structure which applied throughout the plant. Using HAY-MSL techniques, a joint panel representing management and the unions graded 53 different jobs into ten bands. All employees worked an average 39-hour week, and all were on the clock. There was no overtime pay; extra hours were compensated by time off in lieu. Management reported to Incomes Data Services that one of the main advantages of the simplified pay structure was that it substantially reduced personnel staff time in calculating pay and resolving minor pay issues.

Advanced technology played a major part also in the introduction of flexible teamworking, harmonized conditions, and an integrated pay structure at Unigate's[13] new plant located on a greenfield site at Westway in the later 1980s. Unigate Dairies, part of Unigate plc, had around 13,500 employees working in the processing, packaging and distribution of dairy products, with its activities concentrated mainly in the Midlands and the South of England. With progressively keener competitive pressures, Unigate Dairies decided to close its Vauxhall bottling plant, to redevelop its distribution depot in Shepherd's Bush, and to build from scratch a new milk packaging plant at Westway. Westway Dairy, the company claims, was the 'most modern dairy complex in Europe', costing £12 million and producing milk cartons in units from one-third of a pint to 20-litre catering packs. A great deal of research and planning went into the design of both plant and working practices at the new complex. The introduction of teamworking, the use of team briefings, the development of a new grading structure covering all employees from senior management downward, the harmonized payment system and common terms and conditions were all discussed and agreed with the TGWU which represented all employees at Westway.

The personnel aspect of Westway's operation was discussed by a steering group, set up in 1985, whose deliberations focused on the transfer and recruitment of staff, staff training and development, organization of work and working arrangements, and job grading, pay and conditions. Drawing on the experience of other companies which had set up on greenfield sites with the most advanced technology available, Unigate identified what it considered to be the 'transferable best' to adopt and adapt at its own site. Five key elements were to form the basis of working arrangements and personnel policy: (i) teamworking; (ii) a 'flat' grading structure; (iii) harmonized pay and conditions, with all employees on staff status and fixed salaries rather than receiving overtime and other pay supplements; (iv) open and effective communications; and (v) a committed workforce. As management recognized, effective utilization of new technology would require ongoing training, both in technical and craft skills and also in human relations in order to build and maintain efficient teams.

New technology had an effect on production and work organization in some companies whose public image had for a long time been associated with things 'traditional', 'old fashioned', and 'rooted in the past'. Extending operations, by setting up new manufacturing premises on greenfield sites, provided the occasion to go with the flow of new technology for the CWS.[14] Given competitive market pressures on the one hand and the possibilities of advanced technology on the other, the CWS introduced 'radically modern' working practices at its two new sites: at Crewe in the later 1970s and at Shotton on Deeside in the mid-1980s. The greenfield developments represented further stages of a restructuring programme begun in the mid-1970s; and the site-level agreements relating pay to performance at each new location reflected the gradual disintegration of national industry-wide bargaining arrangements. The rationalization of the CWS's food operations involved some closures and concentration of activities at sites with the most advanced technology available. While the decision to establish the new plant at Crewe was motivated by the need for modern equipment and purpose-built premises for tea and coffee packaging in which the CWS was already engaged, and involved the closure of the older Manchester and Glasgow sites, the establishment of the Deeside factory stemmed from the company's determination to move into a new activity: the production of breakfast cereal. The Deeside location was chosen because of its good transport links, its eligibility for Government grant aid as an unemployment blackspot, and the availability of skilled local labour as a result of closures by Metal Box and the BSC and contraction at Cammell Laird.

Both agreements contained clauses for flexible working within and between job grades, which would be enhanced by training and retraining in a 'demarcation-free environment' and corresponding to the needs of new technology. Integrated pay and grading structures, along with harmonized terms and benefits, covered all grades below management level. All employees became 'salaried', and the acceptability of pay by credit transfer was undoubtedly increased by the provision of cash withdrawal facilities on site. The integrated grading structure at Crewe, based on a job-evaluation exercise taking into account job responsibility, job authority, mental demands and physical working environment, contained eleven grades and was sufficiently flexible to permit movement from grade to grade in the event of change in job design and work tasks resulting from further technological advance. The harmonization of terms and conditions was intended to create a closely integrated workforce committed to the commercial success and future development of the company.

It was the move to a new site which enabled Barr & Stroud[15] to improve business performance and provided the occasion for the introduction of harmonized conditions. The Glasgow-based manufacturer of range-finders and submarine telescopic equipment embarked upon a radical restructuring of its operations in 1991. The Ministry of Defence's move to a purchasing strategy based on competitive tendering spurred Barr & Stroud to increase productive efficiency in order to improve price competitiveness. Another pressure came from cuts in defence spending worldwide following the ending of the Cold War, which affected markets and led to falling sales and declining profit margins. A new business strategy was therefore vital to Barr & Stroud's survival.

The company started upon a ten-year business process re-engineering programme in 1991. Up to that time production at Glasgow had been carried out in five Edwardian buildings separated by busy main roads. The need for relocation and purpose-built premises was essential, given the only too obvious unsuitability of the old buildings for new 'high-tech activities, the transportation of precision-engineered components backwards and forwards through heavy traffic, and the duplication of many activities in the five buildings'. Production at the new Linthouse site in Glasgow began in August 1992, with a workforce reduced to roughly 750 from around 2,500 in 1989. The move to the new 'high-tech' site involved also a move to single-table bargaining with the four unions recognized by the company: the AEEU for engineers and electricians, the TGWU for other manual grades, APEX for clerical workers, and MSF for technicians.

The out-sourcing of Barr & Stroud's non-core activities began in 1991 with the implementation of a Computer Integrated Manufacturing (CIM) strategy, which was to transform the company's traditional style of operating into 'one befitting an ultra-modern new plant operating in a high risk, cost-conscious and smaller market-place'. The management team responsible for the CIM initiative took the view that, in organizational and technological change, 'people issues' were pivotal; effective use of new technology required a funda-mental transformation of the way in which operations were carried out. One set of changes required by CIM included team building, employee development, a new managerial style, a new career struc-ture, and a new pay and grading system. Another set of changes under CIM came under Manufacturing Resource Planning (MRPII) which 'directs and schedules materials, machines and people' to be in the right place at the right time to 'build the products which fit the busi-ness plan and meet the customer's requirements'. To ensure that the data used by the MRPII system was completely accurate, each team would take on responsibility for guaranteeing achievement of delivery targets and product quality – which was integral to total quality management (TQM) at Barr and Stroud.

There were extensive discussions with the unions on issues of major concern to employees: stable employment in the future, job satisfaction, a caring environment, open communications and employee involvement, harmonized conditions of employment, and equal opportunities. Those wishing to take up employment at the new Linthouse site would be expected to accept flexibility of working, which would involve fundamental change in working practices and eradication of all union demarcations.

All of this involved a great deal of training, open forum communica-tion, and preparation including selection and training of team leaders. Along with the harmonization of terms and benefits, a new pay and grading structure was adopted to facilitate and reinforce the desired changes in company culture and working practices. A job-evaluation exercise, using the US computer program, Expert Choice, was under-taken, and a joint management-union panel evaluated jobs and designed the new pay and grading system. One effect of this was to create a career structure; individuals can now progress from the shopfloor to a job which permits them to take a part-time occupation-specific degree course. The single-status culture and concept were reflected in provision of one restaurant equally available to all, deseg-regated parking facilities, and abandonment of differently coloured overalls for different grades.

OLD SITE, NEW TECHNOLOGY AND HARMONIZED CONDITIONS

Business restructuring, involving the installation of advanced technology, flexibility, and moves to harmonized conditions, could be accomplished at brownfield sites by streamlining measures which effected a greenfielding of them.

Leyland Trucks,[16] for example, revamped an existing site, updated its productive equipment, and adopted 'Japanese practices' including JIT methods and harmonized conditions.

Production of vehicles at Leyland, near Preston, has a long and sometimes turbulent history dating back to the interwar years. Leyland Trucks was established in June 1993, with a management buy-out of the trucks division of Leyland-DAF. The objective was to undertake a complete restructuring which included new technology, training and re-training, teamworking based on flexible working practices, continuous quality improvement, a manufacturing partnership with supplying companies, harmonized employment conditions, and single-table bargaining – all of which would contribute to the creation of a 'lean enterprise' culture which management believed to be essential to successful operations. With the buy-out, the workforce was reduced from around 2,000 to 630 permanent full-time employees, and an 'austerity package' made provision to contain some costs and to prune others. Amongst other things, the package provided for: the freezing of basic pay rates until January 1995, an unconsolidated profit-related pay supplement of 2.5 per cent dependent on company performance, removal of all allowances (except 'track' allowances and maintenance skill bonus), abolition of the £5.00 per week attendance bonus, removal of sick pay for temporary employees, withdrawal of the subsidy for canteen services, withdrawal of lease cars from all middle management, and downward adjustment of pay for overtime working and of pay guarantee in the event of short-time and temporary lay-off.

With the creation of Leyland Trucks, the Japanese concept of 'lean production', adapted at the former Leyland Assembly plant, was developed further. Traditional batch production was abandoned and replaced by progressive production methods using advanced computer-controlled material supply and 'just-in-time' component delivery. There are now two sets of parallel conveyer-assembly lines for cab and chassis assembly; and assembly is pre-programmed 'with the specifications and building instructions unique to the particular vehicle set out in a computer print-out'. One of the conveyer lines deals with a vehicle's chassis assembly plus fitting of gear box and wheels. While the chassis is being put together, the particular cab to be fitted to it is being assembled on an adjacent but separate conveyer line. The simultaneously completed cab and chassis are then coupled, the mechanical and electrical connections are made, and lastly the vehicle is subjected to a simulated road test and final inspection before being dispatched to the customer/dealer.

Human resources strategy, which underpinned 'lean production' at Leyland Trucks, was based on the concepts of team working, continuous quality improvement, and total quality management. It involved self-managing teams led by key operators, a de-layered management structure to minimize bureaucracy, and employee responsiveness to changing work demands. Development of human resources involved not only technical training to broaden and update skills, but also training in such areas as quality awareness, problem-solving, and team dynamics.

Terms, benefits and employment conditions for all permanent full-time employees at Leyland Trucks are harmonized. All are covered by the same arrangements for sick pay, holidays and pensions; there is no separate 'top hat' pension scheme for executives, and only a few senior managers have company lease cars. All employees have a normal working week of 37 hours. If overtime working is necessary, up to three extra hours per week are 'banked' and credited for payment at basic rates during any future period of low production when actual weekly working hours are less than 37. Up to five further hours per week are paid at new and harmonized premium rates: time-and-a-third for the first two hours and time-and-a-half thereafter for extra weekday hours, time-and-a-half on Saturdays, and double-time on Sundays. For all employees, 70 per cent of base rate is guaranteed for up to four weeks in any four-month period; beyond that, there is no earnings guarantee. In the new pay and grading structure the number of separate grades for staff and production workers was reduced from thirteen to eight. This, in combination with training opportunities for skill acquisition, provides for career development. Although three unions, the GMB, AEEU, and MSF, have bargaining rights, there is complete single-table negotiation through the Employee Representation Committee, and agreement on 'binding arbitration'. The new business was a response to the keenly competitive state of world markets for vehicles; it brought the trucks division of Leyland-DAF out of receivership and kept Leyland Trucks in business.

New technology, flexibility and moves towards harmonized conditions were part of a rescue strategy also at Westland Helicopters[17] in the early 1980s.

At its Milton Keynes plant and its smaller Higham Ferrers plant, Westland manufactured a variety of high precision components for its helicopters, including hydraulics, under-carriages and large quantities of complex parts requiring a high degree of flexibility from the machine tools used to produce them. An examination in 1981 of production costs at the two plants raised the question of the closure of both; but after further investigation it was decided to close the Higham Ferrers plant but to modernize production methods at Milton Keynes. There was an initial £2 million investment in computerized equipment, and operators received training and hands-on experience in its use. The design of the CNC machine tools was such as to permit tools to be programmed by operators who would be responsible for both the programming and the machining of components from start to finish. Production would involve a three-shift system, multi-machine manning, and flexible working practices.

The effect of new technology in manufacturing and in office work would be an estimated annual saving of some £2.5 million, as a result of increased productivity, reduced lead times, less materials waste, and more efficient administration.

Under the new programme, pre-existing cross-skills working was extended on the basis of team activity with a much greater degree of skill overlap in machining and fitting, much less direct supervision, and far more multi-machine manning with three skilled operators responsible for the programming and operation of five machines. Industrial skills were broadened by cross-trade working, and extended to enable multi-skilled workers to cope with production, control and inspection functions. Semi-skilled and unskilled grades accepted new handling techniques throughout the plant when the old hand-pulled trolleys were replaced by new handling equipment. The installation of a central computer function for administrative functions permitted computerization of time and attendance recording and facilitated the extension of payment by credit transfer to manual operators.

One of the main benefits for employees was greater job security for those who remained. The manual/non-manual differential was much reduced, though improvement fell short of complete harmonization. There were still two separate pension schemes and the manual worker's basic working week was one and a half hours longer than the

37.5 hours worked by non-manual grades. Westland did not yet have an integrated pay and grading structure covering all grades. Like other companies with brownfield sites, its policy was to harmonize conditions in the longer term.

The needs of technology were amongst the main incentives also in Metal Box's decision to introduce greater functional flexibility and a radical restructuring of pay, conditions and industrial relations at its brownfield packaging plant at Swindon[18] towards the end of the 1980s. Change was implemented in the context of planned investment and expansion, and was tied to a four-year pay agreement which set out pay rates until 1991. Management at the Swindon plant had had the possibilities of a wide-ranging pay and productivity agreement under consideration for some time, but it was not until the company took the decision to invest some £14 million in an extension to the Swindon site to triple productive capacity that an opportunity arose. The planned expansion involved the building of a new factory close to the existing plant, the recruitment of additional manpower, and the negotiation of an agreement to cover both factories. The agreement was the outcome of single-table bargaining with four unions, the NGA, AEU, EETPU and MSF, and provided an integrated pay and grading structure and unified terms and conditions for all employees.

Teamworking on the shop floor, regarded by Metal Box as a key feature of its approach to flexible working, was integral to the retraining process. The teams would consist of about thirty employees, working without demarcation limits and collectively responsible for the topping-up of machines, the monitoring of the computer-controlled injection-moulding process, the general flow of production, and cover for breakdowns, product changes and absence.

Technological innovation, flexible working and moves towards harmonized conditions were part of survival strategy in the brewing industry also. The Burton, the Whitbread, and the Ansell Breweries faced similar problems of over-capacity in the industry, increasingly competitive and volatile markets, and marked change in market preferences. Difficulties, already encountered in the later 1970s, intensified in the 1980s.

For many years Ind Coope's Burton Brewery[19] had been geared to volume production of a limited range of beers and lagers, but sales were falling with changes in consumer tastes from lager to wines and speciality drinks, and from consumption of large quantities of a small range of beers on licensed premises to purchase of a wide variety of take-home packs from supermarkets. In these market circumstances the company needed to switch to shorter production runs and multiple packaging styles, to reduce production costs, and to have sufficient flexibility to cope with changing and sometimes capricious markets. The layout of the existing 130-year-old 70-acre site necessitated a great deal of site-wide transportation, which was wasteful of time and resources and affected product quality; and to make matters worse, the site was divided into separate parts by the busy A50 trunk road. At the same time, production equipment was outdated, there was little in the way of computer-based technology, and the several office premises scattered around the site caused duplication, hampered unity of purpose, and impeded collaboration.

These physical problems were compounded by a traditional industrial relations system, and by inflexible working practices. There were several closed shops operated by the six unions – the TGWU, AEU, UCATT, EETPU, ACTSS and ASTMS – recognized by the company, and bargaining groups negotiated separately and had different annual settlement dates. Problematic also were the traditionally hierarchical style of management, confrontational industrial relations, and status-related terms, benefits and employment conditions. In the recent past, the company's approach to planning had proved to be neither sufficiently flexible nor radical enough to remedy the situation.

Following the deliberations of a joint working party in 1982, management, led by a newly appointed managing director, decided upon a long-term survival and modernization plan based upon its 'Greenfield Assessment at Burton Brewery'. This was altogether different from its former short-term strategy of mere bush-fire fighting. There was full involvement of the unions at the planning stage in order to secure their co-operation and commitment to the thorough-going changes which were needed to improve business competitiveness. The plan contained six main features: (i) heavy capital investment to replace the existing equipment with the most advanced computer technology currently available; (ii) the centralization of operations, with the closure of one site and streamlining of process runs and traffic flows at the other; (iii) the eradication of demarcations and a new style of negotiation which avoided fragmented bargaining; (iv) retraining of employees for flexible working, and the introduction of payment structures to facilitate flexible labour utilization and deployment; (v) the development of team-working methods, which were regarded as essential to the goal of flexibility; (vi) moves to harmonized terms and conditions to reduce and ultimately eliminate the workplace divide.

There would be savings on production costs by better use of raw materials, higher productivity in the redesigned and re-equipped brewery, and a 20 per cent reduction of the labour force. This last was to become a bone of contention with the unions. However, a combination of natural wastage, early retirement, voluntary redundancy, a freeze on recruitment, and the creation of new areas of work permitting redeployment, helped to resolve the problem of reducing headcount without serious disruption of industrial relations.

The acquiescence of the workforce in the restructuring initiative was assisted by visits of its representatives to breweries overseas, which gave a better understanding of the disparities between Burton's use of new technology and manning levels and its competitors' production methods and working practices. At Burton, new computer-based production equipment would require flexible organization of work within teams and training to broaden and update skills. The payment structure was revised and simplified. Status divisions were tackled with provision for single-status car parking and canteen facilities, common sick pay, pension, holiday and bonus arrangements, and the same form of time-recording for all employees. This did not amount to complete harmonization, but it was a major step in that direction, and an important part of the 'greenfielding' of Burton's brownfield site. By 1988 the company had a six-band salary structure covering all employees up to executive level. Employees in grades one to three worked a basic 40-hour week; the rest, mainly management, worked 'the hours required by the job' – which not infrequently were more than 40.

Whitbread[20] was similarly affected by the wave of new technology, the recession, and volatile markets. Radical change was necessitated at the company's Romsey depot, one of Whitbread's main centres for the packaging and distribution of beers and lagers produced by its major breweries. In the early 1980s it was recognized that greater flexibility was needed to cope with the peaks and troughs characterizing the seasonal nature of a shrinking market.

Until 1983 the company had conducted separate negotiations with each of its two recognized unions, and the two broad occupational groups had had different terms and conditions. Manual workers had received a weekly paid cash wage, whereas non-manual grades were salaried and paid monthly by credit transfer. Manuals had worked a basic 40-hour week extended by high levels of overtime working; non-manuals had a basic 35-hour week and worked extra hours infrequently. For the company the problem of high levels of overtime pay was exacerbated by an incentive bonus scheme whose effectiveness as an incentive had deteriorated. At the same time the site was riven with traditional craft and occupational demarcations, which were jealously guarded as a means of preserving job security and levels of earnings. Technological innovation provided the opportunity and the necessity of changing much of this.

An agreement, negotiated jointly in 1983 with the two unions recognized at the Romsey site, provided for an integrated pay and grading structure, harmonization of most basic terms and conditions, a shorter working week linked to an annualized hours arrangement, the relaxation of demarcations, and reduction of the high levels of overtime worked formerly. The five-band grading structure covered all non-managerial grades and was accompanied by a payment system providing salaries payable monthly by credit transfer.

Change at the Romsey depot was not a completely new departure for Whitbread; in many ways it mirrored innovation which had already occurred at some of the company's breweries. An agreement reached at Whitbread's Luton brewery in 1981 introduced harmonized terms and conditions, flexible working, new shift patterns, an integrated pay and grading system, and annual salaries paid monthly by credit transfer – 'thus bringing it into line with several other Whitbread plants.'

Pressure for change from new technology has not of course, been confined to the manufacturing scene and manual work, but has been strongly felt in the sphere of financial and similar services with their armies of white-collar employees. Banking has been a prime area of technological innovation since the beginning of the 1970s. During the 1980s and 1990s new computer technology, introduced progressively more widely, affected role descriptions, conventional status divisions and industrial relations. For the Midland Bank[21] and many other such organizations, market pressures brought to the fore diversification of business, six-day trading, improved customer service, and more effective product marketing; to these underlying pressures for thoroughgoing change in technology, staffing structures, and terms and conditions of employment were added the effects of legislation in 1986 relating to equal pay for work of equal value, and pressures from the unions for improvement in the pay structure and other terms of employment. The Midland Bank's response to these several pressures involved 'moves to harmonize a diverse workforce of manuals and non-manuals on to common terms and conditions through a process of job evaluation aimed at addressing the equal value concept'.

In the late 1980s the Midland Bank employed around 43,000 people in some 2,000 regional and national centres and was Britain's third largest clearing bank. Prior to integration and harmonization, occupational divisions at Midland were typical of banking in general. There was a variety of grading structures, pay rates, and bargaining groups, and there were differentials in terms and conditions to the disadvantage of manual grades. The seven main groups, separately and differently evaluated for pay purposes, were: clerical, typing and secretarial, technical and services (manual), domestic (catering), data processing, engineering (craft), and managerial. While new technology had affected work tasks and responsibility, job segregation persisted and was reflected in separate evaluation and grading structures for manual and non-manual, which limited the effect of equal pay legislation. The amendment of that legislation in 1986 widened the potential for equal pay claims, and the demands of ASTMS and BIFU, the two TUC-affiliated unions recognized by Midland, were subsequently pressed more strongly.

In collaboration with HAY consultants, an integrated grading structure was devised, covering technician and service employees, catering staff, the various clerical, typing and secretarial grades, and the lowest managerial tier. The new structure contained four basic grades, with pay progression within each grade based on an annual merit-rating procedure. All employees covered by the integrated structure had moved to common terms and conditions by the end of 1987.

Technological change, in affecting job content, work tasks, skill requirements and the organization of employment, was one of the main causes of moves away from traditional pay systems and their replacement by integrated pay and grading structures. In some companies this was a further, and sometimes final, stage of a process of harmonization begun earlier; at greenfield sites it was part of the total package from the outset.

7 Deregulation, Decentralization and Harmonization

INTRODUCTION

It has been an objective of Conservative Government policy from 1979 to 1997 to effect a fundamental transformation of collective bargaining and systems of pay determination. If new technology was a motivator of harmonized terms and conditions of employment, deregulation of the labour market and decentralization of pay determination were facilitators of it. Developments in these areas have been associated with moves to single-union representation and single-table bargaining.

The structure of industry-wide collective bargaining and national agreements, which had been promoted by successive Governments since the time of the First World War, was now to be dismantled in the interests of flexibility, business competitiveness, and economic regeneration.

For much of the present century the British industrial relations scene was characterized by industry-wide bargaining at national level. Most accounts attribute the development of this system to the Whitley Committee's 1917 recommendations on the means to foster fair and peaceable industrial relations. One recommendation was the creation of national joint industrial councils, supported by district and works councils, to permit centralized bargaining to operate in the well-organized industries; another was the extension and strengthening of the system of statutory wage regulation under the authority of Trade Boards in sectors where organization was weak or non-existent. In general, both proposals were greeted favourably; by 1921 73 joint industrial councils had been set up, and the 1918 Trade Boards Act had been passed to enlarge the provisions of the 1909 measure.

The structure and system of national bargaining was weakened by the effects of the interwar depression, but the Second World War witnessed a revival. The joint industrial councils flourished again, and statutory wage regulation was extended through the 1943 Catering

Wages Act, the 1945 Wages Councils Act, and the 1947 Agricultural Wages Act. The general postwar assumption that Britain had a comprehensive system of national collective bargaining was not without substance, therefore; and that supposition prevailed until the 1968 Donovan Report disclosed the significance of local activities. The Report identified a dual system of formal and informal bargaining, the former based on the official institutions which produced national agreements, and the latter operating on the basis of tacit consent, custom, and practice through the activities of shop stewards, managers, and local union officers.

The formal machinery was said to be undermined by the informal system. In consequence, there was a widening gap between industry-wide agreed wage rates and actual earnings, and procedural agreements were failing to cope with disputes arising within factories. The supposition that national collective bargaining was of overriding importance hampered 'the informal system from developing into an effective and orderly method of regulation.'[1]

The situation persisted. During the 1970s it came to be widely recognized by negotiators that national bargaining was concerned with minimum pay rates, and that actual earnings, enhanced as they were by largely informal local settlement, were often well in excess of the nationally agreed basic rates. Some employers were now beginning to find industry-wide multi-employer negotiation progressively less suitable for their particular business needs; and in certain industrial sectors a number of them began to withdraw completely from the national bargaining bodies. This, it has been claimed, represented a decisive break with the past and a marked shift even from the situation described by the Donovan Commission in the 1960s. Brown's investigation[2] led him to conclude that, by the end of the 1970s, single-employer bargaining had become 'the most important means of pay determination for two-thirds of manual workers' in the manufacturing sector.

Multi-employer centralized bargaining tended to persist in sectors characterized by the existence of numerous small firms, for whom the traditional approach to negotiation appeared to provide the most effective means of maintaining control over the unions and of containing potentially damaging competition.[3] The 1980 and 1984 Workplace Industrial Relations Surveys and the CBI's investigations disclosed considerable diversity in collective bargaining practices, but they broadly confirmed that the trend was away from national multi-employer bargaining, particularly in manufacturing industry in the private sector.[4] The average size of those enterprises which had moved more decisively to company or site level settlement of pay and conditions was markedly larger than firms remaining party to national agreements. Decentralization continued during the following years and, as the 1990 WIRS showed, it was now beginning to spread in the public sector.[5]

Government policy was one of several pressures contributing to the restructuring of collective bargaining after 1979. Deregulation of the labour market was furthered by the repeal of the Fair Wages Resolution, the passage of the 1986 Wages Act which weakened the Wages Councils, and the 1993 Trade Union Reform and Employment Rights Act which abolished them; and it was reflected in the Government's early adoption of an economic policy reflecting its belief in the efficacy of reduced Government intervention, the spur of free market forces, and the vigour of private enterprise. One of the most explicit statements advocating decentralized bargaining was made in a White Paper of 1988, which stated that there was 'no uniquely right way of determining pay, but existing approaches...will need to change if we are to achieve the flexibility essential to economic growth'.[6]

One aspect of Conservative Government policy to remove institutionalized rigidities from the labour market was evident in legislation[7] to curb the trade unions, to control industrial action, to abolish the closed shop, to increase the accountability of union leaders, and to democratize the unions' organizational methods and procedures through the required use of secret ballots. The economy was to be released from the stranglehold of collective institutions. Multi-employer bargaining arrangements and national agreements were unfavourably represented as props for lazy employers, and as restricting the downward flexibility of wage rates necessary to promote jobs where regional unemployment was high. The NJICs that been 'chivvied into existence' by Government intervention many decades ago, were at odds with the free enterprise culture of the 1980s.[8] Deregulation and decentralization were furthered by Government policy to privatize publicly-owned industries and utility services. When the water and electricity industries were privatized in 1989 and 1990, the main consideration underlying decisions to withdraw from industry-wide negotiating arrangements was the belief that national-level bargaining was no longer appropriate in industries now consisting of several large separate companies, each of which had its own needs, it own objectives, and its own strategies for operating effectively in the new competitive environment. Efficiency would now rest upon competitive tendering and responsiveness to market forces. Privatization, and the abolition of the Wages Councils which had permitted multi-employer pay determination for around three million workpeople, were closely linked with the decline of long-standing national bargaining arrangements.

Some leading employers had favoured decentralized bargaining long before the adoption of Government policy to promote it, as essential to their business strategies seeking enhanced flexibility, greater use of merit pay, and pay and grading structures more effectively tailored to their own business needs. Withdrawal from industry-wide bargaining systems had been occurring for some time where an employer found it difficult to accommodate nationally agreed job rates when job content and role definitions were changing in response to new technology, where integrated pay and grading structures were being introduced, and where incremental salary systems with progress based on regular performance appraisal were deemed to be the most appropriate means of rewarding responsibility, skill acquisition, and flexible working.

Companies or divisions recently established on greenfield sites, operating in the newer high-technology sectors, and having good market prospects, had no desire to be constrained by the strait-jacket of national agreements which could conceivably impede their growth and development and their ability to respond rapidly to expanding but changing markets. Elsewhere, national negotiations were being abandoned, particularly in industries encountering hard times, as a result of an inability to agree wage increases which were acceptable to the unions but also affordable by all the employers concerned: 'The parlous state of the economy during the early 1990s has imposed severe strains on multi-employer bargaining arrangements.'[9] One of the main problems faced by national negotiating bodies was that a national agreement often covered numerous companies, large and small, with widely varying fortunes; and in troubled economic circumstances any pay increase conceded tended to represent the 'lowest common denominator', affordable by the worst-off employers. This situation was satisfactory to neither employers nor unions and workforces, since it impeded progress for the most efficient companies and imposed strain on others. Many employers were disenchanted with the slow, cumbersome and progressively more unwieldy structures and procedures of industry-wide bargaining when 'rapid reaction' mechanisms were becoming the order of the day. It tended to be in sectors characterized by the presence of numerous small firms that distinct advantages were seen in maintaining industry-wide bargaining: saving on management time in conducting negotiations, avoidance of leapfrogging pay claims, and control of labour costs through the 'lowest common denominator' effect.

Government policy served to accelerate change in the structure of collective bargaining rather than to initiate it, for moves were already underway long before its attack on multi-employer bargaining in the later 1980s. Several studies have shown that there had been a marked change from the practice, common in the 1960s and 1970s, of topping-up industry-wide agreements. The CBI found that only half of the private-sector firms which had augmented national agreements with their own company deals in 1979 were still doing so in 1986. The main move had been to exclusively single-employer bargaining.

Decentralization of pay bargaining has also occurred *within* firms, in association with change in corporate structure. Here, Brown and Walsh emphasize the significance of the shift away from centralized functionally organized corporations (U-form) to multi-divisional structures (M-form). In Britain this was already occurring in the 1960s and 1970s. Hill and Pickering found that by the early 1980s 80 per cent of the 144 large firms covered by their survey were organized on the M-form model.[10] It was the increased size of the enterprise and its diversification into different product markets which led to the emergence of the multi-divisional corporation. M-form organization permitted management to act strategically; responsibility for corporate planning rests with top level management, while lower levels of management are responsible for operational policy at divisions organized along product lines. Monitoring by corporate management enabled them to allocate capital between units according to divisional performance. This gave plant managers some freedom in settling workers' terms and conditions of employment locally, with top management simply setting limits or issuing guidelines on divisional settlements.

In general it has been employers' need to increase their direct control over unit labour costs and to make effective use of a 'something for something' approach to collective bargaining which has increased the tendency to decentralization in the 1980s. Marsden and Thompson assert that decentralized bargaining has enabled firms to negotiate improvements in performance and changes in working practices at establishment level,[11] and this seems likely to have encouraged employers to adopt more active strategies to link pay to performance. Changes in job structures and work organization have led to the restructuring of pay systems and to greater reliance on in-house company-specific training. Technological change is the main means to higher labour productivity, and the nature and speed of recent advance in technology has required 'constantly changing portfolios of skills on the part of labour'. With shortages of certain skills or combinations of skills, employers who have encountered difficulty in recruitment and retention 'have made greater use of merit and performance-related pay'. The intense competition in product markets has accelerated the move to single-employer bargaining and the personnel practices associated with it.

Decentralization of bargaining was associated also with change in the structure of employee representation. In some cases the employer recognized and dealt with a single trade union; in several others the changeover was to single-table bargaining, which meant that the various unions recognized by the employer negotiated as a single body; in some newly established concerns, where no trade union was granted bargaining rights, negotiation was conducted through the agency of a company council or other enterprise-specific body. These changes appear to have been initiated largely by employers, and at first they were greeted with varying degrees of enthusiasm by unions and workforces. Before long, however, some unions were actively seeking single-union deals at new sites and offering single-table negotiations elsewhere.

One or two single-union agreements date from the 1960s and 1970s but it was during the 1980s that they appeared on a scale sufficient to attract the attention of industrial relations practitioners, academics and journalists. The trend was most conspicuous on greenfield sites, especially those owned by Japanese or American companies. The most common reasons given by employers for recognizing only one union were: to enhance flexibility by avoiding trade and skill demarcations; to improve the industrial relations climate by avoiding inter-union disputes; and to maintain the principle of harmonized conditions by avoiding the emergence of differentials that might result if several trade unions were recognized and each had differing bargaining priorities. Dealing with a single union also saved management's time and simplified administration. The total number of single-union agreements in operation by the end of the 1980s was unknown; but the AEU was said to have reached about 60 of them, the EETPU and the TGWU each laid claim to around 40, the GMB admitted to 'at least three dozen', and USDAW, SOGAT, and the NGA each had a few.[12]

Many single-union agreements contained arbitration clauses, some of which provided for 'binding pendulum arbitration' whereby pay claims and other matters unresolved by the company's internal procedures would be referred to an external independent arbitrator who would find in favour of one party or the other without the option of splitting the difference. Clauses attached to other agreements permitted the arbitrator to provide a compromise solution. Arbitration was intended to minimize the risk of strikes and lock-outs. The idea was not new nor of recent origin. Few single-union agreements seem to have been without such peace clauses, however, and the 'binding pendulum' version was more likely to be found in the agreements made by single-union companies. ACAS noted in its 1992 report that single-union recognition had become the rule in organizations that had recognized trade unions for the first time in recent years. The approach has been described as 'controlled unionism', reflecting employers' preparedness to deal with a union, provided they could do so on their own terms.

The 'new style' single-union agreement is said to have been pioneered in Britain by foreign-owned companies setting up mainly on greenfield sites in the 1980s and able to take advantage of the changed climate of industrial relations. The single-union package deal commonly contains features such as: sole bargaining rights for one union; single-status terms and conditions of employment for manual and staff employees below management level, or moves in that direction; elimination of traditional demarcations to permit greater labour flexibility; a highly developed system of employee participation and involvement, usually including a company council; an emphasis on a consensual style of management; a willingness to accept training and to assist in the training of others; 'no-strike' provisions seeking to preclude industrial action; and 'pendulum arbitration' as the final procedural stage in the process of negotiation, under which an independent arbitrator must find in favour of the union's final claim or the employer's final offer.

Many observers and industrial relations practitioners regard the single-union approach as a new consensual and progressive form of industrial relations, promoting industrial peace and prosperity, whilst allowing for the presence of 'responsible' trade unions. Bassett,[13] for example, represents such developments as the 'new industrial relations', imbued with the spirit of co-operation and in stark contrast to the confrontational stances of yesteryear. Critics take a less favourable view, seeing the single-union deal as a potential means of undermining both substantive and procedural standards so that, in practice, trade unions are neutralized and the workforce exploited. None of the individual elements of the 'typical' single-union agreement is new; rather, it is the whole package deal, the combination of the different elements and their inter-relatedness, which is novel and of recent origin.

A significant proportion of establishments in Britain with single-union package deals are foreign-owned, particularly Japanese-owned, but they have spread also in British-owned companies and are to be found in companies with German, American and Dutch ownership. They are generally regarded as having originated in the high-technology sector of electrical and electronic engineering, where they are still concentrated, and to be 'typical' at greenfield sites. Throughout the 1980s and early 1990s, however, they gradually spread into mainstream manufacturing sectors such as vehicles, steel, and glass. It is unsurprising that they should be introduced at greenfield sites where companies were in an ideal position to create an industrial relations environment free from the constraints of traditional practice, but the single-union package has been successfully introduced at brownfield sites with pre-existing industrial relations traditions, mechanisms and procedures – at Eaton's Newton Aycliffe plant and at United Merchant Bar in Scunthorpe. An LSE investigation disclosed that companies with single-union package deals were concentrated in North Wales in the Wrexham area, in the industrial coastal belt in South Wales, and in the North East of England. The regional concentration probably reflects inward investment from abroad, especially from Japan.

Employers with such agreements believe that they help to achieve certain important objectives: avoidance of multi-unionism and the problems caused by inter-union disputes and leapfrogging claims; reduction, if not elimination, of the risk of industrial action and the loss of both production and goodwill as a result of strikes; development of common terms and conditions for all employees regardless of occupational grade, in the interests of fairness, justice, and community spirit; flexibility in the use of labour, and eradication of traditional demarcations which reduce productive efficiency and raise costs; creation of a co-operative and committed workforce, with a sense of corporate identity and common purpose.

Single unionism was not a practical possibility in many longer-established companies where two or more unions already had recognized bargaining rights; but, where a company needed to restructure its operations, to introduce new technology, and to achieve flexibility in a demarcation-free environment, the traditional approach to collective bargaining was inappropriate. A compromise was found in single-table bargaining; this allowed participation by all the company's recognized unions but required them to negotiate as a single bargaining unit. By the end of the 1980s many employers were reviewing their bargaining arrangements. The TUC's Special Review Body was also considering ways and means of surmounting the problems which arose, and of which employers complained, where the recognized unions represented separate bargaining units, each with its own annual settlement date. It was believed that in circumstances of declining union membership, one way of making union involvement more attractive to employers was to accept, or to offer, single-table arrangements. Ideally, both manual and non-manual groups would be represented at the single table for bargaining purposes, but in practice the arrangement more commonly affected manual and some lower-level white-collar grades. The idea seems to have met with some approval; as *IRRR* pointed out in 1989, single-table bargaining was a practical alternative to single-unionism, 'allowing a multi-union environment without the risks of a fragmented bargaining structure'.[14]

The initiative for introducing single-table bargaining has usually come from employers, as in the case of single-unionism. A major advantage cited by employers was the saving of management's time and the avoidance of duplication of effort. Another benefit was that single-table bargaining produced consistency in industrial relations and avoided the problem of 'comparability' and 'leapfrogging' in pay claims. The most important reason for adopting a new style of collective bargaining, however, seems to have been organizational change, particularly when it took the form of decentralization of control from industry to company or from company to division, with an associated need to establish new bargaining arrangements. Several companies appear to have adopted single-table bargaining as the most effective means to reaching agreement on major changes in working practices, involving increased flexibility and reduced demarcations. In this context some companies had introduced single status for manual and non-manual grades; the feeling was that it was more efficient to negotiate common terms and conditions and to eradicate demarcations with a single bargaining unit than by separate negotiations with different unions.

Some recently established companies did not deal with the trade unions for purposes of negotiation. The growth of non-unionism was not necessarily a reflection of employers' increasing hostility to unions and the effect of 'counter-measures' such as 'human resources management' (HRM), though there was some evidence of opportunistic attempts at union avoidance. Investigation of industrial relations developments in the wake of the well-documented decline in union membership and coverage of collective bargaining since 1979 led McLoughlin and Gourlay[15] to the conclusion that the significance of non-unionism and non-union firms was unlikely to diminish in the foreseeable future.

The most frequently cited reasons for non-recognition were: employers' desire to link pay more effectively to individual performance, a belief that collective bargaining was inappropriate in current business circumstances, and low levels of union membership, which implied lack of interest in collective forms of representation and negotiation.

Harmonized conditions, or moves towards them, are frequently found in companies with provision for single-union or single-table bargaining, but they are not confined to companies with such arrangements. They are found in non-union concerns and in enterprises where union de-recognition has occurred. The most frequently cited examples of non-union organizations with common terms and conditions are US-owned 'high-tech' companies such as International Business Machines, Texas Instruments, and Hewlett Packard. Single-union companies with single-status conditions are, again, often foreign-owned; Japanese-owned companies such as Sanyo, Toshiba, Komatsu, Matsushita, Nissan and the US-owned Continental Can Company are frequently cited as typical examples. Single-table bargaining for harmonized conditions is more readily found in established companies with earlier traditions of fragmented bargaining and recognition of a multiplicity of unions, and tends to be associated with the employer's withdrawal from multi-employer bargaining and industry-wide agreements. The publicity which has been given to employment terms and conditions in foreign-owned companies with innovative industrial relations practices has tended to distract attention from developments in British enterprises.

HARMONIZATION WITHOUT UNIONIZATION

J.W. Thornton,[16] a non-unionized family firm engaged in production of high quality chocolate confectionery, made further moves in the

1980s in a harmonization policy which had been adopted some two decades earlier. The firm had never been party to national agreements and industry-wide bargaining.

Thornton had two main production sites, at Belper and Sheffield, and some 150 retail outlets throughout Britain. Given a seasonal pattern of market demand, production was high from August to November in preparation for the Christmas trade and from February to April for Easter. During the busy months casual labour was taken on in order to match production to demand. Nearly three-quarters of the 510 employees at the Belper factory were engaged in production, around 50 in clerical functions, and roughly 80 in managerial and supervisory roles. Although the company had never recognized trade unions for collective bargaining functions, consultation and communication had long been encouraged through the development of a company council. The council's ten members included five employee representatives, elected every two years from each area of the factory, a full-time employee representative, three members from middle and senior management, and one director. The council's functions, through sub-committees where appropriate, were to revise, clarify and change existing policies, to establish a written code of practices covering all conditions of work, and to resolve disputes over employment conditions. At the Belper site earlier moves to harmonize conditions for permanent full-time employees had mainly focused on holiday, sick pay and pension entitlements. In the 1960s the company had also introduced an integrated single-status pay and grading structure, based on the Paterson decision-banding technique, as a logical extension of its harmonization policy. This system was restructured in the 1980s in response to pressures from employees for the re-evaluation of jobs following the introduction of new working methods which had a differential impact on individual and group responsibility. Non-unionism, clearly, had not prevented employee involvement in the decision-making process, nor has it obstructed the firm's ability to maintain communication with its workforce and to respond positively to the demand for change.

While harmonization of terms and conditions took place without the involvement of trade unions at Thornton, moves to eradicate differentials at Tioxide[17] were associated not only with decentralization of industrial relations but also with derecognition of the unions and the introduction of individual employment contracts. In the mid-1980s Tioxide (UK), a member of the Tioxide Group, whose origins date back to the interwar years, was the world's second largest producer of titanium dioxide which was used mainly as a pigment in paints, plastics, textiles, paper, ceramics, and foodstuffs. The company had two main manufacturing sites at Greatham and Grimsby, its TIL organic chemicals division at Billingham, and six subsidiaries overseas.

Tioxide had already become disenchanted with traditional bargaining arrangements when the recession began to bite in the late 1970s, and in 1981, while retaining membership of the Chemical Industries' Association for some purposes, the company withdrew from the industry's national multi-employer negotiating body in order to gain the freedom to develop its own business strategy and personnel policy. At that time the AUEW, EETPU, TGWU and ASTMS all had recognized bargaining rights at Tioxide.

At the Billingham site, when the recession began to ease towards the end of 1982, Tioxide introduced skill training to create quality circles in production, and established new channels of communication with employees; at the same time, issues such as performance appraisal, a progressive grading and salary structure, and opportunities for career development were all under active consideration. Many new ideas had been implemented by the mid-1980s, including 'Juran groups', and employees were encouraged to develop their skills through in-house and external training courses. The objective was to increase productivity through 'greater accountability and flexibility'. Harmonization of terms, benefits and employment conditions, by raising manual grades to staff status, was to be the 'thread which would draw these strands together'.

At the small TIL division, with a workforce of around 100 split into roughly equal numbers of manual and non-manual/managerial employees, it had long been recognized that the traditional workplace divide was an impediment to harmonious working relationships. Moreover, technology required close-knit workgroups, for which harmonized conditions were both appropriate and desirable. After discussions with the workforce, harmonized conditions were applied across the board towards the end of 1986. The advantages of similar moves at the much larger Grimsby factory, with a workforce of almost 1000, would be even greater if the multiplicity of union agreements with their associated restrictive practices could be removed. For some time the manual and craft unions had been pressing for parity with the staff pension scheme, specifically for an accrual rate of one-sixtieth as opposed to one-eightieth of salary per year of service, and life assurance of treble as opposed to double salary. Staff conditions

were favoured by the unions and, linked to changes in working practices, would enable the company to substitute 'unfettered flexibility'
for 'custom and practice'.

Kennedy notes that at the Grimsby site, management had made
three features of the proposed policy very clear from the outset.
Firstly, collective bargaining and formal agreements with the unions
would cease to operate; in effect this meant derecognition of the
signatory unions but not the abandonment of consultation and negotiation as such. Secondly, the existing separate pay systems and
structures would be replaced by a single integrated salary and grading
structure to cover both manual and non-manual grades. Thirdly,
subject to training, all employees would be required to work with
complete flexibility, unrestricted by demarcations and traditional job
rights. A ballot of the workforce met with a 93 per cent turnout and
an overwhelming 76 per cent in favour of the proposed policy. In
January 1987 'single status was declared at Grimsby', and during the
following month over 600 manual workers signed personal contracts
of employment with the company, thereby gaining 'terms and conditions entirely in common with those of monthly salaried staff'.
Employment-related issues, formerly dealt with by collective bargaining conducted with the trade unions, would now be handled by an
all-embracing company council. In 1988 there were demands from the
workforce for the policy's extension to the Greatham site.

HARMONIZATION WITH SINGLE UNIONISM

Harmonization, along with arrangements of one kind or another for
pendulum arbitration, was accomplished in a number of companies,
such as United Merchant Bar, Excel, BICC, and the German-owned
Bosch company, on the basis of single unionism. In reviewing developments in the mid-1980s, *IRRR* observed that 'single-union no-strike
deals' with 'single-status conditions, labour flexibility, and pendulum
arbitration' were now beginning to spread from 'high-tech industry'
into other sectors, including iron and steel.

United Merchant Bar,[18] established on the site of a BSC rod mill
which had closed in the early 1980s, was a new set-up in which the
British Steel Corporation and Caparo Industries had financial stakes
of 25 and 75 per cent respectively. UMB, involved in the processing
of billets from BSC's Scunthorpe works into angles, channels, and
flats, agreed to recognize the ISTC for collective bargaining purposes.

The agreement between UMB and the ISTC contained clauses relating to sole recognition, negotiating procedures with provision for 'no-strike' pendulum arbitration, consultation arrangements, provision for two-year deals in future negotiation, and in-built flexibility and interchangeability of labour. In addition, it contained a harmonized employment package under which all employees would receive the same treatment in respect of pension, working hours, holiday and sick pay. Length of service, regardless of job grade, was the sole qualification for maximum entitlement to some of these benefits, and the arrangements applied equally to all permanent full-time employees, including management. Opportunities for salary progression were created with the introduction of an integrated five-grade pay structure covering everyone up to managerial level. There would be an automatic move to pendulum arbitration in the event of a dispute proving unresolvable by normal negotiating procedures.

A similar single-union package deal was agreed at Excel Wound Components's[19] brownfield site at Harlow in the mid-1980s. Excel, originally set up under the name of Wound Components as part of STC in the 1960s and relocated in 1983, produced transformer coil windings and components for the telecommunications, electronics and power supply industries. Following STC's decision to close Wound Components as part of its rationalization programme in the context of recession, EWC was created with a management buy-out in 1986. Prior to the buy-out both the AEU and EETPU had had bargaining rights, and many terms and conditions of employment had already been harmonized. The EETPU was chosen as the single union to represent the workforce, because it had formerly had majority membership at the site and had recently signed a similar agreement with another Harlow-based electronics firm, the STC Components Relay Unit.

The agreement contained the 'now well-known elements' of single status, single-union representation, flexible working, built-in quality control, training arrangements, a consultative council, and pendulum arbitration. The workforce would be both functionally and numerically flexible. Under the terms of the agreement, a temporary workers' register was set up to enable the company to accommodate fluctuating workloads by drawing on a pool of suitable labour as and when necessary. The intention was to provide a formal contract guaranteeing for temporary workers the same pay rates as permanent employees, access to union membership, and the chance of permanent jobs when vacancies arose. The temporary workers' register was an attempt to deal with the employment and union membership implications of the 'flexible firm' with its core employees buffered by peripheral groups whose interests also had to be accommodated.

BICC's[20] 1987 single-union agreement with MATSA, the GMB's white-collar section, bore some similarities to Excel's deal with the EETPU; the main differences were that BICC wanted functional rather than numerical flexibility of its workforce, and MATSA was resistant to the idea of binding pendulum arbitration though in flavour of new industrial relations practices in line with the GMB's policy to foster new standards for union recognition agreements. The union's recently issued document, *Into 2000*, had outlined a model single-union agreement to promote the GMB's initiative to 'move with the times' and in particular to 'gain single status employment conditions for the manufacturing workers it represented'. For BICC, UK leader in the manufacture of metallic and fibre optics cables, the agreement provided the kind of industrial relations structure that management was keen to introduce in greenfield situations.

In the 1980s fibre optics began rapidly to displace the use of copper-based cables as the new communications medium. Fibre optics described as the use of 'fine silica strands which are made into optical cables through which messages can be passed by being converted into electrical impulses and thence to infra red light pulses, with a reverse decoding process at the other end of the cable', had distinct advantages over metal cables: greater message carrying capacity, less physical bulk, and a higher quality of message transmission. In response to changes in telecommunications and orders from BT, BICC's main customer, the company had moved into fibre optics and had also rationalized its production of metal-based cables. Change in both areas involved some closures, refurbishment of some premises, investment in new sites, retraining for some employees and redundancy for others. By the mid-1980s metal cables production was concentrated at the company's refurbished factory at Blackley near Manchester, and a new optical cables unit had been built on a greenfield site at Whiston on Merseyside.

Production changes were accompanied by a revision of industrial relations procedures and arrangements. Formerly, BICC Cables, the largest company on the employers' side of the Electrical Cable Making JIC which had negotiated basic rates for the industry with the GMB, TGWU and EETPU, had generally settled in line with the JIC national agreement. However, as part of BICC's new business strategy, management wanted to develop plant autonomy as far as possible and to introduce unified bargaining structures at its greenfield sites. The company had already experimented with a single-union arrangement at the new BICC Optical Fibres factory, an independent joint venture formed by BICC and Corning Glass in 1983 at Deeside in North Wales, and in the mid-1980s the largest producer of optical fibres outside the USA. ESSA, the EETPU's staff section, had been granted sole recognition at the Deeside plant. Discussion of industrial relations in the new Whiston site were conducted in 1986 around the time when production at the now completed factory was about to start up. In this context management wanted an industrial relations framework that would emphasize the separate identity of the unit, and believed that this could be most effectively accomplished and reinforced by a single-union agreement. There was accord between MATSA and the company on the principles of single unionism, decentralized bargaining, and single-status terms and conditions.

The agreement, covering all employees up to management level at BICC's Optical Cables Unit, provided an integrated seven-grade salary structure with pay progression based on merit appraisal and salaries paid monthly by credit transfer. Arrangements for sick pay, pension, and holiday entitlement were common to all. Everyone worked a basic 39-hour week except for shift workers who had a basic week of 37.5 hours. The single-status concept applied also to attendance recording and catering amenities; clocking was a requirement for all, and no status distinctions were observed in menus, prices and seating in the dining room.

Management regarded training and flexible working practices as the key to success at the new plant, and skill acquisition was recognized in the incremental salary structure which offered the potential for career development. A 46-week programme for flexible-skill training was designed to transform the engineering maintenance team into a multi-skilled group of individuals with a combination of mechanical, electrical and electronics skills.

MATSA's Whiston agreement with BICC, and two similar agreements the union had recently concluded at the new Pirelli business wires factory at Aberdare and at one of British Cable Service's modernized cable television plants, reflected GMB/MATSA's determination to gain recognition within the 'high tech' sector in company start-ups and reorganizations, and at the same time to secure harmonized conditions for the people it represented.

Like a number of other companies we have considered, Anacomp (formerly Control Data)[21] the American-owned computer media manufacturing company, did not have greenfield conditions when it agreed a single-union package deal at its Brynmawr production site in South Wales in 1984. Single unionism at the Brynmawr site dates from 1976, but the agreement reached at that time was of the conventional procedural type which simply granted bargaining rights to one of the three unions with members on site. The single-union package deal, as such, dates from 1984. Control Data had owned and run the site since 1974 and in 1976 had agreed to recognize the EETPU to represent and negotiate for all operatives employed in the production area. In the early 1980s, following an expansion of plant capacity, the company came to the decision that existing industrial relations arrangements at the plant were outdated and inappropriate for its present and future purposes. A new procedural and substantive agreement was reached with the EETPU in 1984. The substantive part of the agreement provided for a two-year pay deal and a 'harmonization plan' which would phase in single-status terms and conditions of employment, including basic working hours, salaried status with monthly pay by credit transfer, and common holiday, pension and sickness benefit arrangements. Though specific demarcations to be eradicated were not itemized, the agreement contained a general statement of commitment by the company and its employees to 'a flexible attitude to the needs of the production process'.

The German-owned Bosch[22] company, in contrast, had the advantage of starting 'from scratch' on a greenfield site in the Cardiff area in South Wales, with purpose-built premises and industrial relations arrangements to match. It's new high-technology manufacturing unit began production in 1991, with an industrial relations policy embodying a single-union no-strike agreement with the EETPU. The package contained eight main provisions. The electricians' union was recognized as the sole union to represent, and negotiate on behalf of, all manual grades and junior non-manual staff. Production would be based on teamworking, with 'complete flexibility' in the utilization and deployment of labour 'at all levels and across jobs'. A plant council, consisting of management and directly elected workforce representatives, with one seat reserved for an EETPU officer, would function as the main forum for consultation and negotiation. Single-status conditions were to apply from the start-up of operations: payment by credit transfer at monthly intervals, a 39-hour basic working week for all employees, a basic annual holiday entitlement of 25 days, and common sick pay and pension arrangements. All employees to whom the agreement applied were covered by a simple pay and grading structure with no rigid job definitions, and salary progression was linked to performance appraisal. The highly developed communications system included regular team briefings and team problem-solving sessions. A 'peace clause' attached to the agreement provided for unilateral reference to ACAS, with binding pendulum arbitration as the final stage in the procedure for settling a dispute.

HARMONIZATION WITH SINGLE-TABLE BARGAINING

In years when the new approach to industrial relations was taking the form of single-union arrangements in some companies, others streamlined their decentralized systems by adopting single-table bargaining arrangements which simplified negotiations while maintaining multi-union recognition. The latter course was chosen by Reed Corrugated Cases.

Reed Corrugated Cases[23] formally withdrew from industry-wide multi-employer bargaining in 1982, but pressures for change had been building up since the early 1970s. Both management and the unions, SOGAT and GMBATU, believed that they could 'achieve more on their own than through multi-employer bargaining'.

There were four main reasons for Reed's withdrawal from industry-wide negotiations. Firstly, there were increasing difficulties in agreeing an employers' negotiating mandate for the whole industry because of the differing financial effects of a national agreement on different companies. Secondly, delays in concluding national settlements had damaging effects on the morale of the company's workforce and also on customer confidence. Thirdly, changes in the company's pay structure made it difficult to accommodate industry wage rate increases. Fourthly, the achievement of some of the objectives shared by the company and the unions was hampered by the provisions of national agreements.

At its fourteen manufacturing sites throughout Britain, Reed Corrugated Cases, part of the large Reed International Group, produced corrugated fibre-board containers and a range of heavy duty packaging. Reed's 1982 announcement of its intention to withdraw from the fibre-board packaging industry's national agreement on wages and conditions was the culmination of a decade of change in the company.

The overall aims, identified as early as 1973, were: improved company efficiency, reduced unit labour costs, better industrial relations framework, and improved terms, benefits and conditions of employment. Specifically, this meant: a common pay structure across all RCC plants, higher basic wage rates plus adequate incentive pay, greater employment security and a guaranteed week, harmonized terms and employment conditions for all grades, increased labour flexibility, facilities for trade union representatives, and a restructured and fairer system of job grading which would not only iron out pay anomalies but would also facilitate the introduction of new technology and new working methods. Following job evaluation, a new unified pay and grading structure was introduced in 1975 by agreement with the unions, and from then on wage bargaining was to be centrally conducted and the company agreement applied uniformly across all the fourteen sites. At the same time a joint consultation structure was set up, with representation from management and the unions, to discuss issues such as production levels, business performance, investment and new technology, and to produce plans for the future by what the company described as a 'round-table consensus approach'.

For some years following these reforms Reed continued to be party to industry-wide bargaining and national agreements negotiated by the British Fibreboard Packaging Employers' Association with SOGAT and the GMBATU. The national agreement set basic rates of pay, minimum earnings levels, shift and overtime rates, standard working hours, holiday entitlement and holiday pay, and member companies were expected to comply with the terms of the agreement and not to depart from them by local negotiations. A growing problem in the late 1970s was that, although there was a fair degree of standardization of product and process throughout the industry, there were great variations in company size and business viability. Average labour costs, at 25 per cent in the industry as a whole, were not unreasonably high, but for the numerous small firms operating on lower margins, wage costs assumed much greater significance than for large and medium-sized companies. As the recession deepened, the industry's profit margins were eroded generally, but while business was a downhill struggle with redundancies and mergers for some companies, others succeeded in maintaining a viable position.

Members of the employers' association for the industry were encountering ever greater problems in agreeing on their bargaining stance, given increasing divergence in their payment systems; and Reed found it progressively more difficult to adapt the industry's pay award to its own pay structure. It was against this background that in

1981 Reed and its two unions conducted in-depth discussions of the possibility of withdrawing completely from national-level negotiations. All recognized that the company's progressive and innovative employment policies were increasingly pointing in the direction of single-employer bargaining. Some terms and conditions, such as sick pay, pensions and the pay and grading structure had been harmonized, but further advance was hampered by the restrictions of the national agreement. Progressive moves at industry level tended to be impeded by small companies operating on tight labour cost margins. Reed wanted to reduce manual workers' standard working hours, but the proposal had been opposed by small firms. Another of the company's main objectives, that of harmonized terms and conditions of process, maintenance and white-collar employees, was also hampered by the industry agreement. Plans, it was felt, would be more readily achievable through single-employer bargaining, and at the same time, by avoiding the frustrating delays of national settlements, negotiations could be focused on matters specific to the company and issues dispatched without hindrance.

The first company settlement, reached in September 1983 by single-table bargaining, provided for further moves towards harmonization. A shorter working week, to be as far as possible self-financing through productivity off-sets, was agreed, and would be implemented through a gradual reduction in manual grades' 'attended hours' from 40 to 39 in January 1984, to 38 in January 1985 and to 37.5 in January 1986; actual working hours would fall from 37.5 to 36.5, then to 35.5 and finally to 35 over the same period. By 1986 full harmonization of working hours for manual and non-manual grades would be achieved. RCC's management and local union officers believed that, freed from the encumbrance of industry-wide bargaining on which small firms exerted a restrictive influence, the company could continue to prosper.

While RCC's policy sought to enable a relatively prosperous company to do even better, withdrawal from multi-employer negotiation and moves to single-table bargaining and harmonized conditions at BCL, Babcock Power and BICC Cables Blackley formed part of strategies for survival.

BCL,[24] a wholly-owned subsidiary of Courtauld, was founded as British Cellophane in 1935 to manufacture packaging film as part of Courtauld's diversification policy. In the early 1980s a declining global market for cellophane spurred the company to make strategic commercial decisions about its manufacturing operations at its

Barrow site. The package of radical reforms involved investment in new technology, training to create a 'flexible, lean and committed workforce', new shift-working patterns underpinned by an annualized hours system and five-crew working, the use of contract labour for certain maintenance purposes, a new five-band pay and grading structure covering manual grades and white-collar staff, and harmonization of terms and employment conditions in the longer term, beginning with sick pay, pensions and holiday entitlements in 1984 and basic working hours the following year. At the highly unionized Barrow plant, the package was negotiated around a single table at which the TGWU, AEU, EETPU, UCATT, ASTMS and ACTSS were all represented.

Babcock Power's survival plan,[25] like BCL's, involved heavy investment in new equipment, and led to a far-reaching pay and flexibility deal. Part of Babcock International, Babcock Power produced boilers and high-pressure vessels at its heavy engineering works at Renfrew. With the drastic fall-off in power station building in the early 1980s and the consequent drastic reduction of orders, the Renfrew factory had subsisted on small commissions and there had been substantial redundancies. By 1986 new business was concentrated in the areas of defence, oil-related products, and equipment required by British Nuclear Fuel's long-term investment programme. Half of Babcock Power's manufactures went to exports. The innovations of the 1980s were essentially a continuation of the modernization begun in the preceding decade with investment of £28 million to improve flagging competitiveness in a global market increasingly dominated by Japanese, French and German manufacturers. In 1980 and 1981 Babcock invested a further £18 million in a new machine and assembly factory equipped with computer-controlled systems which made it possible to undertake complex machining operations to produce goods at the competitive prices needed for access to new markets. The second phase of the survival plan, embarked upon in 1983, sought to consolidate and build upon the earlier achievements. The aim was further to improve costs, quality and delivery, to increase flexibility to enable the company to meet both current and future market requirements, and to create the most modern medium-heavy engineering facility in the UK. Negotiated round a single table with the nine unions with bargaining rights at the Renfrew site – the AUEW, GMBATU, EETPU, TGWU, FTAT, UCATT, APEX, ASTMS and TASS – the package deal provided for the relaxation and eventual eradication of traditional job and skill demarcations, training to create work teams of multi-skilled operatives, self-supervision of work teams, enhanced pay, and further moves to the 'convergence' of terms and benefits of manual and white-collar groups. Basic working hours and holiday entitlements had already been equalized. In near prospect was harmonization in the areas of sick pay, pensions, and the period and method of pay.

BICC, as we have seen, recognized a single union at its new units for fibre optics and cables at Whiston and Deeside, but at its long-established and refurbished Blackley plant producing metal-based cables, the company settled in 1993 for single-table bargaining with the GMB, AEEU, and MSF, given their recognized bargaining rights and their high levels of membership amongst the Blackley workforce.

The BICC Cables Blackley factory[26] had been manufacturing metallic telecommunications cables, which had been used throughout the national telephone network, for almost a century. In the later 1980s some of the product range was exported, some was purchased by Mercury Telecommunications, but orders from BT had accounted for almost 80 per cent of all sales. With BT's decision gradually to install optical cables throughout the network, its requirement for metallic cables had declined and was expected to decline further from a peak of 190,000 loop kilometres per week in 1990 to some 20,000 in 1997.[27] To make matters worse, with the move to competitive tendering in 1991, BT's orders for metallic cables from BICC fell by 50 per cent as a result of more competitive tenders received by BT from other suppliers. BICC Cables Blackley had no option but drastically to cut costs and raise productivity to survive in the present and improve its position for the future.

The 1993 agreement provided for single-table bargaining, a common disputes procedure, flexible team working, an integrated pay and grading structure covering all employees up to management level, and salaried status plus harmonized terms and benefits.

Most terms and conditions were harmonized for all groups. Notice periods for process and craft workers were increased from two weeks to one month, in line with non-manual employees. All employees were already covered by the same pension fund but there had been differences in contributions and entitlements; with harmonization all calculations would be based on grade salaries. Sick pay arrangements and accident benefits for process and craft employees were improved and aligned with arrangements for staff. Weekly working hours for white-collar staff were increased by half an hour to equalize with process and craft employees at 37.5 hours. Arrangements for payment for periods of authorized absence were standardized for all employees. Like many other companes moving to single status, BICC Cables transferred all employees to monthly cashless pay. With the cost and price reductions which were achieved BICC's next tender brought a contract to supply 40 per cent of BT's metallic cable requirement until 1997, compared with only 17 per cent under the previous contract.

Decentralization of pay determination, withdrawal from multi-employer bargaining, and the decline of industry-wide negotiations, have removed many restrictions imposed by national agreements upon management and workforces at company level, and have facilitated the harmonization of conditions in many companies with progressive managerial outlooks. Government policy, actively fostering deregulation of the labour market and a wider variety of approaches to the settlement of terms and conditions of employment, has indirectly encouraged harmonization in companies seeking to innovate and having the financial and organizational means to do so. Government policy and legislation, favouring advance where it was affordable, avoided imposing the financial cost of innovation on firms which could not yet find the necessary resources.

8 Payment Structures and Harmonization

INTRODUCTION

Dissimilarity in payment systems, the pay period and method of pay has been one of the most deep-rooted and persistent features of the manual/non-manual workplace divide. There were some moves to provide 'manual salaries' in a number of companies introducing staff status arrangements for manual grades in the 1950s and 1960s, but it is only relatively recently that change has occurred on a scale sufficient to attract the attention of researchers and commentators. Many, though by no means all, of the developments in payment structures have been part of more general moves to harmonize conditions, often featuring as the final stage of a process begun much earlier.

Many observers regard the emergence of integrated pay and grading structures as one of the most important of all the developments in remuneration systems since the beginning of the century, and one which has facilitated the high degree of labour flexibility required by new technology and innovative ways of organizing production and employment. Such changes were claimed to represent 'the final step in eliminating the manual worker's traditionally second-class employment status'.[1]

Traditional payment structures for non-manual staffs have usually been based on an annual salary, which seldom permitted overtime pay. By the end of the 1970s there was some variation in the salary structures found in private-sector companies: for senior management, junior management, and clerical and technical staffs.[2] Generally, for senior management there were open-ended salary bands with discretionary progression, often linked to some form of appraisal system. Other levels of management were paid according to fixed salary bands, again, with discretionary progression often closely tied to performance appraisal of some kind. For clerical and technical staff there were fixed-range salary bands, sometimes giving set increments up to the mid-point in the band with flexible increments beyond; again, progression might be based on performance appraisal. In the public sector the type of salary structure most commonly found provided incremental scales for all staff, with individual progression by regular and specified steps. In addition to these approaches, there were some non-incremental salary structures, which tended to apply to junior clerical, technical and supervisory grades whose jobs were more narrowly defined and involved limited variation in work tasks. Much of this persists today.

Many salaried staff have long had a monthly pay period, although in some cases salary might be paid fortnightly or weekly. The method of pay some time ago was generally by cashable cheque, but this came to be largely replaced by a system of credit transfer directly to the individual's bank or other savings account and pay-statement notification that the transaction had been completed. For recipients, the main financial advantages of salaried status are stability, dependability and predictability of earnings, progressively rising income where salary is incremental, access to bank and building society financial services, and relative ease of acquiring a mortgage or other large loan – given the salary earner's repayment prospects.

All of this was in stark contrast to the situation of most manual workers. Until relatively recently, most received a wage, usually paid weekly by cash in the pay packet. Earnings were based on various kinds of payment-by-results schemes (PBR) geared to the amount produced. Other schemes were based on some form of measured day work (MDW). Where time-rates applied, there was a basic hourly rate or a basic weekly wage related to normal weekly working hours. In the general absence of incremental pay progression, pay increases were a matter of collective bargaining, nationally and/or locally. Basic pay might be enhanced by bonuses, various kinds of special supplements, shift premia, and overtime rates which varied according to the amount worked and the day on which it was worked. Many of these payment systems were, and still are, highly complex and produce levels of take-home pay which fluctuate from week to week.

The operation of different and separate payment systems for manual and non-manual grades made sense in circumstances prevailing in times past, but in many companies change in production processes and the organization of work has rendered the traditional approach both inappropriate and inefficient. New technology, in affecting the job content, work tasks, responsibilities and working methods of manual workers, technicians and office staffs, is eroding the differences and blurring the boundaries between manual and white-collar jobs in many industries and services; and robotics and other computer-controlled machinery have created a demand for broader skills to be deployed flexibly. Technological advance, Grayson observed in 1984, would have an 'impact upon payment systems' by requiring the 'development of white-collar rather than blue-collar type payment structures'.[3] Pay and grading systems would need to be updated corresponding to changes in working practices, skill requirements, and job responsibilities.

Another incentive for an employer to integrate pay and grading structures was the trend to harmonized conditions. Where a firm proposed, or had already implemented, a policy to harmonize terms and benefits, negotiation and discussion would inevitably at some stage focus on 'methods of payment, levels of pay, the merging of grade and payment structure, and career progression'.[4] The trend reflected the 'continuing interest in removing the "them and us" syndrome of UK industries'.[5]

In some circumstances PBR and MDW systems might be suitable in revised and more flexible forms; and profit-sharing, share-ownership, gain-sharing and similar kinds of incentive schemes might be put to effective use as financial motivators. Many employers, however, were recognizing a growing need for manual pay structures which would facilitate flexible utilization and deployment of labour, and at the same time accommodate skill acquisition and permit pay and career progression. An integrated pay and grading system offered a potentially more effective means of motivating and rewarding effort. The likely spread in Britain of the company-wide job evaluation schemes being developed in Europe in the early 1980s provided another part of the explanation for British employers' growing interest in simple unified pay systems. Another pressure came from management's efforts to rationalize the firm's fragmented bargaining structure into a more cohesive unit, involving a common annual settlement date and a common negotiating forum; a unified bargaining system suggested the logic of a unified pay and grading structure. There were distinct advantages flowing from such moves, in terms of ease of administration and control, and a saving on the time and cost involved in operating different payment systems. Another important consideration in the 1980s was the influence of legislation requiring equal pay for work of equal value, which provided good reason for introducing a single pay and grading system covering all or most employees.

In its most advanced form, an integrated structure covers the company's entire workforce up to and including management. Of the schemes introduced in the 1980s, the most common were those covering all manual grades; some covered manual and lower white-collar grades, and others all grades except management. Relatively few included all managerial grades.

In an integrated grading structure all jobs, regardless of their traditional collar-colour labels, are evaluated and placed in one or other of a small number of main bands or grades, each of which may contain both manual and non-manual jobs assessed to be of equal value. This means that an operative and a clerical employee may be in the same grade and receiving the same amount of basic pay. There is the opportunity for salary progression within each band, with advance based on proficiency and performance, and also for progression from one band to the next with the acquisition of additional or higher skills and knowledge. An integrated grading and salary system can provide the individual with stability and predictability of pay, a structured means to pay progression, and, with arrangements for training and retraining, real opportunities for career development. This is a major step forward for the manual worker, for it provides access to an employment condition which was an advantage traditionally associated with non-manual employment. Such policies are said to establish equity between task levels, and to create improved career paths by widening promotion opportunities from the shopfloor and removing traditional limitations on advancement. For the employer, a unified pay and grading structure offers the means to resolve problems relating to the interface between separate payment systems based on different principles when the boundaries between them have been blurred by changed working practices and requirements of new technology; and it has flexibility in permitting movement both within and between pay bands.

On recent greenfield sites integrated payment systems have operated from the commencement of operations, in support of business strategies and personnel policies in which traditional job and skill boundaries have been largely irrelevant from the outset. In other longer established companies both management and unions have come to recognize the need for change in payment structures where innovation in production methods and technology have rendered the traditional separate payment systems unsuitable; in such cases, Grayson argues, an integrated pay structure has been a major contributor to improved company performance by facilitating new working methods and reducing costs through the opportunities provided for continuous improvement in individual and group skills. All existing integrated payment systems are 'under-pinned by a belief in single-status terms and conditions of employment'. Harmonization of conditions, including a unified payment structure, might be an 'expression of company philosophy about how people should be treated' or a 'pragmatic recognition' that the 'reduction or elimination of differentials' is an 'immense encouragement to mutually supportive individual, team, and company-wide effort' and a means to 'create more positive attitudes to work'.[6]

In the 1980s the increasing use of flexible payment systems, in line with the increased demand for flexible working, seemed likely to bring to the fore the issue of individual appraisal and merit-rating. Integrated payment structures tend to go hand in hand with systems of performance appraisal. Merit pay based on systematic perfor- mance review was relatively uncommon for manual workers, but with the growing sophistication of payment systems and moves to harmon- ized conditions it was likely to feature more prominently in the future. Forms of merit pay for manual grades had been in existence, notably in the engineering industry, since the mid-1960s, but unions and workforces had tended to be suspicious of them, mainly because merit tended to be subjectively assessed. The idea of merit pay was re- emerging in the early 1980s, however. The main difference between the old discredited approach and its reconstructed form was that the latter was based upon 'systematic assessment against predetermined criteria'.[7]

IRRR's 1987 review of pay and grading systems in six single-status companies – Hewlett Packard, Digital, National Semiconductor, Inmos, Sanyo, and ICL Mainframe Systems – disclosed that each regularly and systematically appraised employees' performance against predetermined criteria. The IPM's 1986 investigation[8] found 'substantial recent growth' in the practice of applying such systems to manual grades; 24 per cent of the companies surveyed now used performance appraisal compared with only 2 per cent in 1977. This 'phenomenal increase in performance review among skilled manual workers' was said to be the result of growing management interest in flexible work practices and the creation of a multi-skilled manual grade, the wider use of job evaluation which tended to equate multi- skilled and flexible craft grades with some non-manual and technician grades for whom methods of performance appraisal had been in operation for some time, and also 'changing social attitudes and or- ganizational moves towards harmonization of conditions for all non-management employees'. In all the companies covered by *IRRR*'s 1987 survey the process of performance appraisal was found to be not only 'retrospective' in reviewing past performance, but also 'developmental' in setting future goals. The manufacture or utilization of new technology was a common feature of these companies.

If the spread of integrated payment structures and methods of performance appraisal were reducing the differential between non-manual and some manual groups, the gradual move to 'cashless' pay furthered the process. The beginnings of change were evident in the 1970s. Incomes Data Services noted that in 1969 89 per cent of manual workers were paid in cash, that the proportion had fallen to 78 per cent by 1979, and that there had been 'slow but steady progress' during the following three years.[9] Moves tended to be initiated by employers, and were later encouraged and facilitated by Government policy. Since unions and workforces were not enthusiastic at first, inducements were needed to secure their acceptance of pay by credit transfer, sometimes linked to a move to a monthly pay period. The inducements variously offered by employers included a period of free banking, one-off interest-free loans, a cash lump sum, extra holiday entitlement, a special bonus, better pensions, and even a pay rise.[10]

Employers' reasons for seeking change are readily identifiable. The financial advantages forthcoming to the company in paying all employees monthly by credit transfer include: savings on security costs for transportation of cash, protection of staff, storage of pay packets, cash in transit to pay points, and insurance premiums; savings of staff and staff time in payroll sections; savings on employees' time in collecting pay during working hours; savings on bank charges for withdrawal of cash; savings on pay packet stationery; savings on cash handling equipment; possible savings on systems overheads.[11] In effect, for the company cashless pay and a monthly pay period for all permitted greater efficiency, reduced costs, and discouragement of pay packet theft and violent crime. It was invariably cheaper and administratively simpler to pay earnings directly into employees' bank accounts; and the larger the workforce, the greater the savings.

Britain was far behind other developed countries in matters of payment method and frequency of pay. At the beginning of the 1980s over 95 per cent of the working populations were paid through banks in France, West Germany, the Netherlands, Canada, and the USA. Britain's relative backwardness was attributable partly to legislation relating to payment of manual workers' wages and partly to entrenched habit. Truck Acts, dating from the nineteenth century, laid down that workmen's wages must be paid in the current coin of the realm. The 1960 Payment of Wages Act permitted payment by cheque or credit transfer, but only if the worker so requested or agreed, and the individual retained the right to revert to cash pay. Local authorities were keen to change to cashless pay in view of the estimated cost-saving which could be made. The Local Government Chief Inspector of Audit suggested in his 1980 report that the current annual administrative cost of paying the wages and salaries of local authority employees was over £25 million, that this amount could be halved by moving to credit transfer for all, and that the cost could be reduced to less than £3 million if all employees were paid monthly.[12]

The banks, unsurprisingly, were very much in favour of the idea of wage payment directly into bank accounts, and twelve of them mounted a campaign in the early 1980s to encourage the adoption of the idea. Employers' organizations, by and large, were also in favour.

The TUC and its affiliated unions were not adamantly opposed, but they took the line that individual workers should have free choice in the matter. The general feeling amongst the unions, and the official view of the TUC, was that the Truck Acts should be retained as protection against exploitation, yet the inevitability of the spread of cashless pay, particularly where it was part of moves to improve the manual worker's status, was fully understood. Electricity Supply's 1981 national agreement contained a clause expressing the unions' support for change: 'The trade unions' members support and encourage the payment of NJIC members by cheque or credit transfer on a monthly basis'.

The most obvious advantages for workpeople in receiving pay by bank transfer – which for many meant opening a bank account for the first time – were avoidance of pay packet theft and access to bank facilities such as loans, overdrafts, interest-bearing accounts, financial advice, and payment of bills by cheque or, later, by standing order or direct debit.

There were some disadvantages, however, and these go some way in explaining the slow rate of change in the 1970s and early 1980s. Given the manual worker's daily and weekly working hours, there might be difficulty in withdrawing cash from banks whose opening times were limited, especially if the bank was some distance from the worker's place of employment. There was also the problem of bank charges and unfamiliarity in managing a bank account and writing cheques. At the same time, many male workers were reluctant to allow details of their earnings to become known to their wives. Deeply engrained habits presented cultural barriers to workpeople's eagerness to embrace change in the method of pay.

The other main impediment lay in the Truck Acts of 1831–1940, which preserved the right of a manual worker paid by bank transfer to revert to receiving his or her pay in cash on request. These Acts were being reviewed by the Government in the early 1980s, and consultative documents, issued in July 1983 and October 1984, outlined legislation to repeal them and to provide new statutory protection against 'unlawful deductions' from pay. The 1986 Wages Act repealed the Truck Acts and associated legislation, with effect from January 1987. This meant that employers were no longer under an obligation to pay manual workers in the coin of the realm, but, where the worker's right to be paid in cash was written into a contract of employment, that right remained unless the worker agreed to a change of contract. The most important change made by the 1986 Act was the withdrawal of the manual worker's right to revert to cash pay once having accepted cashless pay. By 1990 only about one quarter of the British workforce, mainly lower socio-economic groups and older workers, were still paid in cash.[13] Undoubtedly the 'sweeteners', which employers were prepared to give, encouraged the move to credit transfer and, in a growing number of cases, the associated acceptance of a monthly pay period. Change was facilitated also by the activities of banks and building societies in providing cash dispensers with instant and constant access to cash, and by the wider use of credit cards and the Switch system of paying for purchases. As *IRRR* observed in 1990: 'Moving the entire workforce to cashless pay is frequently a feature of harmonization programmes, and can be claimed to enhance industrial relations and flexibility by treating the whole workforce equally and removing status barriers.'[14]

HARMONIZATION OF PAY SYSTEMS, METHODS AND FREQUENCY OF PAY

Change in the structure, method and frequency of pay and the application of performance appraisal were closely linked with companies' harmonization policies. Progress was more readily discernible in the private sector than in public employment where innovation occurred more slowly.

Some of the most advanced practices were to be found in non-union companies. That unified grading systems, in combination with other common terms and conditions of employment, had been successfully introduced in non-unionized environments is not altogether surprising, given that the workforces in question were generally less affected by institutionalized divisions separating bargaining groups. The situation was markedly apparent in companies owned by foreign multi-nationals, especially where the production, servicing and sales of new technology and largely American ownership were involved, as in the case of Hewlett Packard, Digital and National Semiconductor operating in Scotland's 'silicon glen'. The fact that all three were recently established on greenfield sites is as important as US influence in explaining their advanced and highly distinctive personnel policies: 'Operating in the main from greenfield sites, the companies have had the opportunity to introduce model industrial relations practices, unfettered by the weight of tradition'.[15] At Hewlett Packard and Digital a single grading arrangement covered all employees except senior executives by the mid-1980s; at National Semiconductor the unified pay and grading arrangement covered manual and administrative personnel, but not management and senior professional staff. In all three companies salary progression at all levels was based entirely on merit, as assessed by regular performance reviews; and non-pay employment terms were fully harmonized, with level of pay as the only key differential.

Hewlett Packard had a 12-grade job-evaluated pay structure in the mid-1980s, with a wide salary range for each pay grade, which provided a difference of 35 per cent between the minimum and maximum salary levels for the grade. Salary progression was based entirely on performance, and overall salary ranges were raised annually in line with market forces. Two factors, performance appraisal and ranking against comparable workers, determined the individual's position in the salary range for his or her grade. Supervisors' decisions concerning performance were subject to 'fine tuning' by senior managers and the personnel department to ensure consistency of treatment across the whole workforce. The appraisal took the form of a 45-minute discussion between the employee and the immediate supervisor and was based on a four-page standard form. Given the importance of merit-rating, supervisors were prepared for their appraisal role by regular in-house training sessions. The appraisal process served two interlinked purposes, the assessment of past performance and the identification of objectives for future development, reflecting the company's philosophy of 'management by objectives'. There were six criteria against which performance was measured: work quality, work quantity, judgment, initiative, teamwork, and dependability. The overall performance rating determined within which of the four quartile pay bands in the salary range the individual's salary was located.

Digital's merit appraisal system was similar to Hewlett Packard's in its underlying principles. Here, also, pay ranges were raised annually in line with market forces, but all individual salary movement was tied to performance, and the merit element was more significant than at Hewlett Packard. At Digital there was a gap of at least 50 per cent between the minimum and maximum salary points for each grade. For senior employees the gap was as wide as 80 per cent. All employees, except for very senior managers, were covered by an eleven-grade job-evaluated pay structure. Each grade, as at Hewlett Packard, had a salary range divided into four broad bands corresponding to different performance levels. On the basis of performance appraisal employees were rated as FMR (fails to meet requirements), RD (requires development), MR (meets requirements), UER (usually exceeds requirements), and AER (always exceeds requirements). In practice the FMR classification was used very rarely and was not reflected in the pay banding structure. Individual salaries, as at Hewlett Packard, were based partly on performance appraisal and partly on an annual ranking by supervisors. The appraisal system operated by Digital was an elaborate three-stage process, known as 'job planning and performance review'. The immediate supervisor and the employee would jointly agree a job plan for the year at the beginning of the annual cycle. The job plan consisted of agreed 'core responsibilities' and also agreed 'job goals', which were concerned with ways of improving basic competence and means of enlarging the scope for individual development. This process typically took four hours or more. An interim review of progress was held subsequently, when any special support plans necessary to meet targets might be agreed. The final review in the cycle took place six months later. As at Hewlett Packard, job evaluation only determined the individual's broad pay band, leaving considerable scope for merit-rating by the supervisor.

National Semiconductor, in contrast, gave general increases in pay rates as well as purely performance-linked rises, and the system of rewarding merit was quite different in that it was based on a matrix of performance points. In the case of manual workers' jobs there was an eight-grade structure, with five pay steps within each grade and progression dependent on performance. The individual's performance was reviewed twice each year by supervisors, who, as at Digital and Hewlett Packard, received special in-house training for their role in the appraisal system. Each employee was awarded points, out of one hundred, against specified criteria. The amount of merit pay was based on the average number of points scored in appraisal conducted twice each year. Merit rises were more difficult to achieve once the individual had reached the upper levels of the pay range.

Integrated payment structures in combination with other harmonized terms and conditions were spreading also in single-union companies and they were introduced in some of the employing enterprises moving to single-table bargaining. Almost invariably, a monthly pay period and pay by credit transfer were brought in at the same time or before long.

Continental Can (UK)'s[16] agreement with the TGWU in 1980, covering all employees below managerial level at its Wrexham greenfield site, provided for a unified nine-band grading structure as part of its single-status policy. Accounts clerks and machine operators were placed in Band C, following a comprehensive job evaluation exercise; assistant buyers, electricians, and tooling inspectors shared Band E(2). The entire workforce was paid monthly by credit transfer. Duracell,[17] the British subsidiary of the US-based corporation Duracell Inc., itself a subsidiary of the multi-national Kraft Group, had introduced performance appraisal to operate in association with its integrated pay and grading system and other broadly harmonized conditions by 1987 on the basis of its single-union deal with the AEU. Similar moves were evident at Inmos,[18] a joint Anglo-American enterprise set up in Britain in 1978 with substantial investment funds from the National Enterprise Board to produce a new generation of microchips with which the company could prospectively gain a sizeable share of a rapidly expanding global market for such products.

Production was scheduled to commence in the early-1980s at Inmos's purpose-built factory at Newport in South Wales. A high degree of employee motivation and flexible working were essential to enable the company to compete with the exacting productivity and quality standards of its mainly Japanese rivals. Amongst the main priorities of its industrial relations policy were effective communication channels, arrangements for the rapid resolution of disputes, continuous training for the constantly changing needs of production, and single-status terms and conditions to promote and reinforce a sense of common purpose. Basic working hours, holiday entitlement, provision for sick pay and pensions, canteen and car parking facilities, and private medical cover, were the same for all employees. An integrated pay and grading system, performance appraisal, and monthly payment of salary by credit transfer were basic elements of the single-status policy. For each grade there were minimum and maximum salary points, with progression based on merit as assessed during the formal appraisal process. Under the system, still being developed in the early 1980s, there was an annual agreement on the total amount to be allocated for pay increases; part of the total was paid as a general increase to all staff, and the remainder apportioned as merit pay.

Holset Engineering[19] introduced its integrated pay and grading system on the basis of single-table bargaining with its recognized unions, the AUEW, ASTMS, and TASS, representing some 1,400 employees at the company's Halifax and Huddersfield sites. With the move to full harmonization towards the end of 1984, the separate grading structures were replaced by a unified five-band system, with six incremental steps within each pay band. The company adopted a skill development programme, designed to enable employees to progress to their grade maximum through successful completion of one skill module per year. Other main elements of Holset's harmonization policy were a basic 35-hour working week for all, common holiday, sick pay and pension entitlements, the abolition of clocking, and payment by credit transfer at monthly intervals.

In Electricity Supply[20] further development of policy dating from the 1960s took the form of a totally new pay and grading structure with incremental scales and opportunity for career progression, and the creation of a new negotiating forum bringing together in one body representatives from each of the formerly separate bargaining units. By the end of the 1970s harmonization had been achieved in the areas of annual salaries, basic working hours, clocking, sick pay, pensions, and annual leave. The industry also provided subsidized single-status canteen facilities at major power stations, engineering maintenance depots and administrative locations; and subsistence allowances, removal expenses, and car and motor cycle allowances.

The need to rationalize the pay and grading structure was recognized in the 1978 NJIC agreement, which stated that the time was 'now opportune for a joint review of the NJIC salary structure with a view to simplification whilst preserving the efficiency with which staff are utilized in the industry'. After extensive joint discussions, agreement on the changes to be implemented was reached in 1981.

The new grading structure rationalized over 76 existing job duties into five broad salary bands, the fifth of which created a new level of 'enhanced craftsman'. Each band had a four-point incremental scale and contained jobs evaluated as roughly comparable in terms of skill level and responsibility. In Band 1 were general assistants in labouring, security and catering functions, who were described as 'staff carrying out a range of manual and other basic duties'. Band 2 contained craft attendants, security guards, drivers, and cooks, all of whom were deemed to have 'duties requiring skills for a limited area of work'. In Band 3 were boiler operators, plant attendants, laggers, and storekeepers, who were assessed as having 'sufficient skills to perform duties in a substantial area of work and to take significant responsibility'. Electrical and mechanical fitters, overhead line men, and instrument mechanics, described as 'staff with basic craft and skill responsibilities' were placed in Band 4. Band 5 contained 'enhanced grades of craftsmen' who had 'extended skill, experience, knowledge and training' and who were 'capable of undertaking higher levels of craftwork with minimum supervision'.

Clearly this was not a fully integrated pay and grading structure for it did not extend to non-industrial staff. It did have the effect, however, of rationalizing a multiplicity of job duties and plus payments, and of providing a framework for career progression for industrial employees, many of whom would spend the greater part of their working lives in the industry. In that sense, *IRRR* observes, 'it mirrors the career structure open to non-industrials'; opportunity for career development was a feature of many kinds of non-manual employment and, at the beginning of the 1980s 'a relatively neglected aspect of the whole staff-status/harmonization concept'.[21] Under the terms of the agreement, Electricity Supply's management would provide training opportunities for industrial grades in order to facilitate upward mobility through the career structure: 'It is a basic intention of the revised structure to provide meaningful opportunities for career progression'.

In contrast to Electricity Supply's somewhat truncated grading structure, the form adopted by Pilkington Insulation[22] covered all employees up to middle management. An integrated payment system and the harmonization of other terms and conditions were implemented by Pilkington in the context of moves to divisional bargaining and single-table negotiation. In the 1980s the activities of Pilkington's 32 different locations throughout the UK extended from the production of basic glass goods to the development and marketing of products for science, medicine, defence, leisure and agriculture.

In the aftermath of a major strike in 1970 the company had set up a new bargaining structure with five central but separate negotiating committees covering manual groups, craft grades, non-manual staff, foremen, and drivers. Of a total workforce of around 23,500, nearly 20,000 came within the scope of the centralized system for pay determination, which continued to operate until December 1983. By this time the company had expanded to become a diverse organization with separate divisions and functions, producing for many different markets and utilizing many different technologies. For some time activities had been commercially decentralized, with each product-based division forming a separate profit centre with a degree of autonomy.

Divisionalization of industrial relations had been discussed from time to time since 1976, but it was not until December 1983 that the company moved to plant-by-plant bargaining. The new policy had three main objectives: firstly, 'site identity' which would combine the team spirit approach with local cost centres; secondly, an integrated payment structure which would be fundamental to the elimination of unnecessary differentials and the harmonization of conditions of employment; and thirdly, single-table bargaining which would merge separate bargaining units at site level so that all staff and manual unions would negotiate in one forum.

At the Ravenhead site in St Helen's, Pilkington Insulation introduced a nine-grade integrated payment structure, based on Hay-MSL principles of job evaluation. In effect, Pilkington transferred to an established plant many of the conditions introduced four years earlier at its 'show piece' Greengate works which had had the advantage of a greenfield site and full harmonization of terms and benefits from the outset.

Swan Hunter,[23] the shipbuilding firm, adopted single-table bargaining in a major move to harmonize its payment structure for manual, craft, technical and clerical staff in 1990. Other terms of employment were to be harmonized as part of a deal which left scope for further development in the future.

The British shipbuilding industry is all too often assumed to have declined largely as a result of demarcation-dominated working methods, outmoded and inflexible working practices and its turbulent industrial relations history; but in the early 1990s the Newcastle-based Swan Hunter could justifiably claim to be 'in the vanguard of change' in the steps it took to compete in a global economy. The company, whose origins date back to the nineteenth century, became part of British Shipbuilders in 1977 when the Labour Government nationalized the shipbuilding industry. The complex, diverse and inconsistent range of pay rates and payment systems which British Shipbuilders inherited caused numerous strikes over pay comparabilities. Agreement between British Shipbuilders and the CSEU to resolve existing anomalies and introduce flexible working was overtaken by the Conservative Government's decision to privatize the industry in 1984.

At Swan Hunter privatization was followed by a management buy-out in 1986. By this time the company's workforce had declined from 13,500 in 1976 to 3,500 as a result of the world recession, and further job losses followed. An agreement of 1988–9 provided for further moves towards fully flexible working, harmonized conditions, and a single integrated pay structure. Sick pay and holiday entitlements for manual workers were equalized.

Under the 1990 agreement all employees were to receive an annual salary, based on a five-band payment structure. Previously, only non-manual staff had had incremental merit-pay progression, but this was to be extended to manual and craft grades who, under new arrangement, would move on to a system of annual appraisal similar to the staff. The existing system for non-manual staff provided annual service-based increments up to a bar within the salary range for the grade, with merit increases linked to annual appraisal results thereafter. With an hours reduction for manual grades, basic working time was harmonized at a 37-hour 4.5-day week for all. However, this was to be partially financed by agreed change in working practice, including the elimination of the 15-minute morning teabreak, bell-to-bell working, the maintenance of current staffing levels within the terms of a 'versatility agreement' implemented two years earlier, team working, and the phased introduction of a new training programme to replace the traditional apprenticeship scheme.

The workforce had co-operated with management in the modernization and rationalization of production methods in the company's shipyards, but none of the changes prevented Swan Hunter from going into receivership in 1993, when its bid for the contract to build a Royal Navy helicopter carrier was rejected in favour of a more competitive tender from Vickers Shipbuilding and Engineering.

A similar long-term deal, providing leeway for future development in both procedural and substantive matters, was reached at Scottish & Newcastle Breweries[24] in the early 1980s. The three-year agreement of 1982 not only laid down a policy to harmonize the basic terms and benefits of manual grades and white-collar staff, but set in motion the complete overhaul of the fragmented bargaining structure with a view to bringing together the TGWU, AUEW, EETPU and ACTSS into one negotiating body with a common annual settlement date, and at the same time initiated the rationalization of the pay and grading system.

During the years prior to the changes begun in 1982, the company had used an outdated method of job evaluation and had had a pay and grading structure which produced inter-group conflict over earnings differentials. Craftsmen, believing themselves to be undervalued by the company, were seeking rights to staff conditions, and were voicing their concern about the impact of new technology on traditional craft practices and the implications for craftsmen's skill and status. Staff employees and supervisors were becoming restive about the decline of their pay relativities *vis-à-vis* other grades and about the erosion of their non-pay differentials as a result of improved fringe benefits for manual workers. All of this was having an adverse effect on the company's production costs, productivity, and industrial relations climate.

In 1982, after in-depth discussions with the unions, a package was agreed which embodied a trade-off between the company's aims and the unions' objectives. The company wanted to streamline the pay and grading structure and to establish single-table bargaining; and, in order to improve its business performance, it needed a relaxation of traditional craft demarcations and acceptance of flexible working. As management recognized, however, none of these changes were likely to be countenanced by the unions unless the problem of resentment over pay differentials could be resolved, the manual workers' claims for improved fringe benefits could be satisfied, and the non-manual staff's discontent about the erosion of their accustomed privileges could be appeased by financial compensation which might be built into the new company-wide pay and grading system.

For several years in annual settlements the manual unions had been whittling away differences between manual grades and non-manual staff in non-pay areas such as holiday entitlement, sick pay, pensions and working hours. So far, these had been one-off concessions rather than part of an overall strategy to harmonize conditions; but now the time had come for moving more methodically and deliberately along a path which would ultimately lead to full harmonization, with an integrated pay and grading structure and monthly pay by credit transfer as the first of many steps to be taken.

A number of other major brewing companies were also revising their personnel policies along similar lines in these years. At

Whitbread's long-established Romsey site in Hampshire, for example, an agreement reached in 1983 with the TGWU and ACTSS introduced a unified five-grade payment structure as part of the company's new integrated approach to terms, benefits and employment conditions. Overtime, bonus and other pay supplements were abolished, leaving premiums for shift workers and chargehands as the only additions to salary. The agreement established flexible working practices across the site. Each employee was committed to work up to a specified number of hours daily and weekly, which might involve weekend working in some cases, under an annualized hours arrangement. With basic terms and conditions broadly harmonized, all employees would receive an annual salary related to job grade and his or her annual hours commitment.

It was around this time also that BP Chemicals at Barry, by agreement with its recognized unions, introduced a salary payment structure for manual grades, with salary progression based on performance appraisal, as a further stage of a harmonization policy dating from the 1960s. Change was broadly similar at Shell's Stanlow refinery. Here, three new process grades were created, with progression within each grade based on merit assessment and skill acquisition.

The Wellcome Foundation and Metal Box both revised their pay and grading systems, by agreement with the several unions recognized for collective bargaining purposes, in 1986 and 1987 respectively.

Wellcome,[25] a major producer of pharmaceutical products, with headquarters in London and research and manufacturing sites in Beckenham, Dartford, Crewe, Royton and Berkhamsted, employed a large workforce of technicians, scientists, managers, clerks, secretaries, and manual operatives, who were variously represented by ASTMS, the TGWU, AEU, EETPU, UCATT and other unions at individual locations. By 1986 the non-pay conditions of industrial and non-industrial staff were already harmonized. In the early 1970s the existing PBR system covering industrial grades had been replaced by an MDW system based on a high day-rate. That system had been revised by an agreement reached in 1978 to introduce a job evaluation scheme to cover all manual grades, including craft workers; the effect was to reduce the number of grades from ten to eight. The next major change occurred in 1986 at a time when management was seeking greater labour flexibility and some overlap between skilled and semi-skilled functions by the removal of traditional craft and trade demarcations. An agreement, based on the principles of harmonization and flexibility, sought to create an industrial relations climate conducive to employees' acquiescence in ongoing change. It introduced annual performance appraisal based on the same principles for all employees, in combination with an integrated pay and grading structure with four salary bands within each new job grade. Wellcome subsequently reported 'slow but perceptible change in attitudes', which was manifest in higher productivity and greater harmony in industrial relations because 'all employees are now treated in the same manner'. As in other companies adopting systems of performance assessment, supervisors received training for their roles as appraisers. The appraisal process became the means of improving employees' performance of work tasks and of developing career paths.

Harmonized terms and benefits at Metal Box's Braunstone plant[26] near Leicester were also the outcome of negotiation in a multi-union context at a site with highly automated processes for production of cans for the food and beverage industry. Despite a multi-union structure involving the GMB, AEU, NGA, EETPU and ASTMS, the site had had single-status conditions from the time of its greenfield start-up in 1978. Six-monthly appraisals to assess past performance and developmental needs had also been conducted from the outset. In 1987 the appraisal process did not directly govern incremental pay progression; instead, higher than average performance was rewarded by means of a highly developed system of internal promotion.

In the 1990s the rationalization of pay and grading systems and the use of performance appraisal were beginning to feature more prominently in companies' harmonization policies. Harmonization involved a whole package of reforms which were often only feasible in a decentralized bargaining context which permitted the company or division to develop its own business strategy and personnel policy unconstrained by national agreements. It is unsurprising that harmonized conditions should be found in non-union and single-union companies and at sites with single-table bargaining.

If change in payment systems and bargaining structures were to the fore in initial, further or final moves to harmonized conditions, the requirements of new technology and the quest for flexibility, efficiency and business competitiveness were the main motivating forces. The linking of pay to performance, the extension of new incremental salary structures to manual grades, and the creation of opportunities for manual career development served further to erode, and possibly to erase, the traditional workplace divide.

In the mid-1980s, in line with the Government-endorsed principle linking reward to effort, appraisal schemes were spreading, as a means of raising employees' productivity and a company's overall performance. *IRRR* noted in 1986[27] that appraisal was becoming a 'subject of growing importance' in the 'determination of the individual's pay and career development'. The kind of pay and grading systems which were already well-established for non-manual and professional grades in the finance sector were spreading elsewhere and beginning to be extended to manual workforces. The shift in the centre of gravity of collective bargaining, from national industry-wide level to the company, the division or the site, was claimed by the Institute of Personnel Management in 1990 to be one of the most conspicuous features of recent changes in industrial relations. The main impetus for change was said to be employers' desire to tie pay more closely to performance. Employers wanted the freedom not only to determine pay rates and increases, but to introduce new pay structures tailored to suit their business strategies.[28]

Breaking free from multi-employer bargaining and national agreements has given employers greater scope to gain concessions on flexible working from the unions, and to fashion the total remuneration package to suit their own needs and circumstances. The removal of the constraints of industry-wide settlements forms part of the explanation for the spread of harmonized conditions, accompanied progressively more often by integrated payment structure, performance appraisal, and monthly pay by credit transfer.

9 In Retrospect

INTRODUCTION

The traditional differentials in the terms, benefits and conditions of employment of manual and non-manual employees have been steadily eroded since the Second World War. By the beginning of the 1980s many companies, entire industries even, had done much to break down the timeworn workplace divide which had buttressed class consciousness and become widely recognized both as a barrier to innovation in industry and as a constraint on economic performance. In 1981 the CBI[1] strongly urged that: 'Management should encourage a steady movement towards harmonization of status and conditions between staff and shop floor... British industry still suffers from too many social divisions.'

THE CAUSES OF CHANGE AND EMPLOYEES' REACTIONS

An important influence on personnel policy has been change in non-manual employment. Arthurs[2] argues, convincingly, that the 'feminization and unionization' of non-manual employment have contributed during the course of time to the 'gradual development of a different relationship with employers'. The vast increase in numbers, the routinization of much of the work done, the depersonalization of the relationship with the employer, increased union membership and the tendency of white-collar unions to emulate the strategies and tactics of manual unions are all well-documented. The declining relevance of some of the underlying historical reasons for treating non-manual grades preferentially goes some way in explaining employers' willingness to consider dismantling the conventional barriers of yesteryear.

While the justification for rewarding office staffs with a superior total remuneration package has diminished, the reasons for improving manual workers' terms and benefits and for aligning them with staff conditions have become more pressing. Some kinds of manual work, and the associated job content, responsibility and skill requirements, have changed beyond all recognition. Work measurement and job evaluation exercises have disclosed that the value to the company of some kinds of manual work is equal to, or greater than, that of the more routine clerical and administrative functions. Recognition of the key role of 'well-trained, reliable production and maintenance workers' has caused employers to search for ways to make them 'stable, loyal, and well-motivated'. Where manual work increasingly required a high degree of skill, concentration and judgment, the 'artificiality and anachronistic character' of the traditional workplace divide became self-evident.[3] As a statement submitted to the Donovan Commission by the AEU in the 1960s claimed:

> There is still concern... over the workman's status in the industrial unit, and his position *vis-à-vis* the staff. The increased skill demanded by new industrial conditions and the onset of automation mean that many workmen are not only skilled and dextrous but need academic ability to accomplish the necessary theoretical work... The average workman is not encouraged to have any sense of belonging to his firm since the staff are maintained as a separate and favoured group... enjoying privileges he does not have. The traditional dichotomy between the white collar and the cloth cap, if continued, will increase friction and diminish efficiency, especially as the two groups are now drawing together in the realms of skill and educational attainment... Management could do much to avoid the 'red carpet' complex, to mitigate the sense of remoteness.[4]

Some employers, already aware of the problem, sought to remedy the sense of alienation by raising manual workers to staff status.

For employers, the attraction and retention of labour was difficult in circumstances of tight labour markets in the 1960s, and the problem of recruiting and retaining *suitable* people did not disappear with the sharp rise in the number of unemployed job-seekers in the 1980s. The need was for workpeople who already possessed, or with training could acquire, appropriate practical skills, but who were also capable of developing the desired attitudes of commitment, loyalty, and co-operation in the achievement of the firm's business objectives. Technological innovation necessitates training and retraining, often in an enterprise-specific package of skills; and even in semi-skilled functions employees' experience and dependability count for something in the achievement of production targets. Many managers understood perfectly well that the productivity improvements, for which government ministers and economists clamoured in the 1980s, could not readily be achieved without stable well-knit and effectively motivated work groups. Having recruited people of a suitable calibre, and expended time, effort and hard cash in training them up, employers have been reluctant to lose them.

The more sophisticated the technology and the greater the firm's investment in its human resources, the greater is the incentive to retain trained, experienced and reliable employees rather than continually to recruit new people. As White[5] has argued, where a company encounters the need for high investment in training, it pays to provide 'job security, career development, good pay and conditions, anything that will lock in valuable personnel and prevent the investment being wasted through job mobility'. Employers who used staff status for manual workers or harmonized conditions to that end, reported that such arrangements helped to bring about 'profound improvement in the working climate, better employee self-esteem...and a greater sense of purpose and involvement with the prosperity and development of the organization'.[6] Exploitation of more generous sick pay arrangements, the abandonment of clocking and discontinuation of pay deductions for lateness tended to be short-lived; persistent abuse by a few was now dealt with by supervisors.

One of the main objectives of employers who upgraded manual groups to staff status and more recently harmonized their terms and benefits with those of office staffs was to transform characteristically oppositional shopfloor postures into the kind of attitudes which Sykes[7] showed to be typical of white-collar workers in the 1960s. Staff employees' concept of the employment relationship, their view of their role within the firm's occupational structure, and their attitude to their work, the employing enterprise and management, were quite different in certain significant respects from the socio-cultural values generally displayed by the manual workforce. Unlike their manual counterparts on the shopfloor, office clerks identified with the interests of the firm; the two broad manual and non-manual classes each had a different ethos. Pay had top priority for manual workers, and in the general absence of opportunities for promotion to higher paid positions, their standard of living expectations were pinned on hard bargaining which often involved confrontational stances against management. Clerical and other white-collar employees, in contrast, believed that their career prospects were favourable, and many were prepared to study for qualifications to better their promotion chances. With a climbable career ladder, the office staffs identified with the employing enterprise and adopted management's interest as their own.

Staff status arrangements for manual workers and the more recent schemes for harmonization, especially where the latter came to embrace an integrated pay and grading structure in combination with provision for training, offered an individualistic solution to the problems of low status and sense of inferiority. At the same time, greater functional flexibility of labour helped to further fluidity in the social structure of the workplace, thereby assisting the mollification of attitudes produced by the traditionally rigid socio-economic workplace barriers which had blocked the advance of a whole class. Opportunities for career development, in times past a non-manual privilege, are more widely available for manual grades in companies whose harmonization policies include an integrated pay and grading structure. The same arrangements may also improve lower-grade white-collar workers' prospects of climbing a career ladder whose upper rungs were either out of reach or obstructed a quarter of a century ago when employers began to recruit university graduates directly on to the higher levels.

The innovations in personnel policy, management of human resources, bargaining styles, and the total remuneration package were part and parcel of business strategy for improved company performance and greater competitiveness in domestic and global markets. Employers sought higher productivity, lower production costs, better quality products, and sufficient flexibility to enable the company to respond readily to the changing demands of markets. An ability to recruit, retain, motivate and control labour was essential to the achievement of their business objectives; the commitment, dependability and co-operation of the workforce was a necessary condition of the business enterprise's success.

Many personnel managers, Roberts[8] argues, have consistently favoured the removal of most differentials, on philosophical grounds; the only justifiable disparities, in their view, were in money earnings which reflected levels of work responsibility and the measurable value of the work tasks undertaken; and, in so far as some people had better benefits than others, such as longer periods of paid holiday and sick leave, the differential should be a function of length of service with the company rather than of collar colour. During the third quarter of the present century, society's concepts of fairness and justice were changing. Social, economic and political influences began to challenge traditional industrial practices and attitudes. Expectations were affected by rising standards of living, improvements in education based on equal opportunity, better communication, higher purchasing power, travel abroad, welfare statism and progress in social security. Socio-cultural horizons widened; aspirations rose. In such circumstances some employers came to the conclusion that 'there is now no moral justification for having different sets of conditions of service for manual and staff employees doing work of equivalent value, and that such differences are an anachronism'.[9] Company philosophy, changing attitudes about 'fairness, justice and equity' in the treatment of different categories of employees were amongst the explicit reasons given by some employers for their adoption of harmonization policies.

There were, of course, important pragmatic reasons for reducing differentials, even in firms where company philosophy was a major influence. During two and a half decades of near-full employment following the Second World War, when tight labour markets made it difficult to increase the numbers employed, the means to greater production lay in increased labour productivity, and achievement of it depended to a great extent on employees' co-operation and goodwill.

The practical objective of gaining manual workers' acceptance of changes desired by management has been one of the most frequently cited reasons for upgrading their conditions. This reason was foremost in the status agreements reached in the 1960s and early 1970s in the process of productivity bargaining, which was encouraged by successive Governments' incomes policies, and which enabled at least some employers to secure a relaxation of demarcations and restrictive practices, reduction of excessive overtime working, and changes in manning levels. In the 1980s and 1990s the accelerating trend to harmonized conditions was characterized by a tendency to do so 'for pragmatic rather than for purely philosophical reasons'. Agreements on harmonized conditions almost invariably contain clauses relating to flexible working, including mobility within and between departments. The cost of improving manual workers' conditions would be offset by the higher productivity and reduced unit costs permitted by employees' acceptance of flexible working, which was the price they were required to pay for their improved benefits. Roberts expresses this in terms of the 'selling price': 'Employers attempt to ensure that there is a productivity improvement as the *quid pro quo* of harmonization.'[10]

The changes in workpeople's attitudes which employers desired, it was generally recognized, could not be accomplished overnight by the simple expedient of provision for career development and better terms, benefits and employment conditions. In the longer term, however, where traditionally accepted hierarchies are broken down, the social barriers which they buttressed tend to crumble and new attitudes and relationships are the more likely to develop. In 1987 the final report of a CBI working party was unequivocally in favour of single-status terms and conditions as a means to realizing the full potential of companies' workforces;[11] but, as observers had been pointing out for some time, given a long pre-history of confrontation and adversarial stances in industrial relations, manual workers might be suspicious of a company's motives in introducing changes, believing them to be subtle or devious attempts to reduce their earnings when overtime is to be phased out, or seeing them as threats to future security and accustomed job rights when flexible working and more efficient labour utilization are to be implemented. It is a truism that people feel comfortable and secure with what is familiar, and feel threatened by change when the motives of its initiators are unclear and the effects upon groups and individuals are uncertain. There may be caution, cynicism or hostility when innovation is intended to bring about fundamental changes in traditional roles and relationships in the workplace.

The peaceable industrial relations which employers sought as one of several objectives in reducing and ultimately eradicating differentials, sometimes proved elusive, especially earlier in the period when unfamiliarity with the whole idea of staff status for manual workers caused them to question the price they were expected to pay for it, and when the knock-on effect of disturbed inter-group relativities in pay, terms and benefits produced discord rather than harmony in the workplace. There was little trouble when individuals or small groups were upgraded selectively; but the wholesale approach affecting the densely unionized majority sometimes produced reactions unwanted by management. Such skirmishes as occurred should have been, and sometimes were, anticipated.

Craftsmen sometimes had deep reservations about their move to staff status but, where one group of skilled tradesmen had been upgraded, other skilled groups were likely to seek parity. For electricians staff status soon became a symbol of their elitism and a means of separating themselves from production workers for negotiating purposes. While eager to move into the ranks above, they had little desire to be accompanied in that move by the ranks below. Where staff conditions were offered in return for surrendered job and skill demarcations, craftsmen were sometimes hostile at the prospect of encroachment by non-craft workers on their traditional job preserves.

Fear of the erosion of craft status caused industrial relations problems for both ICI and Electricity Supply in the 1960s.

Technical and white-collar staff were also affected when Electricity Supply's manual workers were upgraded wholesale. The grievance in both cases was the uncompensated erosion of their differentials relative to manual grades. The technical staff pointed out also that, since they were required to supervise manual workers, they were directly and equally affected by changes in manual working practices but they had not been equally compensated for increased responsibility. To placate technical staff, who were threatening industrial action on this score, an agreement had to be reached giving an annual supplement to 'buy out' the 'voluntary nature of their overtime'. Electricity Supply's clerical and administrative staff put up their own argument. Their main grievance concerned pay; the new payment structure, introduced as part of the status agreement, disturbed their pay relativities *vis-à-vis* both technical and industrial grades, and the 'co-operation payments' provided for industrials caused further distortion. Office staff asserted that they had been fully and voluntarily co-operative in the interest of the industry's efficiency for many years, and had never received any recompense for their compliance. They now demanded what they viewed as 'deserved' equivalence of treatment. Again, it took the threat of industrial action and reference to arbitration to settle the matter.[12]

White-collar workers felt that they had been too accommodating in the past and were now paying the price with the erosion of their differentials. The rise in manual workers' wage rates during the past decade and a half meant that most hourly paid groups received higher pay than some white-collar grades, and staff status arrangements providing access to staff benefits brought further encroachment. Non-manual staff were expected to share their own privileges with manuals but were being denied manual advantages such as overtime pay in return.

These more militant attitudes certainly produced some results. In the BEA pact, for example, in which maintenance engineers were paid large increases for dropping an incentive bonus scheme in association with the status agreement, a third of these increases were paid to non-manual grades. Mobil Oil also increased the pay of office staff when its staff status deal for manual grades was agreed in March 1965. Similarly, the Electricity Council gave increases of 'at least 8 per cent' to office staff; the National Board for Prices and Incomes officially sanctioned this concession as a 'disturbance allowance –

compensation to non-manuals for sharing their traditional benefits with manuals'.[13]

White-collar unionists were not opposed in principle to gains for other grades, but they were becoming increasingly alarmed to see their status advantages dwindle away. The changes underway, and fears about the non-manual worker's situation in the social structure of the workplace, probably contributed to the growth of white-collar unionism and militancy in the 1960s and 1970s. That *IRRR* found relatively few and only minor disturbances on the score of eroded differentials in the late 1980s and the 1990s may be attributable to greater familiarity amongst workpeople with the idea of harmonized conditions and to pre-emptive action by employers to provide acceptable compensation for the groups likely to be aggrieved by the extension of their former privileges to many, if not all and sundry, in regular full-time employment. Something may be owed also to the chastening experience of the recession and the persistence of unemployment, which diverted the focus of attention from differentials to job security. Older workers bore the brunt of redundancy. This, and early retirement, left many companies with younger workforces; and younger recruits into employment had been neither habituated nor acculturated to the workplace systems which structured the working lives of former generations. As Arthurs has observed, the dismantling of status barriers in British industry has now become 'part of the conventional wisdom of good employee relations'.

GOVERNMENT POLICY AND LEGISLATION

Harmonization of the employment conditions of manual and non-manual employees has been favoured by successive Governments for many years, but the removal of differentials in terms and benefits has, for the most part, been regarded as a matter for voluntary agreement between employers and their workforces. Several of the reports produced by the National Board for Prices and Incomes in the later 1960s advocated the elimination of 'invidious distinctions'.[14] In this, Crouch has argued, the NBPI's intention was to establish 'an income hierarchy based on skill and responsibility and not on status factors such as white-collar versus blue-collar, and to secure united effort by all sections of industry and the workforce in the search for increased efficiency and productivity'.[15]

In years when Britain was seeking entry to the EEC, each of the three major political parties was advocating the elimination of non-pay differentials. The Labour Government's White Paper of 1969[16] urged employers to consider sympathetically the possibility of removing out-dated distinctions between the salaried and the waged, which were an avoidable source of ill-feeling. In the early 1970s the Liberal Party was pressing for a comprehensive programme of legislation with harmonization of terms, benefits and conditions of employment as the ultimate objective. The Conservative Government's Code of Practice, issued as a supportive document to the 1971 Industrial Relations Act, urged the need progressively to remove differences in employment conditions which were not based on job requirement. Similarly, practically all the major institutions concerned with British industrial relations have urged the reduction of differentials during the past twenty-five years, but, as Arthurs has pointed out, at no time has any Government even contemplated legislation with the explicit intention of removing the manual/non-manual distinction.

In the 1960s and 1970s the main political influence came from legislation applying to all employees regardless of occupational grade, which established minimum standards in areas such as notice of dismissal, redundancy, maternity leave, contracted-out occupational pensions, and health and safety. The effect of the establishment of a 'floor of rights' was to improve certain conditions for manual workers and to bring them more into line with those of non-manual employees; but in the general absence of a 'ceiling of entitlements', employers could, and frequently did, continue to treat non-manual staff preferentially. Similarly, during roughly two decades of incomes policy, when constraints were advised or imposed on pay increases, negotiators were expected to settle for wage rises within the pay limits and for improvements in benefits to the extent that incomes policy allowed. The effect was to improve holiday entitlement, pensions and sick pay for manual workers, thereby reducing the manual/non-manual differential. However, taxation policy encouraged employers to find ways of circumventing liability to income tax by shifting the focus from pay increases to increases in non-pay benefits, the effect of which was to widen the differential between senior management and the rest. It was during the period of incomes policy, and the associated spread of productivity bargaining, that significant numbers of agreements were reached providing staff status for manual workers.

The eighties decade was characterized not only by economic recession and persistently high levels of unemployment but also by the abandonment of national incomes policy and a fundamental shift towards free market economics in government policy. The Conservative Government's policies relating to the labour market and industrial relations reflect the view that trade unions are a hindrance to the proper operation of labour market forces. A spate of legislation to curb the unions sought to: terminate the statutory supports and political encouragement for the extension of collective bargaining; free employees from institutionalized constraints which 'force' them to be union members for reasons other than positive choice; depoliticize trade unions through a weakening of their links with the Labour Party, by requiring compulsory ballots on the political levy and by illegalizing 'political' and 'solidarity' strikes; weaken the power of trade union leaders by a statutory requirement to ballot members prior to industrial action; restrict the scope of trade unions to organize and engage in industrial action; and exclude the unions from most spheres of state policy-making.[17]

There has been a contraction in the extent of collective industrial relations since 1979, but how far this is directly attributable to the reforms embodied in legislation is in some doubt. More legislation was enacted or proposed in the early 1990s: to restrict strikes in essential services; to revise procedures governing union check-off agreements; and to make it lawful for employers to offer superior pay and conditions to employees agreeing to accept a personal contract rather than coverage by collective agreements.[18] Observers have referred to a 'retreat from collective bargaining', to 'de-unionization', and to companies' moves from multi-employer industry-wide arrangements for pay determination.

These developments in collective bargaining and industrial relations have been regretted by some and welcomed by others. The effect upon the spread of harmonized conditions is largely a matter of conjecture. To the extent that the constraints imposed on the trade unions by Government policy and legislation have weakened their power to secure improvements in terms and benefits in the process of collective bargaining, piecemeal progress on the basis of gains item by item in the pay round is likely to have been impeded.

However, since harmonization policies are usually employer-initiated, are not usually the subject of industry-wide, multi-employer bargaining at national level, and can be more readily implemented at the level of the company, the division or the plant, Government policy and legislation may have had the indirect effect of encouraging the spread of such arrangements by freeing employers from certain institutional constraints and giving them greater scope for innovation in human resources management. In recent questionnaire surveys of harmonization, employers did not cite Government policy and legislation as restraining factors; by far the most frequently cited impediment was cost. It is significant that about half of the eighty-three companies surveyed by *IRRR* in 1989 had implemented their harmonization policies during the preceding five years, that the majority had phased in common terms and conditions over a period of years, and that most of the changes had involved discussion and negotiation with the trade unions. Most companies expected that the pressures for further harmonization would increase in the 1990s. Internal pressures were foreseen as being the necessity of reducing production costs, the quest for flexibility, and the need to recruit and retain the type of staff required; the most significant of the external pressures was given as the creation of the European single market. Two-thirds of the employers believed that the pace of harmonization would accelerate, while all the rest, with one exception, thought that the current pace of progress would be maintained.[19]

HARMONIZED CONDITIONS, BUT 'ONLY AT THE LEADING EDGE'?

The practice of extending staff conditions to manual workers was on the increase in the 1960s, but such practices were not randomly scattered throughout all industries and services. At the beginning of the 1970s, Robinson's investigations disclosed a distinct association between various types of staff status schemes and companies with certain characteristics.[20] Such schemes appeared to predominate in the south-east of England, and were usually to be found in large companies. In general, very large multi-plant concerns tended to offer a wider range of benefits to their manual workers than did small firms, and it is unsurprising therefore that staff status schemes were found to predominate 'amongst the giants'. One possible explanation for this is that their highly structured personnel policies and personnel management departments were better equipped to implement and administer unconventional arrangements. In addition, it seems likely that, in terms of sheer financial size and profitability, a large organization had an advantage in initiating ambitious but expensive policies when some of the returns would be realized only in the longer term. Also, company size tends to correlate directly with capital intensiveness, and the application of advanced highly automated processes based on new technology provides a motive for upgrading manual workers where skill requirement and responsibility increase.

Robinson found that staff status practices were becoming firmly entrenched in chemicals, engineering and the aerospace industry. The apparent clustering of staff status arrangements in the South East probably reflected the regional distribution of expanding and progressive light industry at that time. Employers were said to encounter less resistance to such policies in regions where the old staple industries with their traditional deeply engrained socio-cultural divisions had never been widespread and strongly rooted. That the industries in the South East were more recently established, were often newer growth industries, and tended to recruit younger managers and workforces, may have facilitated the introduction of innovative personnel policy. Many of the companies employed disproportionately large numbers of non-manual employees relative to manual workers, and had relatively large administrative, technical, research and development departments.

Many of the early characteristics of organizations at the 'leading edge' were still present in the mid-1970s. Murlis and Grist observed that the incidence of single status rose with company size; companies with one thousand or more employees were more likely than smaller firms to have advanced personnel policies. Companies which had introduced staff status or single status had one or more of the following characteristics: good profit and growth records, capital-intensive structures, new production technologies, new sites away from areas of established traditional practice in employment conditions, good industrial relations, and US or European ownership. Such practices were more frequently found in 'profitable industries such as electronics, electrical engineering, petrochemicals, and pharmaceuticals'. Typical characteristics of industries with few or no staff status schemes were: average or poor profit and growth records, labour-intensive production methods, difficult industrial relations, and traditional hierarchical working relationships with differentials in benefits and privileges accepted as the 'social norm'. For companies in industries with these characteristics, 'the cost of single status would be prohibitive, and negotiation difficult if it has to take place with several different unions at once, each bargaining over long-established demarcations and work practices', which would 'slow down any attempted change and make all but piecemeal improvement difficult'.[21]

Progress continued, however, despite the very real difficulties faced by employers, and it was not confined to the private sector. Innovation in the public sector had already occurred in Electricity Supply in the mid-1960s and was followed by further moves in that industry in the 1970s and 1980s; and first steps were taken in water supply, the Civil Service and the Atomic Energy Authority, and somewhat later in the gas industry and local authority services.[22] There is little to suggest that the trend was subsequently reversed by privatization of nationalized industries and services.

Arthurs's observation, that the labour market pressures, which had spurred employers to introduce staff status for manual workers during the years of markedly low unemployment in the 1960s and early 1970s, were no longer present during the recession of the 1980s, implies that there was a deceleration of the trend to align manual workers' conditions with those of non-manual staffs. In point of fact, however, there has been a distinct acceleration of the trend since 1979. Product market pressures, technological advance, and the quest for flexibility and greater competitiveness appear to have been more influential than the general state of the labour market in employers' decisions to harmonize conditions. Even with a persistently high unemployment rate, there were tight labour markets for certain kinds of labour; employers wanted new skills, overlapping skills, or enterprise-specific packages of skills which were not readily found in a generally slack external labour market.

An investigation conducted by *IRRR* in the early 1980s disclosed that harmonization was occurring across 'a wide spectrum' of public and private sector organizations, on greenfield sites and in companies 'more traditional and long-established', and in firms which were capital-intensive and others which were labour-intensive.[23] Evans claimed in 1980 that industries 'like electronics, electrical engineering, aircraft, chemicals, petroleum and pharmaceuticals' had been 'quick to move with the trend' but that 'industries with relatively traditional methods and technology operating at existing locations for long periods of time and with less favourable industrial relations histories' had been 'much slower off the mark'.[24] Practice, even so, was no longer confined to a few companies in half a dozen industries, but was spreading elsewhere, into glass, confectionery, steel, shipbuilding, distribution, and brewing, for example. Single status was typical of companies with US, Japanese, or European parentage, many of which began with the advantage of greenfield locations. In the challenging economic environment of the 1980s British companies in the new and expanding industries introduced harmonized conditions as part of a business plan opportunistically to gain market advantages; and many established companies were spurred into action as part of a survival strategy. In 1989 *IRRR* found 'no sign that harmonization is the preserve of new greenfield sites'.

Companies with harmonized conditions today are no longer to be found almost exclusively in the South East; many Japanese, American and other foreign-owned firms have established sites in South Wales, the North East of England, and in Scotland's 'silicon glen', and more British companies with long-established sites in the traditional industrial regions have adopted harmonization policies. It is true, as Price and Price argue, that such conditions are to be found mainly in large companies, and that the numerous small firms which have been set up during the last decade and a half have made only slow progress towards harmonization. As Storey[25] has disclosed, in 1994 over 95 per cent of firms in the European economy could be officially classified as small, yet they collectively provided only 'over half' of all jobs. If a mere 5 per cent of all firms may be described as large, they are likely to offer harmonized conditions for the very large minority of employees holding the 'rather less than half', which they provide, of all European jobs.

The view of harmonized employment conditions taken by Price and Price in 1994, and by Arthurs before them, tends to err on the side of caution, and even pessimism. The implication is that such conditions are not at all widespread. Price and Price argue that recent survey evidence 'presents a picture of practice at the "leading edge" of industry', and that in so far as harmonization practices apply in Britain, they are to be found in a manufacturing/industrial sector which has shrunk dramatically since 1970. Three points need to be made here. Firstly, as long ago as 1981, non-manual employees, comprising 52 per cent of the labour force, out-numbered manual workers; and to the extent that the steadily enlarging numbers of non-manual employees have permanent full-time work, they will, by definition, have 'staff conditions'. Secondly, harmonization practices are not confined to private-sector manufacturing industry; as we have seen, they are to be found also in public-sector services, in distribution, and in privatized utility services. Thirdly, in many companies without a harmonization policy as such, there have been gradual piecemeal improvements in the terms and benefits of manual grades in regular full-time work, which have had the effect of eroding traditional differentials.

HAS THE BOURGEOIS WORKER ARRIVED AT LONG LAST?

The terms 'bourgeois' and bourgeoisie' have taken on such different meanings and acquired such differing connotations that they have lost any clarity they may have had in the first place. The term, bourgeoisie, is perhaps most appropriately applied to the social group made up of entrepreneurs, merchants and industrialists who were active in the early stages of industrialization. In time, it came to be used loosely by left-wing theorists to describe the middle or ruling classes in capitalist society, who were said to have a vested interest in preserving the capitalist *status quo* in a struggle with the working class over the distribution of surplus value. 'Bourgeois' may simply be defined as 'of or relating to the property-owning middle class' or, from a Marxist perspective as 'of or relating to the middle or ruling classes who, by virtue of their ownership and control of the means of production, exploit the property-less working class'. In a derogatory sense, bourgeois may be used to describe someone who is unimaginative, or conventionally respectable, or conservative in tastes, attitudes and ideas, or overly concerned with material possessions and social status. Clearly, the allegedly bourgeois worker of the 1960s was not being represented, by those who claimed to have identified the type, as moving into the ranks of the entrepreneurial, merchant-trading and industrialist middle classes; nor was he or she rising into the professions. It was the consumption patterns and standard of living of white-collar and non-manual groups, which the inaptly styled 'bourgeois worker' was claimed to be emulating.

Another part of the controversy surrounding the embourgeoisement thesis was whether affluent manual workers saw themselves as middle class, and whether they were accepted by others as having middle-class status. Status, again, is an elastic term which has been stretched to fit so many different situations as to have lost its shape and clarity. It may simply refer to what a person is or does. Its dictionary definition is variously given as: condition, consequence, distinction, eminence, grade, position, prestige, rank, or standing; or as a person's social, legal or professional position in relation to others. It is used as a synonym for honour or prestige, when social status denotes the relative position of a person on a publicly recognized scale or hierarchy of social worth. Status is to do not only with a person's self-perceived identity, but with other people's perceptions of that identity. Much depends on current concepts of class, rank, and worth, bearing in mind that perceptions alter as society and its priorities change and develop in the course of time.

It is symbolically significant that the terms used to describe the upgrading of conditions have also changed. In the earlier stages, manual workers were put on 'staff grade' or 'staff status', possibly because the employer wished to convey the idea that he valued the manual workers in question equally with the office staff, and wanted to raise the former's sense of self-worth and self-perceived identity. The terms reflect the class attitudes of the era. 'Staff status' has connotations of snobbery, pretentiousness and divisiveness. It strikes a discordant note, and it is unsurprising that many manual workers were cynical about the status implications, and suspicious about the employer's motives. Staff status is a divisive 'us and them' term; some may have had the good fortune to be elevated to the ranks of 'us', but 'them' are still out there somewhere. The term 'single status' is somewhat problematic. It may give the idea that the employee is solitary or unattached, which is hardly appropriate if the employer seeks to create a sense of belonging or community, especially where quality circles and team working are involved. On the other hand, it may give the suggestion of being unique, or distinct, or particular – the idea that each employee, though receiving similar terms and conditions, is recognized and valued as an individual in his or her own right. The expression 'common terms and conditions of employment', favoured by Wickens,[26] has something to recommend it, clumsy though it is; but even this term is slightly off-key in that it may give the wrong impression. 'Common' may be intended to mean general or standard, but colloquially it is used to describe something which is low, vulgar, or even coarse – which is not how manual workers wish to see themselves. Recent literature contains the more straightforward terms: 'harmonization' or 'harmonized conditions'. In many ways these terms are preferable to any of the earlier alternatives. 'Harmonized conditions' conveys the idea that terms and benefits are being blended, co-ordinated and aligned, and there is the associated suggestion of voices or instruments which are 'in-tune'. Harmonious relationships are agreeable, amicable, and compatible; there is rapport, goodwill and understanding. These are amongst the objectives of human resources management. There are undertones of commitment and involvement, though there is the danger that, in focusing on the importance of the group, the significance of the individual may become submerged.

Goldthorpe and his co-researchers argued in the 1960s that the case for the existence of the bourgeois worker was 'not proven'; it rested largely on evidence of consumer behaviour, and the proponents of the embourgeoisement thesis had overlooked the crucial significance of people's occupations and work situations for their class position in the social structure. A degree of 'convergence' between the most affluent manual workers and some of those in the more routine kinds of white-collar work did not amount to a process of embourgeoisement. Yet, even at the time when Wedderburn and Craig were asserting that the 'great divide' at work was that which separated manual from non-manual, change was occurring, and the worker's role as producer in the workplace has changed a great deal more since then. It cannot be convincingly argued, however, that the alignment of manual workers' terms, benefits and conditions of employment with those of non-manual grades has caused the emergence at long last of the bourgois worker or the embourgeoisement of the working class. Terminology and concepts which were bizarre in the 1960s are no less eccentric in the 1990s.

A NEW DIVIDE IN THE WORKPLACE?

The traditional manual/non-manual workplace divide was markedly evident during the quarter century following the Second World War, but signs of change were already identifiable. The affluence of certain sectors of the manual workforce raised questions about their class position, and, while some saw them as moving into the middle class, others found the changes to be less extreme and more subtle than the proponents of the embourgeoisement thesis alleged.

The affluent workers of the 1960s had strong economic aspirations for a continually improving standard of living; their jobs, union membership, and votes in parliamentary elections were instrumental means to standard-of-living objectives. Goldthorpe and Lockwood claimed that the social change which was underway was not the assimilation of manual workers and their families into the middle class, but rather a 'much less dramatic process of *convergence*'. The effect of economic and industrial change had been to 'weaken simultaneously *both* the traditional "collectivism" of manual wage earners *and* the traditional "individualism" of non-manual employees'. Convergence did not imply identity, however; while the affluent manual worker had overwhelmingly economic goals, the non-manual employee was primarily concerned with 'status differentiation'.[27]

The predominant ideas which had spread in postwar society had been those of collectivism 'based on a sense of common interest... and the intervention of Government to guide the economy...'[28] Much of this had changed by the 1980s, however. The vast majority of employees, irrespective of occupational grade, became primarily concerned with the economic goal of improving, or at least maintaining, their standard of living. Britain's declining economic competitiveness brought the principles and practices of collectivism into question. In what Phelps Brown refers to as the 'counter-revolution of our time', the practices of the welfare state and planned economy were pruned or reversed.[29] Collectivism fell out of favour, to be replaced by the principles of individualism. To the fore came 'self-reliance, acquisitive individualism, the curtailment of public expenditure, the play of market forces instead of the restraints and directives of public policy, the prerogatives of management instead of the power of trade unions.' For large sections of society the promises of collectivism lost much of their attractiveness, and social solidarity was undermined by acquisitive individualism. People today tend to see their economic well-being as less dependent on the institutionalized class power wielded by the trade unions in national negotiations, and more bound up with the fortunes of the individual employing enterprise.

The emergence both of core sectors with relatively secure employment and enterprise-specific career ladders, and of fringe sectors with impermanent or part-time jobs, has contributed to the weakening of the trade unions' collectivist hold. The traditional staple industries, which were formerly trade union strongholds, have suffered contraction. Expansion has occurred in 'high-tech' employment and the services, which are generally organized in smaller units. These do not lend themselves to strong trade unionism, either because the unions find it difficult to recruit those who work in small widely dispersed groups, or because employees in such circumstances do not see themselves in an inherently adversarial relationship with management. Phelps Brown asserts that changes in the kind of work in which much of the working population is engaged have 'affected both the social structure and the attitudes that are linked with it'.

The vestiges of the traditional class structure remain, but the concepts of class identity, class grievance, class solidarity and class action have lost much of their energizing potency. Major pressure groups, espousing such causes as ecological awareness, children in need, age concern, gay rights, protection of animals, equality for women, famine relief, alternative technology, and many more, are not class-based in the sense of being working-class or middle-class movements seeking class-specific objectives. The kind of working-class solidarity which produced mass action in the past has slowly crumbled away. The route to higher material living standards today runs mostly through negotiations at the level of the individual company, or division, or site; and the 'effect of localization is even stronger' where a core of the labour force is distinguished by the 'prospects... of security and advancement within the firm', that localization offers.[30]

The most significant workplace divide can no longer be claimed to be the traditional manual/non-manual separation. More distinct is the division between people who have relatively secure full-time employment and the one-third or more of the total working population who may be described as temporary, part-time or self-employed. Yet neither of these two broad groups have 'class solidarity' or a 'class ideology'. Core sectors of employment, where jobs are relatively secure and full-time, contain manual, white-collar, professional, and managerial employees; in common they are likely to have career prospects, a range of often harmonized fringe benefits, some of which increase with years of service, training opportunities, and earnings which rise predictably with skill acquisition and responsibility. Manual workers no longer labour in the mass on the shopfloor. The interests of core workers, whatever the colour of their collars might be, are bound up with the interests of the company, the division, or the site, rather than with a monolithic social class. Likewise, the vastly increased numbers in self-employment, and in work which is temporary or part-time, cannot be said to comprise a cohesive class. Peripheral groups are not engaged exclusively in menial low-paid manual work; they may contain highly qualified computer programmers and university lecturers at one extreme and minimally qualified kitchen hands and cleaners at the other. While many receive very low rates of pay, others are highly remunerated.

The presence of numerically flexible peripheral workers permits and reinforces job security for those in the core; but security of employment can no longer be equated with non-manual work, nor job insecurity and vulnerability to redundancy with manual employment. Harmonized conditions are likely to spread further amongst the 'insiders' in core employment. Linked as many of the benefits are to long service with the same employer, they are unlikely to be extended wholesale for temporary workers, and, though permanent part-timers may have a *pro rata* entitlement to paid holidays and sick pay, it is rare for employers to provide opportunities for career development for anyone outside the core.

If the core/peripheral separation is accepted to be the most distinct workplace divide today, it remains to consider whether it can be described as 'new'. There is nothing novel, of course, about the practice of employing people on a temporary, part-time or sub-contractual basis; nor is self-employment a recent invention. The social surveys of the late nineteenth and early twentieth centuries have shown that casual and irregular work was the lot of many, that self-employment was not unusual, and that various sub-contracting systems were used in agriculture, mining and building. Though permanent full-time employment may have existed as an 'ideal' for many generations past, it did not become the 'norm' until the third quarter of the present century, with a generally low unemployment rate, tight labour markets, and full employment as an explicit objective of Government policy. To this extent, there is nothing fundamentally new about the present workplace divide.

There are two main differences, however. Firstly, the peripheral sector now contains white-collar, non-manual, and professional groups who had good prospects of secure employment in the past. Many of the work tasks, functions, and kinds of expertise required of them have changed beyond all recognition, but their occupations no longer carry any assurance of permanent full-time employment. Secondly, in the past and especially during the quarter century following the Second World War when, with a very low unemployment rate, permanent full-time work became the general 'standard' or 'norm', the manual/non-manual distinction was otherwise predominant. The vast majority of companies may have offered permanent employment, but most provided preferential terms and benefits for their permanent non-manual staffs than for their permanent manual workforces. Today, however, it has become common for an employer to provide the same conditions for all those with sustainable employment in the firm's central or key activities. To this extent, today's workplace divide is new.

None of this is to deny that there are other divisions. The persistence of gender and racial inequalities is well-documented; and income inequalities have widened recently. While many people receive abysmally low rates of pay, the huge salaries and vastly superior benefits of executives, directors and top management give them an exceptionally privileged position in the occupational structure.

The latter are no less advantaged than Wedderburn and Craig showed them to be a generation ago.

The class attitudes of yesteryear are fast disappearing, along with the class structure which produced and buttressed them. Manual workers are no longer engaged in large numbers in factory employment. Changes in the production process, in productive equipment, and in the organization of employment have produced diversity; flexible working, cell manufacture, teamwork, quality circles, JIT methods have all contributed in various ways to the disappearance of the 1960s-style of workplace, with its vast armies of overalled workers engaged in standardized mass production and subject to its associated divisions of labour. Diversity is now characteristic in both core and peripheral sectors. Appraisal systems, performance-related pay progression, and opportunities for career development and advancement for manual workers permit a degree of fluidity in the social structure of the workplace, which is in stark contrast to the rigid class lines of the old occupational hierarchies. There is no longer a situation where a whole class is blocked, and left with a brutally confrontational industrial relations stance as the only means to improving pay and conditions.

The cynic will attribute the gradual pacification of industrial relations and the decline in the number of days lost through headline-hitting strikes in recent years to a persisting fear of unemployment, a numerically weaker trade union movement, and Government-imposed curbs on trade unions' actions and procedures. These influences cannot be discounted; but much is owed also to the changing nature of employment and its increasing heterogeneity in both core and peripheral sectors, to greater involvement, participation and communication, and moves towards harmonized terms, benefits and conditions. With the encouragement of Government grant-aid, Japanese, American and other foreign-owned companies have successfully established subsidiaries in some of the districts where traditional class structure and class culture were most deeply embedded. Yet the migrants have gained acceptance, and their personnel policies, industrial relations frameworks, and single-status packages have contributed both to the healing of old class-inflicted wounds and to the amelioration of attitudes. In contributing to the regeneration of regional economies, the inward-investors also helped to emancipate regional communities from the old class system and its associated indignities.

There are still wide social inequalities in income, standard of living, and quality of life; but the class structure and class identities of the mid-twentieth century are long gone. The class system was beginning to weaken in the 1970s when Roberts[31] detected a process of fragmentation. In the 1990s Pakulski and Waters[32] have proclaimed 'the death of class'. There are few who will lament its passing and weep at the graveside.

Notes

CHAPTER 1: INTRODUCTION

1. Pakulski, J. and Waters, M. (1996), *The Death of Class*, London, Sage.
2. Zweig, F. (1961), *The Worker in an Affluent Society*, London, Heinemann; Millar, R. (1966), *The New Classes*, London, Longman; Turner, G. (1963), *The Car Makers*, London, Eyre & Spottiswoode.
3. The foremost of these was Titmuss, R.M. (1962), *Income Distribution and Social Change*, London, Unwin.
4. Goldthorpe, J.H., Lockwood, D., et al. (1969), *The Affluent Worker in the Class Structure*, Cambridge, University Press; Goldthorpe, J.H. and Lockwood, D. (1963), 'Affluence and the British Class Structure', *Sociological Review*, Vol. 11, No. 2, pp. 133–66.
5. Price, L. and Price, R. (1994), 'Change and Continuity in the Status Divide', in Sisson, K., ed., *Personnel Management: A Comprehensive Guide to Theory and Practice in Britain*, Oxford, Blackwell, pp. 527–61.
6. Lockwood, D. (1958), *The Blackcoated Worker: A Study in Class Consciousness*, London, Allen & Unwin.
7. Braverman, H. (1974), *Labor and Monopoly Capitalism: The Degradation of Work in the Twentieth Century*, New York, Monthly Review Press.
8. Anderson, G. (1976), *The Victorian Clerk*, Manchester, University Press; Lockwood, D., op cit.
9. Abercrombie, N. and Urry, J. (1983), *Capital, Labour, and the Middle Classes*, London, Allen & Unwin.
10. Orwell, G. (1961), *England Your England, and Other Essays*, London, Secker & Warburg, p. 223.
11. Carr Saunders, A.M. and Caradog Jones, D. (1937), *A Survey of the Social Structure of England and Wales*, Oxford, University Press, 2nd ed., p. 67.
12. *The Economist* (1948), 24 January.
13. Central Office of Information, 'Social Change in Britain', extracts printed in *New Society* (1962), 24 December.
14. Routh, G. (1965), *Occupation and Pay in Great Britain, 1906–60*, Cambridge, University Press.
15. Abrams, M. (1959), *The Changing Pattern of Consumer Spending*, London, Press Exchange; Zweig, F., op. cit.; Turner, G., op. cit.; Millar, R., op. cit.
16. Abrams, M. (1960), 'New Roots of Working Class Conservatism', *Encounter*, May.
17. Butler, D. and Stokes, D. (1969), *Political Changes in Britain*, Basingstoke, Macmillan.
18. Nordlinger, A.E. (1967), *The Working Class Tories*, London, MacGibbon & Kee; McKenzie, R. and Silver, A. (1968), *Angels in Marble*, London, Longman.

19. Crosland, C.A.R. (1960), *Can Labour Win?* Fabian Tract No. 324, London, Fabian Society.
20. Goldthorpe, J.H., Lockwood, D. et al., op. cit. pp. 24–6.
21. Wedderburn, D. and Craig, C. (1974), 'Relative Deprivation in Work' in Wedderburn, D. ed., *Poverty, Inequality and Class Structure*, Cambridge, University Press; Wedderburn, D. (1970), 'Workplace Inequality', *New Society*, 9 April.
22. Russell, A. (1991), *The Growth of Occupational Welfare in Britain: Evolution and Harmonization of Modern Personnel Practice*, Aldershot, Gower, ch. 10.
23. Bugler, J. 1965), 'Shopfloor Struggle for Status', *New Society*, 25 November, pp. 19–22.
24. Committee on Holidays with Pay (1938), *Report*, Cmd. 5724.
25. Government Actuary (1958), *Occupational Pension Schemes: A Survey*, London, HMSO. Further surveys were published by HMSO in 1966, 1968, 1972, 1978, 1981, and 1986.
26. Ministry of Labour (1964), *Sick Pay Schemes, 1961*, London, HMSO; Central Statistical Office (1971), *New Earnings Survey, 1970*, London, HMSO, section F.
27. Reader, W.J. (1975), *Imperial Chemical Industries: A History*, Oxford, University Press, Vol. 2, pp. 62–8.

CHAPTER 2: THE ECONOMIC CONTEXT, GOVERNMENT POLICY AND PROBLEMS FOR EMPLOYERS

1. Pollard, S. (1992), *The Development of the British Economy, 1914–1990*, London, Edward Arnold, chs 7, 9.
2. Roeber, R.J.C. (1975), *Social Change at Work: The ICI Weekly Staff Agreement*, London, Duckworth, chs 1, 2.
3. Coopey, R. and Woodward, N., eds (1996), *Britain in the 1970s: The Troubled Economy*, London, UCL Press, chs 1, 4, 5, 12.
4. Pelling, H. (1992), *A History of British Trade Unionism*, Harmondsworth, Penguin, statistical table, pp. 301–5; Trades Union Congress (1996), *General Council Report*, London, TUC Publications.
5. Towers, B. (1988), 'Forward' in Oliver, N. and Wilkinson, B., *The Japanization of British Industry*, London, Blackwell; Wickens, P. (1988), *The Road to Nissan: Flexibility, Quality, Teamwork*, Basingstoke, Macmillan.
6. Peters, T. and Waterman, R. (1982), *In Search of Excellence*, New York, Harper & Row.
7. Oliver, N. and Wilkinson, B., op. cit.
8. Schonberger, R. (1982), *Japanese Manufacturing Techniques*, New York, Free Press, cited ibid., p. 30.
9. Feigenbaum, A. (1983), *Total Quality Control*, New York, McGraw Hill, p. 7.
10. Fortune, J. and Oliver, N. (1986), *Human Aspects of Quality*, Milton Keynes, Open University Press, p. 24.
11. Briggs, P. (1988), 'The Japanese at Work: Illusions of the Ideal',

Industrial Relations Journal, Vol. 19, No. 1, pp. 24–30.

12. Yap, F. (1984), *A Guide to Quality Control Circles and Work Improvement Teams*, Singapore, Aequitas Management Consultants, cited in Oliver, N. and Wilkinson, B., op. cit., p. 10.

13. Schonberger, R., op. cit., p. 16.

14. Sugimore, Y., et al. (1977), 'Toyota Production System and Kanban System: Materialization of Just-In-Time and Respect-For-Human System', *International Journal of Production Research*, Vol. 15, No. 6, pp. 553–64; Bicheno, J. (1987), 'A Framework for JIT Implementation', in Voss, C., ed., *Just-In-Time Manufacture*, London, IFS, pp. 191–204.

15. Royal Commission on Trade Unions and Employers' Associations (1968), *Report*, Cmnd. 3623.

16. Phelps Brown, H. (1971), 'Forward' in Edwards, R. and Roberts, R.D.V., *Status, Productivity and Pay, A Major Experiment: A Study of the Electricity Supply Industry's Agreements and their Outcomes, 1961–1971*, Basingstoke, Macmillan.

17. Braverman, H. (1974), *Labor and Monopoly Capitalism: The Degradation of Work in the Twentieth Century*, New York, Monthly Review Press; Littler, C.R. (1982), *The Development of the Labour Process in Capitalist Societies*, London, Heinemann.

18. Retrospective comment in Cross, M. (1984), *Towards the Flexible Craftsman*, London, Technical Change Centre; Jones, B. (1982), 'Distribution or Redistribution of Engineering Skills? The Case of Numerical Control' in Wood, S., ed, *The Degradation of Work? Skill, Deskilling and the Labour Process*, London, Hutchinson, pp. 179–200.

19. Roeber, R.J.C., op. cit., chs 1, 2.

20. McKersie, R. and Hunter, L. (1973), *Pay, Productivity, and Collective Bargaining*, Basingstoke, Macmillan.

21. Government White Paper (1965), *Prices and Incomes Policy*, Cmnd. 2639, and (1965), *Prices and Incomes Policy: An 'Early Warning' System*, Cmnd. 2808.

22. Flanders, A. (1970), *Management and Unions: The Theory and Reform of Industrial Relations*, London, Faber.

23. Royal Commission on Trade Unions and Employers' Associations, op. cit., p. 17.

24. Ibid. (1967), Research Papers (4), *Restrictive Labour Practices*, p. 17.

25. Clegg, H.A. (1964), *Socialist Commentary*, December.

26. Stettner, N. (1969), *Productivity Bargaining and Structural Change*, London, Pergamon, p. 39.

27. Ibid., p. 43.

28. Cited and quoted ibid., p. 3.

29. Bugler, J. (1965), 'Shopfloor Struggle for Status', *New Society*, 25 November, pp. 19–22.

30. 'Flexibility of Labour', *IRRR*, No. 166 (December 1977), pp. 2–8.

31. Atkinson, J. (1984), *Manning for Uncertainty: Some Emerging UK Work Practices*, IMS Research Paper, Sussex, Institute of Manpower Studies.

32. NEDO (1986), *Changing Work Patterns: How Companies Achieve Flexibility to Meet New Needs*, London, National Economic Development Office.

33. Ibid., p. 5.
34. Cited and quoted in Wickens, P., op. cit., p. 41.
35. NEDO, op. cit.; Incomes Data Services (1984), *Craft Flexibility*, Study No. 322, London, IDS.
36. Quoted in Wickens, P., op. cit., pp. 40–1.
37. Ibid.
38. Cited in 'Flexible Employment Strategies', *IRRR*, No. 325, (August 1984), pp. 13–16.
39. Kirosingh, M. (1989), 'Changed Working Practices', *Employment Gazette*, August, pp. 422–9.
40. 'Productivity Offsets for Shorter Hours in Engineering', *IRRR*, No. 464, (May 1990), pp. 7–11.
41. Incomes Data Services (1982), *Harmonization of Conditions*, Study No. 273, London, IDS, pp. 6–7.
42. Hakim, C. (1987), 'Trends in the Flexible Workforce', *Employment Gazette*, November, pp. 549–59.
43. Hunter, L. and MacInnes, J. (1992), 'Employers and Labour Flexibility: The Evidence from Case Studies', *Employment Gazette*, June, pp. 307–15; McGregor, A. and Sproull, A. (1992), 'Employers and the Flexible Workforce', *Employment Gazette*, May, pp. 225–34.

CHAPTER 3: STAFF STATUS AND HARMONIZED CONDITIONS

1. Hand, M. (1968), *Staff Status for Manual Workers*, London, Pergamon, p. 17.
2. A detailed account is given in ibid.
3. Incomes Data Services (1974), *Staff Status for Manual Workers: Part 2*, Study No. 77, London, IDS, pp. 5, 10.
4. Industrial Society (1970), *Status Differences and Moves towards Single Status*, London, IS, pp. 7–8.
5. Ibid., p. 17.
6. Incomes Data Services, op. cit., p. 3; Robinson, T. (1972), *Staff Status for Manual Workers*, London, Kogan Page, pp. 36, 42, 67; Roeber, J. (1975), *Social Change at Work: The ICI Weekly Staff Agreement*, London, Duckworth, chs 3, 4.
7. Incomes Data Services, op. cit., pp. 5, 8, 10.
8. 'Sweet Harmony: A Single Status Survey', *IRRR* (November 1993), No. 548, pp 7–11.
9. Bugler, J. (25 November 1965), 'Shopfloor Struggle for Status', *New Society*, pp. 19–22.
10. Edwards, R.S. and Roberts, R.D.V. (1971), *Status, Productivity and Pay, A Major Experiment: A Study of the Electricity Supply Industry's Agreements and their Outcomes, 1961–71*, London, Macmillan.
11. Incomes Data Services, op. cit., pp. 14–15.
12. National Board for Prices and Incomes (1966), *Pay of Industrial Civil Servants*, Report No. 18, Cmnd. 3034, and (1970), *Pay and Conditions of Industrial Civil Servants*, Report No. 146, Cmnd. 4351.
13. Quoted in Incomes Data Services, op. cit., p. 15.

14. Ibid., pp. 14–15.
15. National Board for Prices and Incomes (1968), *Pay and Productivity of Industrial Employees of the United Kingdom Atomic Energy Authority*, Report No. 51, Cmnd 3499.
16. Incomes Data Services, op. cit., p. 14.
17. 'Staff Status: British Airports Authority', *IRRR* (April 1981), No. 245, pp. 10–13.
18. Roberts, C., ed. (1985), *Harmonization: Whys and Wherefores*, London, Institute of Personnel Management, pp. 118–25.
19. 'People-Centred Policy in Sheffield', *IRRR* (February 1985), No. 338, pp. 20–7.
20. 'Braintree District Council: Total Quality in Local Government', *IRRR* (July 1994), No. 563, pp. 7–11.
21. 'Sweet Harmony: A Single Status Survey', *IRRR* (November 1993), No. 548, pp. 7–11.
22. 'From Public to Private Sector: A New Deal at BREL', *IRRR* (April 1990), No. 461, pp. 10–14.
23. 'Industrial Relations Developments in the Water Industry', *IRRR* (July 1992), No. 516, pp 6–15; 'Thames Water: The "Employee Project"', *IRRR* (September 1992), No. 420, pp. 4–7; 'Partnership and Restructuring at Severn Trent Water', *IRRR* (November 1994), No. 571, pp. 7–11.
24. Edwards, R.S. and Roberts, R.D.V., op cit.; National Board for Prices and Incomes (1967), *Pay of Electricity Supply Workers*, Cmnd. 3405; 'Staff Status: Electricity Supply', *IRRR* (May 1981), No. 247, pp. 6–12; 'Staff Status: Issues and Trends', *IRRR* (May 1981), No. 248, pp. 2–8.
25. 'Reforming Industrial Relations in Electricity Supply', *IRRR* (October 1992), No. 521, pp. 6–12.

CHAPTER 4: SINGLE STATUS IN BRITAIN: THE AMERICAN MODELS?

1. Robinson, T. (1972), *Staff Status for Manual Workers*, London, Kogan Page, pp. 35, 37, 54, 86; Incomes Data Services (1974), *Staff Status for Manual Workers: Part 2*, Study No. 77, London, IDS, p. 11.
2. Detailed information on TI (UK) in Incomes Data Services (1980), *Staff Status*, Study No. 227, London IDS, p. 15; Robinson T., op. cit.
3. Ibid.
4. Maslow, A.H. (1970), *Motivation and Personality*, New York, Harper & Row, 2nd Edn; Herzberg, F. et al. (1959), *The Motivation to Work*, New York, Wiley.
5. Cited and quoted in Incomes Data Services (1980), op. cit., pp. 11, 15.
6. Hand, M. (1968), *Staff Status for Manual Workers*, London, Pergamon, pp. 14–15.
7. Quoted ibid.
8. 'Staff Status: E.R. Squibb & Sons', *IRRR* (January 1981), No. 239, pp. 6–8; 'Staff Status: Issues and Trends', *IRRR* (May 1981), No. 248, pp. 2–8; Roberts, C., ed. (1985), *Harmonization: Whys and Wherefores*, London, Institute of Personnel Management, pp. 123–7.

9. Details on these two companies in 'Staff Status Revisited: Porvair', *IRRR* (October 1980), No. 234, pp. 7–11; Incomes Data Services (1974), op cit., pp. 7, 11 and (1980), p. 13.

10. 'Single-Status Bargaining at Beckman Instruments', *IRRR* (August 1979), No. 206, pp. 5–7.

11. 'Eaton Deal Precludes Strike Action', *IRRR* (March 1986), No. 364, pp. 10–13.

12. 'Johnson & Johnson's Integrated Payment Structure', *IRRR* (October 1986), No. 378, pp. 2–8.

13. 'Staff Status: Continental Can Company Ltd', *IRRR* (December 1980) No. 237, pp. 2–6; 'Integrated Job Evaluation at Continental Can', *IRRR* (March 1983), No. 279, pp. 9–15.

14. Institute of Personnel Management (1977), *Staff Status for All*, London, IPM, pp. 23–5.

CHAPTER 5: SINGLE STATUS IN BRITAIN: THE JAPANESE MODELS?

1. Towers, B. (1988), 'Forward', in Oliver, N. and Wilkinson, B., *The Japanization of British Industry*, Oxford, Blackwell, p. xi.

2. Rayback, J.G. (1966), *History of American Labor*, London, Collier Macmillan.

3. Graham, I. (1988), 'Japanization as Mythology', *Industrial Relations Journal*, Vol. 29, No. 1, pp. 69–75.

4. Oliver, N. and Wilkinson, B., op. cit., p. 4.

5. Peters, T. and Waterman, R. (1982), *In Search of Excellence*, New York, Harper & Row.

6. Russell, A. (1991), *The Growth of Occupational Welfare in Britain: Evolution and Harmonization of Modern Personnel Practice*, Aldershot, Gower.

7. Oliver, N. and Wilkinson, B., op. cit., p. 16.

8. Dore, R. (1973), *Origins of the Japanese Employment System*, London, Allen & Unwin.

9. Littler, C.R. (1982), *The Development of the Labour Process in Capitalist Societies*, London, Heinemann.

10. Pascale, R. and Athos, A. (1982), *The Art of Japanese Management*, Harmondsworth, Penguin.

11. Briggs, P. (1988), 'The Japanese at Work: Illusions of the Ideal', *Industrial Relations Journal*, Vol. 19, No. 1, pp. 24–30.

12. Pang, K.K. and Oliver, N. (1988), 'Personnel Strategy in Eleven Japanese Manufacturing Companies in the UK', *Personnel Review*, 17 March, pp. 16–21.

13. ACAS Wales (1986), *Successful Industrial Relations: The Experience of Overseas Companies in Wales*, Cardiff, ACAS Wales.

14. 'IR in Foreign-Owned Firms in Wales', *IRRR* (January 1987), No. 383, p. 13.

15. 'The Japanese in Britain: Employment Policies and Practice', *IRRR* (August 1990), No. 470, pp. 6–11.

16. Quoted in Pang, K.K. and Oliver, N. op cit., p. 20.
17. Wickens, P. (1988), *The Road to Nissan: Flexibility, Quality, Teamwork*, Basingstoke, Macmillan; see also the framework agreement with the AUEW: *Nissan Motor Manufacturing (UK) Limited: Agreement and Conditions of Employment*.
18. Leese, J. (August 1985), 'The Nissan Agreement: A Work Philosophy', *Employment Gazette*, pp. 326–7; 'Nissan: A Deal for Teamwork and Flexibility?', *IRRR* (May 1985), No. 344, pp. 2–7.
19. 'Toshiba Consumer Products (UK) Ltd: New Start, New Industrial Relations', *IRRR* (August 1981), No. 253, pp. 2–6.
20. Quoted ibid., p. 2.
21. Toshiba, *Company Handbook* and *Recognition Agreement*.
22. 'Komatsu: The First Year of a New Start', *IRRR* (May 1987), No. 391, pp. 2–6; Komatsu, *Company Handbook* and *Recognition Agreement*.
23. Oliver, N. and Wilkinson, B., op. cit., p. 67.
24. 'The Japanese in Britain: Employment Policies and Practice', *IRRR* (August 1990), No. 470, pp. 6–11.
25. Work Research Unit (1986), *Learning from Japan*, London, WRU, Department of Employment.
26. 'Lessons from Japan', *IRRR* (June 1984), No. 321, p. 12.
27. Vliet, A. (1986), 'Where Lucas Sees the Light', *Management Today*, June, pp. 38–45; Oliver, N. and Wilkinson, B., op. cit., pp. 45–54.
28. 'Nissan: A Catalyst for Change?', *IRRR* (November 1986), No. 379, pp. 9–12.
29. Smith, D. (1988), 'The Japanese Example in South West Birmingham', *Industrial Relations Journal*, Vol. 19, No. 1, pp. 41–50.
30. Marsden, D. et. al. (1985), *The Car Industry: Labour Relations and Industrial Adjustment*, London, Tavistock.
31. 'Leyland Trucks: Quality Teams in Gear', *IRRR* (February 1994), No. 554, pp. 13–16.
32. 'Thorn Lights the Way to World Class Manufacturing', *IRRR* (July 1992), No. 515, pp. 12–15.
33. 'Just-in-Time Working', *IRRR* (January 1990), No 456, pp. 7–10.
34. Ibid.
35. 'New Employee Relations at Dundee Textiles', *IRRR* (March 1990), No. 459, pp. 12–14.
36. Oliver, N. and Wilkinson, B., op. cit., ch. 4, 'The Emulators'.
37. Wood, S. (1993), 'Are Human Resource Practices in Japanese Transplants Truly Different?', paper given at the British Universities Industrial Relations Association Annual Conference; 'Japanese Employment Policies', *IRRR* (September 1993), No. 544, pp. 3–4.
38. Oliver, N. and Wilkinson, B. (1992), *The Japanization of British Industry: New Developments in the 1990s*, Oxford, Blackwell.
39. 'The Impact of Japanese Firms on Working and Employment Practices', *IRRR* (July 1993), No. 540, pp. 4–16.

CHAPTER 6: NEW TECHNOLOGY AND HARMONIZATION

1. McLoughlin, I. and Clark, J. (1988), *Technological Change at Work*, Milton Keynes, Open University Press, p. 6; see also Rada, J. (1980), *The Impact of Microelectronics*, Geneva, ILO; Forester, T., ed. (1987), *High Technology Society*, Oxford, Blackwell; Forester T., ed. (1980), *The Microelectronics Revolution*, Oxford, Blackwell; Forester, T. (1985), *The Information Technology Revolution*, Oxford, Blackwell.

2. McLoughlin, I. and Clark, J., op. cit., p. 13; Bylinsky, G. and Hills Moore, A. (1987), 'Flexible Manufacturing Systems', in Forester, T., ed., op. cit.

3. Braverman, H. (1974), *Labor and Monopoly Capitalism: The Degradation of Work in the Twentieth Century*, New York, Monthly Review Press.

4. Buchanan, D. (1987), 'Using New Technology' in Forester, T., ed., op. cit.

5. Wilkinson, B. (1983), *The Shop Floor Politics of New Technology*, London, Heinemann; Child, J. (1984), *Organization: A Guide to Problems and Practice*, London, Harper & Row; Martin, R. (1988), 'The Management of Industrial Relations and New Technology', in Marginson, P. et al., eds, *Beyond the Workplace*, Oxford, Blackwell.

6. McLoughlin, I. and Clark, J., op. cit., p. 183.

7. Buchanan, D., op. cit.

8. Barnett, C. (1986), *Audit of War*, Basingstoke, Macmillan, quoted and cited in Daniel, W. (1987), *Workplace Industrial Relations and Technical Change*, London, Pinter.

9. Willman, P. (1986), *Technological Change, Collective Bargaining, and Industrial Efficiency*, Oxford, University Press, p. 253.

10. Buchanan, D. and Boddy, D. (1983), *Organizations in the Computer Age: Technological Imperatives and Strategic Choice*, Aldershot, Gower; Clark, J. et al. (1988), *The Process of Technological Change: New Technology and Social Choice in the Workplace*, Cambridge, University Press.

11. Child, J. (1985), 'Managerial Strategies, New Technology, and the Labour Process' in Knights, D. et al., eds, *Job Redesign: Critical Perspectives on the Labour Process*, Aldershot, Gower, pp. 107–111.

12. 'Decentralized Bargaining at Pilkington', *IRRR* (April 1985), No. 341, pp. 2–5.

13. 'Flexible Team Working at Unigate's Greenfield Site', *IRRR* (December 1988), No. 430, pp. 8–11.

14. 'Change in a Traditional Environment: The CWS Experience', *IRRR* (February 1986), No. 361, pp. 10–17.

15. 'Re-Engineering Industrial Relations at Barr & Stroud', *IRRR* (March 1994), No. 555, pp. 3–7.

16. 'Leyland Trucks: Quality Teams in Gear', *IRRR* (February 1994), No. 554, pp. 13–16.

17. 'Re-Skilling at Westland's Milton Keynes Plant', *IRRR* (January 1985), No. 336, pp. 6–8.

18. 'Packaging Flexibility at Metal Box', *IRRR* (September 1988), pp. 8–11.

19. 'A Greenfield Strategy for Ind Coope's Burton Brewery', *IRRR* (January 1987), No. 394, pp. 2–8; 'Labour Flexibility Re-Assessed', *IRRR* (November 1989), No. 415, pp. 7–10.
20. 'Rationalization and Flexibility of Labour at Whitbread's Luton Brewery', *IRRR* (July 1981), No. 251, pp. 7–11; 'Whitbread Romsey: New Approach to Working Time', *IRRR* (June 1985), No. 364, pp. 9–14.
21. 'Integration and Equality at Midland Bank', *IRRR* (January 1988), No. 407, pp. 7–14.

CHAPTER 7: DEREGULATION, DECENTRALIZATION AND HARMONIZATION

1. Royal Commission on Trade Unions and Employers' Associations, (1968), Report, Cmnd. 3623, p. 12.
2. Brown, W. (1981), *The Changing Contours of Industrial Relations in Britain*, Oxford, Blackwell.
3. Purcell, J. and Sisson, K. (1983), 'Strategies and Practices in the Management of Industrial Relations' in Bain, G. S., ed. *Industrial Relations in Britain*, Oxford, Blackwell.
4. Daniel, W.W. and Millward, N. (1983), *Workplace Industrial Relations in Britain: The DES/PSI/ESRC Survey*, London, Heinemann, pp. 290–1; Confederation of British Industry (1983), *The Structure and Processes of Pay Determination in the Private Sector, 1979–86*, London, CBI Publications, pp. 34–5.
5. Brown, W. and Walsh, J. (1991), 'Pay Determination in Britain in the 1980s: The Anatomy of Decentralization', *Oxford Review of Economic Policy*, Vol. 7, No. 1, pp. 44–58.
6. Department of Employment (1988), *Employment for the 1990s*, London, HMSO.
7. Kessler, S. and Bayliss, F. (1995), *Contemporary British Industrial Relations*, Basingstoke, Macmillan, lists, and summarizes the main provisions of, the relevant Acts up to 1993.
8. Brown, W. and Walsh, J., op. cit.
9. 'Decline of Multi-Employer Bargaining Charted', *IRRR* (September 1993), No. 544, pp. 7–11.
10. Hill, C.S.W. and Pickering, J.F. (1988), 'Divisionalization, Decentralization, and Performance of Large UK Companies', *Journal of Management Studies*, No. 23, pp. 28–47.
11. Marsden, D. and Thompson, M. (1990), 'Flexibility Agreements and their Significance in Productivity in British Manufacturing since 1980', *Work, Employment and Society*, Vol. 4, No. 1, pp. 83–104.
12. 'Single-Union Deals', *IRRR* (June 1989), No. 442, pp. 5–11; 'Single-Union Deals in Perspective', *IRRR* (November 1992), No. 523, pp. 6–15; 'Single-Union Deals Survey: 1', *IRRR* (January 1993), No. 528, pp. 3–15; 'Single-Union Deals Survey: 2', *IRRR* (February 1993), No. 529, pp. 4–12.
13. Bassett, P. (1986), *Strike-Free: New Industrial Relations in Britain*, Basingstoke, Macmillan.

14. 'Unions Explore Single-Table Bargaining', *IRRR* (June 1989), No. 441, pp. 3–4; 'Single-Table Bargaining: a Survey', *IRRR* (May 1990), No. 463, pp. 5–11.
15. McLoughlin, I. and Gourlay, S. (1994), *Enterprise Without Unions: Industrial Relations in the Non-Union Firm*, Buckingham, Open University; 'Managing Employee Relations in Non-Union Firms', *IRRR* (October 1994), No. 580, pp. 2–3; 'Union De-recognition and Personal Contracts', *IRRR* (February 1994), No. 553, pp. 6–13.
16. 'Single-Status Job Evaluation at Thornton', *IRRR* (May 1983), No. 295, pp. 2–6.
17. Kennedy, G. (February 1988), 'Single Status as the Key to Flexibility', *Personnel Management*, pp. 51–3.
18. 'Single-Status No Strike Deals Spread into Steel', *IRRR* (May 1986), No. 368, pp. 6–10.
19. 'Temporary Workers Register Agreed in Excel's Strike-Free Deal', *IRRR* (December 1986), No. 381, pp. 6–10.
20. 'BICC Optical Cables Unit Goes "Into 2000"', *IRRR* (August 1987), No. 398, pp. 12–17.
21. 'Single-Union Deals in Perspective', *IRRR* (November 1992), No. 523, p. 8.
22. Ibid., p. 13.
23. 'Bargaining Moves at Reed Corrugated Cases', *IRRR* (March 1984), No. 316, pp. 10–14.
24. 'BCL Looks to the Future', *IRRR* (August 1986), No. 374, pp. 7–11.
25. 'Babcock Power: Long Term Survival Plan', *IRRR* (May 1986), No. 367, pp. 7–11.
26. 'Re-structuring for Survival at BICC Cables Blackley', *IRRR* (September 1993), No. 544, pp. 11–16.
27. Ibid., p. 12.

CHAPTER 8: PAYMENT STRUCTURES AND HARMONIZATION

1. 'Integrated Payment Structures', *IRRR* (May 1986), No. 367, pp. 2–6.
2. Grayson, D. (February 1984), *Progressive Payment Systems*, Occasional Paper 28, Work Research Unit, Department of Employment, p. 4; Grayson, D. (April 1984), 'The Shape of Payment Systems to Come', *Employment Gazette,* pp. 175–81.
3. Grayson, D. (February 1984), op. cit., p. 8.
4. Ibid., p. 9; see also Incomes Data Services (1982), *Harmonization of Conditions*, Study No. 273, London, IDS; Grayson, D. (July 1986), *The Integrated Payment System in Practice*, Occasional Paper 35, London, Work Research Unit, ACAS.
5. Long, P. (1986), *Performance Appraisal Revisited*, London, Institute of Personnel Management, p. 76.
6. Grayson, D. (September 1982), *Job Evaluation and Changing Technology*, Occasional Paper 23, London, Work Research Unit, Department of Employment; Grayson, D. (January 1987), *Job Evaluation in Transition*, Occasional Paper 36, Work Research Unit, ACAS.

7. 'Merit Pay for Manual Workers', *IRRR* (May 1984), No. 319, pp. 2–7.
8. Long, P., op. cit.; 'Manual Workers' Appraisal: A Growing Trend Surveyed', *IRRR* (August 1987), No. 398, pp. 2–8.
9. Incomes Data Services, op. cit., p. 9.
10. 'Payment Systems: From Cash to Bank Transfer', *IRRR* (May 1981), No. 247, pp. 2–6; Association for Payment Clearing Services (December 1984), *Consumer Payments and Financial Behaviour*, Research Brief, London, APCS; 'Cashless Pay: An End to the Weekly Wage Packet?', *IRRR* (March 1990), No. 460, pp. 5–9.
11. Listed in Incomes Data Services, op. cit., pp. 3–4.
12. *IRRR* (May 1981), op. cit., p. 2.
13. Kessler, S. and Bayliss, F. (1995), *Contemporary British Industrial Relations*, Basingstoke, Macmillan, p. 73.
14. *IRRR* (March 1990), op. cit., p. 6.
15. *IRRR* (May 1984), op. cit., gives details of payment structures in Hewlett Packard, Digital, and National Semiconductor.
16. 'Staff Status: Continental Can Company (UK) Ltd', *IRRR* (December 1980), No. 237, pp. 2–6; 'Integrated Job Evaluation at Continental Can', *IRRR* (March 1983), No. 279, pp. 9–15.
17. 'Manual Workers Appraisal: A Growing Trend Surveyed', *IRRR* (August 1987), No. 398, pp. 2–12.
18. 'Binding Arbitration at Inmos', *IRRR* (July 1983), No. 299, pp. 8–12; 'No-Strike Deals in Perspective', *IRRR* (July 1984), No. 324, pp. 8–12.
19. 'Holset Moves to Full Harmonization', *IRRR* (March 1985), No. 339, pp. 2–3.
20. 'Staff Status: Electricity Supply', *IRRR* (May 1981), No. 247, pp. 6–12.
21. Ibid., p. 12.
22. 'Integrated Payment Structures', *IRRR* (May 1986), No. 367, pp. 5–6; 'Decentralized Bargaining in Practice: 1', *IRRR* (December 1989), No. 454, pp. 6–10.
23. 'Flexible Working Practices Secure Neither Jobs Nor Work for Swan Hunter', *IRRR* (November 1993), No. 547, pp. 7–11.
24. 'Scottish & Newcastle: Long Term Deal Masks Radical Package', *IRRR* (April 1983), No. 293, pp. 5–11.
25. *IRRR* (August 1987), op. cit., p. 6.
26. Ibid., p. 10; 'Packaging Flexibility at Metal Box', *IRRR* (September 1988), No. 424, pp. 8–11.
27. *IRRR* (May 1986), op. cit.
28. Institute of Personnel Management (1990), *Determining Pay: A Guide to the Issues*, London, IPM.

CHAPTER 9: IN RETROSPECT

1. Confederation of British Industry (1981), *The Will to Win: Britain Must Mean Business*, London, CBI Publications.
2. Arthurs, A. (1985), 'Towards Single Status?', *Journal of General Management*, Vol. II, No. 1, pp. 16–28.

3.   Institute of Personnel Management (1977), *Staff Status for All*, London, IPM.
4.   Cited and quoted ibid., p. 12.
5.   White, M. (1988), 'What's New in Pay?', *Personnel Management*, Vol. 17, No. 2, pp. 20–3.
6.   Murlis, H. and Grist. J. (1976), *Towards Single Status: Current Developments in Conditions of Employment for Manual and Non-Manual Employees*, London, British Institute of Management, p. 17.
7.   Sykes, A.J.M. (1965), 'Some Differences in the Attitudes of Clerical and Manual Workers', *Sociological Review*, Vol. 18, No. 3, pp. 297–310.
8.   Roberts, C., ed. (1985), *Harmonization: Whys and Wherefores*, London, IPM, p. 35.
9.   Murlis, H. and Grist, J., op. cit.
10. Roberts, C., op. cit., p. 31.
11. CBI, *Programme for Action: Final Report of the CBI Vision 2010 Group*, London, CBI Publications.
12. 'Staff Status: Electricity Supply', *IRRR* (May 1981), No. 247, pp. 2–12.
13. Cited in Bugler, J. (25 November 1965), 'Shopfloor Struggle for Status', *New Society*, pp. 19–21.
14. NBPI (1968 to 1970), *Reports* Nos. 51, 123, 132, 164.
15. Crouch, C. (1977), *Class Conflict and the Industrial Relations Crisis*, London, Heinemann, p. 99.
16. Government White Paper (1969), *In Place of Strife: A Policy for Industrial Relations*, Cmnd. 3888, London, HMSO.
17. Kessler, S. and Bayliss, F. (1995), *Contemporary British Industrial Relations*, Basingstoke, Macmillan, ch. 5.
18. Smith, P. and Morton, G. (1994), 'Union Exclusion: Next Steps', *Industrial Relations Journal*, Vol. 25, No. 1, pp. 3–14; Hanson, G.C. (1991), *Taming the Trade Unions: A Guide to the Thatcher Government's Employment Reforms, 1980–90*, Basingstoke, Macmillan.
19. 'Harmonization: A Single-Status Surge?', *IRRR* (August 1989), No. 445, pp. 5–10; 'Harmonization 2: Pressures for Change', *IRRR* (November 1989), No. 452, pp. 13–14.
20. Robinson, T. (1972), *Staff Status for Manual Workers*, London, Kogan Page, pp. 74–7.
21. Murlis, H. and Grist, J., op. cit., p. 16.
22. Russell, A. (1991), *The Growth of Occupational Welfare in Britain: Evolution and Harmonization of Modern Personnel Practice*, Aldershot, Gower, pp. 145–51.
23. 'Staff Status: Issues and Trends', *IRRR* (May 1981), No. 248, pp. 2–8.
24. Evans, A. (February 1980), 'Single Status: How the Great Divide is Slowly Fading Away', *Chief Executive*, pp. 53–4.
25. Storey, D.J. (1994), *Understanding the Small Business Sector*, London, Routledge.
26. Wickens, P. (1987), *The Road to Nissan: Flexibility, Quality Consciousness, Teamwork*, Basingstoke, Macmillan.
27. Goldthorpe, J.H., Lockwood, D., et. al. (1969), *The Affluent Worker in the Class Structure*, Cambridge, University Press, pp. 25, 26–7.
28. Phelps Brown, H. (1990), 'The Counter-Revolution of Our Time',

Industrial Relations, Vol. 29, No. 1, pp. 1–14.

29.　Ibid.
30.　Ibid.
31.　Roberts, K., et. al. (1977), *The Fragmentary Class Structure*, London, Heinemann.
32.　Pakulski, J. and Waters, M. (1996), *The Death of Class*, London, Sage.

Select Bibliography

Abercrombie, N. and Urry, J. (1983), *Capital, Labour and the Middle Classes*, London, Allen & Unwin.

Abrams, M. (1959), *The Changing Pattern of Consumer Spending*, London, Press Exchange.

—— (May 1960), 'New Roots of Working Class Conservatism', *Encounter*.

Advisory, Conciliation and Arbitration Service (1982), *Developments in Harmonization*, Discussion Paper No. 1, London, ACAS.

ACAS WALES (1986), *Successful Industrial Relations: The Experience of Overseas Companies in Wales*, Cardiff, ACAS Wales.

Argyris, C. (1964), *Integrating the Individual and the Organization*, New York, Wiley.

Arthurs, A. (1985), 'Towards Single Status?', *Journal of General Management*, Vol. 11, No. 1.

Atkinson, J. (1984), *Manning for Uncertainty: Some Emerging Workplace Patterns*, IMS Research Paper, Sussex, Institute of Manpower Studies.

—— (1984), 'Manpower Strategies for Flexible Organizations', *Personnel Management*, August, pp. 28-9.

Atkinson, J. and Meager, N. (1988), 'Flexibility Just a Flash in the Pan?', *Personnel Management*, September.

Barna, T. (1962), *Investment and Growth Policies in British Industrial Firms*, Cambridge, University Press.

Bichena, J. (1987), ' A Framework for JIT Implementation' in Voss, C. ed., *Just-In-Time Manufacture*, London, IFS.

Booth, A. (1989), 'The Bargaining Structure of British Establishments', *British Journal of Industrial Relations*, Vol. 27, No. 2.

Braverman, H. (1974), *Labor and Monopoly Capitalism: The Degradation of Work in the Twentieth Century*, New York, Monthly Review Press.

Briggs, R. (1988), 'The Japanese at Work: Illusions of the Ideal', *Industrial Relations Journal*, Vol. 19, No. 1.

British Institute of Management (1974), *Employee Benefits Today*, London, BIM.

—— (1978) *Employee Benefits*, London, BIM.

Brown, W. (1981), *The Changing Contours of Industrial Relations in Britain: A Survey of Manufacturing Industry*, Oxford, Blackwell.

—— (1983), 'Britain's Unions: New Pressures and Shifting Loyalties', *Personnel Management*, October.

Brown, W. and Wadhwani, S. (1990), 'The Economic Effects of Industrial Legislation since 1979', *National Institute Economic Review*, No. 131.

Brown, W. and Walsh, J. (1991), 'Pay Determination in Britain in the 1980s: The Anatomy of Decentralization', *Oxford Review of Economic Policy*, Vol. 17, No. 1.

Buchanan, D. (1980), 'Using New Technology' in Forester, T. ed., *The Microelectronics Revolution*, Oxford, Blackwell.

Buchanan, D. and Boddy, D. (1983), *Organization in the Computer Age: Technological Imperatives and Strategic Choice*, Aldershot, Gower.

Bugler, J. (1965), 'Shopfloor Struggle for Status', *New Society*, 25 November.

Butler, D. and Stokes, D. (1969), *Political Change in Britain*, Basingstoke, Macmillan.

Bylinsky, G. and Hills Moore, A. (1980), 'Flexible Manufacturing Systems' in Forester, T. ed., *The Microelectronics Revolution*, Oxford, Blackwell.

Cave, A. (1994), *Managing Change in the Workplace: New Approaches to Employee Relations*, London, Kogan Page.

Child, J. (1984), *Organizations: A Guide to Problems and Practice*, London, Harper & Row.

—— (1985), 'Managerial Strategies, New Technology and the Labour Process' in Knights, D. ed., *Job Redesign: Critical Perspectives in the Labour Process*, Aldershot, Gower.

Clark, J. et al. (1988), *The Process of Technological Change: New Technology and Social Choice in the Workplace*, Cambridge, University Press.

Coates, D. and Hillard, J. ed. (1986), *The Decline of Modern Britain*, Brighton, Harvester.

Committee on Holidays with Pay (1938), *Report*, Cmnd. 5724.

Confederation of British Industry (1981), *The Will to Win: Britain Must Mean Business*, London, CBI.

—— (1987), *Programme for Action: Final Report of the CBI Vision 2010 Group*, London, CBI.

—— (1988), *The Structure and Processes of Pay Determination in the Private Sector, 1979–86*, London, CBI.

Crosland, C.A.R. (1960), *Can Labour Win?*, Fabian Tract No. 324, London, Fabian Society.

Cross, M. (1984), *Towards the Flexible Craftsman*, London, Technical Change Centre.

—— (1988), 'Changes in Working Practices in UK Manufacturing, 1981–88', *Industrial Relations Review and Report*, No. 415, May.

Crouch, C. (1977), *Class Conflict and the Industrial Relations Crisis*, London, Heinemann.

Daniel, W.W. (1970), *Beyond the Wage Work Bargain*, PEP Broadsheet, No. 519.

—— (1987), *Workplace Industrial Relations and Technical Change*, London, Pinter.

Daniel, W.W. and Millward, N. (1983), *Workplace Industrial Relations in Britain: The DES/PSI/ESRC Survey*, London, Heinemann.

Dickens, P. and Savage, M. (1988), 'The Japanization of British Industry? Instances from a High Growth Area', *Industrial Relations Journal*, Vol. 19, No. 1.

Dore, R. (1973), *British Factory, Japanese Factory*, London, Allen & Unwin.

—— (1973), *Origins of the Japanese Employment System*, London, Allen & Unwin.

Eales, R. (1969), 'ICI Abolishes "The Worker" in Pay/Productivity Bargain', *International Management*, Vol. 24, No. 1.

Edwards, R.S. and Roberts, R.D.V. (1971), *Status, Productivity and Pay, A Major Experiment: A Study of the Electricity Supply Industry's Agreements and their Outcomes, 1961–71*, Basingstoke, Macmillan.

Evans, A. (1980), 'Single Status: How the Great Divide is Fading Away', *Chief Executive*, February.

Feigenbaum, A. (1983), *Total Quality Control*, New York, McGraw-Hill.

Flanders, A. (1964), *The Fawley Productivity Agreements: A Case Study of Management Collective Bargaining*, London, Faber.

—— (1965), *Industrial Relations: What is Wrong With the System?*, London, Faber.

—— (1967), *Collective Bargaining: Prescription for Change*, London, Faber.

Forester, T. ed. (1980), *The Microelectronics Revolution*, Oxford, Blackwell.

—— (1985), *The Information Technology Revolution*, Oxford, Blackwell.

—— (1987), *High Technology Society*, Oxford, Blackwell.

Fortune, J. and Oliver, N. (1986), *Human Aspects of Quality*, Milton Keynes, Open University Press.

Goldthorpe, J. H. and Lockwood, D. (1963), 'Affluence and the British Class Structure', *Sociological Review*, Vol. II, No. 2.

Goldthorpe, J. H. et al. (1969), *The Affluent Worker in the Class Structure*, Cambridge, University Press.

Government Actuary (1985), *Occupational Pension Schemes: A Survey*, London, HMSO.

—— (1966), *Occupational Pension Schemes, 1963–4: A New Survey*, London, HMSO.

—— (1968), *Occupational Pension Schemes: A Third Survey*, London, HMSO.

—— (1972), *Occupational Pension Schemes, 1971: A Fourth Survey*, London, HMSO.

—— (1978), *Occupational Pension Schemes, 1975: A Fifth Survey*, London, HMSO.

—— (1981), *Occupational Pension Schemes, 1979: A Sixth Survey*, London, HMSO.

—— (1986), *Occupational Pension Schemes, 1983: A Seventh Survey*, London, HMSO.

Government White Paper (1969), *In Place of Strife: A Policy for Industrial Relations*, Cmnd. 3888.

Graham, I. (1988), 'Japanization as Mythology', *Industrial Relations Journal*, Vol. 29, No. 1.

Grayson, D. (1982), *Job Evaluation and Changing Technology*, WRU Occasional Paper 23, London, Department of Employment.

—— (1984), *Progressive Payment Systems*, WRU Occasional Paper 28, London, Department of Employment.

—— (1984), 'Shape of Payment Systems to Come', *Employment Gazette*, April.

—— (1986), *The Integrated Payment System in Practice*, WRU Occasional Paper 35, London, Department of Employment.

—— (1987), *Job Evaluation in Transition*, WRU Occasional Paper 36, London, Department of Employment.

Hakim, C. (1987), 'Trends in the Flexible Workforce', *Employment Gazette*, November.

Hand, M. (1968), *Staff Status for Manual Workers*, London, Pergamon.

Hanson, G.C. (1991), *Taming the Trade Unions: A Guide to the Thatcher*

Government's Employment Reforms, 1980–90, Basingstoke, Macmillan/ Adam Smith Institute.

Herzberg, F. et al. (1959), *The Motivation to Work*, New York, Wiley.

Hill, C.W.L. and Pickering, J.F. (1988), 'Divisionalization, Decentralization, and Performance of Large UK Companies', *Journal of Management Studies*, No. 23.

Hillard, J. (1986), *The Economic Decline of Modern Britain*, Brighton, Harvester.

Hunter, L. (1988), 'Unemployment and Industrial Relations', *British Journal of Industrial Relations*, Vol. 26, No. 2.

Hunter, L. and MacInnes, J. (1992), 'Employers and Labour Flexibility: The Evidence from Case Studies', *Employment Gazette*, June.

Hutton, G. and Henessey, J. (1964), *Source Book on Restrictive Practices in Britain*, London, Institute of Economic Affairs.

Incomes Data Services (1974), *Staff Status for Manual Workers: Part 1*, Study No. 73, London, IDS.

—— (1974), *Staff Status for Manual Workers: Part 2*, Study No 77, London, IDS.

—— (1980), *Staff Status*, Study No. 227, London, IDS.

—— (1982), *Harmonization of Conditions*, Study No. 273, London, IDS.

—— (1984), *Productivity and Working Time*, Study No. 312, London, IDS.

—— (1984), *Craft Flexibility*, Study No. 322, London, IDS.

Industrial Relations Review and Report: contains numerous case studies of companies with staff status and harmonization policies in the 1980s and 1990s.

Industrial Society (1966), *Status and Benefits in Industry*, London, IS.

—— (1970), *Status Differences and Moves towards Single Status*, London, IS.

Institute of Manpower Studies (1981), *Staff Status for Manual Workers*, Commentary No. 9, London, IMS.

Institute of Personnel Management (1977), *Staff Status for All*, London, IPM.

—— (1990) *Determining Pay: A Guide to the Issues*, London, IPM.

Jackson, M.P. et al. (1993), *Decentralization of Collective Bargaining: An Analysis of Recent Experience in the UK*, Basingstoke, Macmillan.

Jones, K. and Golding, J. (1966), *Productivity Bargaining*, Fabian Research Series No. 257, London, Fabian Society.

Kendall, W. (1984), 'Why Japanese Factories Work', *Management Today*, January.

Kennedy, G. (1988), 'Single Status as the Key to Flexibility', *Personnel Management*, February.

Kessler, S. and Bayliss, F. (1992), *Contemporary British Industrial Relations*, Basingstoke, Macmillan.

Kirosingh, M. (1989), 'Changed Working Patterns', *Employment Gazette*, August.

Leese, J. (1985), 'The Nissan Agreement: A Work Philosophy?', *Employment Gazette*, August.

Likert, R. (1961), *New Patterns of Management*, New York, McGraw-Hill.

Littler, C.R. (1982), *The Development of the Labour Process in Capitalist Societies*, London, Heinemann.

Lockwood, D. (1958), *The Blackcoated Worker: A Study in Class*

Consciousness, London, Allen & Unwin.

—— (1960), 'The New Working Class', *European Journal of Sociology*, Vol. 1, No. 2.

Long, P. (1986), *Performance Appraisal Revisited*, London, IPM.

Marsden, D. et al. (1985), *The Car Industry: Labour Relations and Industrial Adjustment*, London, Tavistock Press.

Marsden, D. and Thompson, M. (1990), 'Flexibility Agreements and their Significance in Productivity in British Manufacturing since 1980', *Work, Employment and Society*, Vol. 4, No. 1.

Maslow, A.H. (1970 edn), *Motivation and Personality*, New York, Harper & Row.

May, T. (1993), *An Economic and Social History of Britain, 1760–1970*, London, Longman.

MacGregor, D. (1960), *The Human Side of Enterprise*, New York, McGraw-Hill.

McGregor, A. and Sproull, A. (1992), 'Employers and the Flexible Workforce', *Employment Gazette*, May.

McKersie, R. and Hunter, L. (1973), *Pay, Productivity and Collective Bargaining*, Basingstoke, Macmillan.

McLoughlin, I. and Clark, J. (1994), *Technological Change at Work*, Buckingham, Open University.

McLoughlin, I. and Gourlay, S. (1994), *Enterprise Without Unions: Industrial Relations in the Non-Union Firm*, Buckingham, Open University.

Meager, N. (1986), *Temporary Work in Britain: Its Growth and Rationales*, Sussex, Institute of Manpower Studies.

Millar, R. (1966), *The New Classes*, London, Longman.

Millward, N. and Stephens, M. (1986), *British Workplace Industrial Relations, 1980–84*, Aldershot, Gower.

Morris, J. (1988), 'The Who,Why, and Where of Japanese Manufacturing Investment in the UK', *Industrial Relations Journal*, Vol. 19, No. 1.

Mullins, T. (1986), 'Harmonization: The Benefits and the Lessons', *Personnel Management*, Vol. 18, No. 3.

Murlis, H. and Grist, J. (1976), *Towards Single Status: Current Developments in Conditions of Employment for Manual and Non-Manual Employees*, London, BIM.

National Board for Prices and Incomes (1966), *Pay of Industrial Civil Servants*, Cmnd. 3034.

—— (1967), *Productivity Agreements*, Cmnd. 3311.

—— (1967), *Pay of Electricity Supply Workers*, Cmnd. 3405.

—— (1968), *Pay and Productivity of Industrial Employees of the United Kingdom Atomic Energy Authority*, Cmnd 3499.

—— (1969), *Pay of General Workers and Craftsmen at Imperial Chemical Industries Limited*, Cmnd. 3941.

—— (1970), *Pay and Conditions of Industrial Civil Servants*, Cmnd. 4351.

National Economic Development Office (1986), *Changing Working Patterns: How Companies Achieve Flexibility to Meet New Needs*, London, NEDO.

Oliver, N. and Wilkinson, B. (1988), *The Japanization of British Industry*, Oxford, Blackwell.

—— (1992), *The Japanization of British Industry: Developments in the 1990s*, Oxford, Blackwell.

Pakulski, J. and Waters, M. (1996), *The Death of Class*, London, Sage.

Pang, K.K. and Oliver, N. (1988), 'Personnel Strategy in Eleven Japanese Manufacturing Companies in the UK', *Personnel Review*, March.

Pascale, R. and Athos, A. (1982), *The Art of Japanese Management*, Harmondsworth, Penguin.

Pelling, H. (1992), *A History of British Trade Unionism*, Harmondsworth, Penguin.

Peters, T. and Waterman, R. (1982), *In Search of Excellence*, New York, Harper & Row.

Phelps Brown, H. (1971), 'Forward' in Edwards, R.S. and Roberts, R.D.V., *Status, Productivity, and Pay, A Major Experiment: A Study of the Electricity Supply Industry's Agreements and their Outcomes, 1961–71*, Basingstoke, Macmillan.

―― (1990), 'The Counter-Revolution of our Time', *Industrial Relations*, Vol. 29, No. 1.

Pollard, S. (1992), *The Development of the British Economy, 1914–1990*, London, Edward Arnold.

Pollert, A. (1988), 'The Flexible Firm: Fixation or Fact?', *Work, Employment, and Society*, Vol. V, No. 1.

Price, L. and Price, R. (1994), 'Change and Continuity in the Status Divide' in Sisson, K. ed., *Personnel Management: A Comprehensive Guide to Theory and Practice*, Oxford, Blackwell.

Purcell, J. and Sisson, K. (1983), 'Strategies and Practices in the Management of Industrial Relations' in Bain, G.S. ed., *Industrial Relations in Britain*, Oxford, Blackwell.

Rada, J.(1980), *The Impact of Microelectronics*, Geneva, ILO.

Reader, W.J. (1975), *Imperial Chemical Industries: A History*, Oxford, University Press.

Rifkin, J. (1995), *The End of Work: The Decline of the Global Labor Force and the Dawn of the Post-Market Era*, New York, Tarcher Putnam.

Roberts, C. ed. (1985), *Harmonization: Whys and Wherefores*, London, Institute of Personnel Management.

Roberts, K. (1977), *The Fragmentary Class Structure*, London, Heinemann.

Robinson, T. (1972), *Staff Status for Manual Workers*, London, Kogan Page.

Roeber, R.J.C. (1975), *Social Change at Work: The ICI Weekly Staff Agreement*, London, Duckworth.

Royal Commission on Trade Unions and Employers' Associations, (1968), *Report*, Cmnd. 3623.

Rubinstein, W.D. (1993), *Capitalism, Culture, and Decline in Britain, 1750–1990*, London, Routledge.

Russell, A. (1991), *The Growth of Occupational Welfare in Britain: Evolution and Harmonization of Modern Personnel Practice*, Aldershot, Gower.

Schonberger, R. (1982), *Japanese Manufacturing Techniques*, New York, Free Press.

Smith, D. (1994), 'The Japanese Example in South West Birmingham', *Industrial Relations Journal*, Vol. 25, No. 1.

Stettner, N. (1969), *Productivity Bargaining and Structural Change*, London, Pergamon.

Storey, D.J. (1994), *Understanding the Small Business Sector*, London, Routledge.

Sugimore, Y. et al. (1977), 'Toyota Production System and Kanban: Materialization of Just-In-Time and Respect-For-Human System', *International Journal of Production Research*, Vol. 15, No. 6.

Sykes, A.J.M. (1965), 'Some Differences in the Attitudes of Clerical and Manual Workers', *Sociological Review*, Vol. 18, No. 3.

Titmuss, R.M. (1962), *Income Distribution and Social Change*, London, Unwin.

Towers, B. et al. (1973), *Bargaining for Change*, London, Allen & Unwin.

Turner, G. (1963), *The Car Makers*, London, Eyre & Spottiswoode.

Vliet, A. (1986), 'Where Lucas Sees the Light', *Management Today*, June.

Wedderburn, D. (1970), 'Workplace Inequality', *New Society*, 9 April.

Wedderburn, D. and Craig, C. (1974), 'Relative Deprivation in Work' in Wedderburn, D. ed., *Poverty, Inequality, and Class Structure*, Cambridge, University Press.

Wickens, P. (1988), *Road the Nissan: Flexibility, Quality, Teamwork*, Basingstoke, Macmillan.

Willman, P. (1986), *Technological Change, Collective Bargaining and Industrial Efficiency*, Oxford, University Press.

Wilson, J.F. (1995), *British Business History, 1720–1994*, Manchester, University Press.

Work Research Unit (1986), *Learning from Japan*, London, Department of Employment, HMSO.

Zweig, F. (1952), *The British Worker*, Harmondsworth, Penguin.

—— (1961), *The Worker in an Affluent Society*, Harmondsworth, Penguin.

Index